Jade

Jade Goody

Jade

How It All Began

My First Book

JOHN BLAKE

Published by John Blake Publishing Ltd,
3 Bramber Court, 2 Bramber Road,
London W14 9PB, England

www.johnblakepublishing.co.uk

First published in hardback in 2006 by *HarperCollinsEntertainment*,
an imprint of HarperCollins*Publishers*

This edition published in paperback in 2009

ISBN: 978-1-84454-753-1

British Library Cataloguing-in-Publication Data:

A catalogue record for this book is available from the British Library.

Design by www.envydesign.co.uk

Printed in Great Britain by CPI Bookmarque, Croydon, CR0 4TD

1 3 5 7 9 10 8 6 4 2

Papers used by John Blake Publishing are natural, recyclable products made
from wood grown in sustainable forests. The manufacturing processes conform
to the environmental regulations of the country of origin.

Every attempt has been made to contact the relevant copyright-holders,
but some were unobtainable. We would be grateful if the appropriate people
could contact us.

For my two special boys,
Bobby and Freddy.

Acknowledgements

Thanks to my mum for loving me unconditionally and supporting me throughout everything in my life. To Dan Haywood and Simon Bridger for inspiring me to actually put my life down on paper in the first place, and to Lucie Cave for all of your hard work and words of wisdom.

Contents

Prologue

Phil Edgar–Jones, Executive Producer of *Big Brother*
Jade Goody applied for *Big Brother* in 2002. It was at the time when the selection process required people to send a video of themselves along with a great big application form that we'd asked them to fill in. We got about ten thousand entries that year. I'll always remember Jade's video. She was standing in front of this weird airbrushed picture in her house and she was talking nineteen to the dozen. I couldn't understand a bloody word she said, and for some reason she was putting herself through an elastic band (she cited this as one of her 'skills'). She was unlike anybody we'd ever had on *Big Brother* before. We had to put her through to the next stage.

She was invited to one of our audition days in London. We made the contestants play all sorts of games – such as someone being blindfolded and the other person having to steer them round an assault course. On that day, despite there being a large number of people in the room (including her future *Big Brother* housemate, Kate Lawler), the only person you could really notice was Jade. It still makes me laugh now. Literally, all you could hear was Jade's voice because: a) her decibel level was higher than most other people's, b) her laugh was the loudest I'd ever heard, and c) she just didn't shut up.

The producers were slightly divided about Jade, and not everyone was convinced about her potential as a housemate. I thought she was fantastic but some thought she was too loud, too in your face, and that the public wouldn't like her or like watching her. That's the thing about Jade – you either love her or hate her. I wanted to meet her properly, face to face, to see for myself. So we invited her for an interview.

There was just something about Jade; it's an indefinable quality. When she walked into the room she lit it up. And she was fascinating. When I first met her she was only 20 years old, but she'd had such an interesting life. She'd looked after her mum since her mum's accident, her dad was in prison, she'd been done for theft, she had a dodgy boyfriend – she'd really been through the mill. But in spite of all these hardships, she was still an incredibly grounded, normal, very robust person. I remember her interview to this day. I just didn't want her to leave the room because I felt like I could continue talking to her for hours. And if I felt like that, then people would want to keep watching her. I definitely wanted her in the house.

I was the person who made the phone call to Jade to tell her she'd got in. It was a weird conversation. I said, 'I'd like to invite you to be in the *Big Brother* house.' She started hyperventilating, then she screamed, then she dropped the phone. There was a clunk and a silence until she eventually came back on the line. 'Oh, sorry, I fell over,' she told me. I said, 'The important thing is, Jade, you must not tell anybody.' Of course, I knew that as soon as she got off that phone she'd be telling everyone she met. There was a feeling among most people that Jade wouldn't last longer than a week in the *Big Brother* house. But she proved her critics wrong and was there right to the final. She came fourth in the end, but Jade was the true winner of *Big Brother 3*. She was the biggest star, the most memorable person, and she's had the most longevity because she has that extra little something. She's a pretty smart girl too. She might not have known where East Anglia was, but Jade knows who she is, what she's good at, and what she wants.

Introduction

I've just spent two days in Manchester recording a *Celebrity Stars in Their Eyes* special. I won. Can you believe it? Apparently, Jade Goody can actually sing. Bet you never imagined that. I wanted to be Mariah Carey at first – she's my favourite singer of all time. I love her nearly as much as I love my Jimmy Choos. Jeff took me to see her in concert at Wembley about two years ago when I was pregnant with Freddy. People knew who I was by then, but I didn't care. I was crying my eyes out at every song – tears streaming down my cheeks like an idiot. I *loved* her. This woman beside me kept looking at me as if to say 'Calm yourself, love', but I was oblivious. I was standing up on my chair, screaming out loud, 'Oh my God!' Mariah came down this walkway in front of our row and I reached out and started stroking her hand. I was looking at her like she was God or something. Jeff just stood there letting me get on with it. Then Mariah threw these big ball things that she'd signed her name on out into the crowd. I caught one. The woman next to me said, 'You don't need that! You can get one any time.' I just looked at her with the devil in my eyes and replied, 'No. It's mine.' I was not letting go. It was the best concert I've ever been to in my life. Much better than East 17 (*and* I fancied Brian Harvey).

In the end I wasn't Mariah on *Stars in Their Eyes*. I don't think I could've done her justice really. I was a country and western singer called Lynn Anderson instead. Obviously I didn't have a clue that that was her actual name, I just knew I liked the song, 'Rose Garden'. I had learnt the lyrics off by heart, that was the easy part, but trying to sing in her American accent did my head in. I'd already forgotten it was Cat Deeley who hosted the show and said, 'Tonight, Matthew, I'm going to be...' in rehearsals by mistake. It was a mad experience, though, and I could tell nobody was expecting me to be any good. When I first walked out onto the stage I could see two women in the front row rolling their eyes. They looked disgusted. They were clearly convinced I wasn't going to pull it off. But once I opened my mouth the whole audience started standing up and clapping. I couldn't believe I won. People were coming up to me afterwards saying, 'Jade, your voice is amazing – you should get a record contract.'

I thought the radio DJ Neil Fox was going to walk it. He was Dean Martin and he was really good. Martin Offiah, the rugby player, was on it too. He took himself so seriously it cracked me up. He wasn't blessed with a good voice but he's so competitive, he'd had loads of singing lessons beforehand. He was in the changing room practising his scales and warming up his vocal cords, and I was shouting through the wall, 'Oh shut up, Martin!' And guess who else was there? Lucy Ewing – the poison dwarf from *Dallas!* Charlene Tilton's her real name. She was Madonna. It was all very surreal to see everyone in their costumes. I looked a right state. I had a long blonde wig, pink satin trousers, a pink satin shirt and white cowboy boots. If you'd squinted your eyes you might've thought it was me four years ago. I looked exactly the same as I did when I came out of the *Big Brother* house. It was spooky, like I'd gone back in time. It just reminded me of those chants of 'Burn the Pig' – ouch!

* * *

26 July 2002
9.01 p.m.
'Jade – you are the ninth person to leave the *Big Brother* house.'

That's it. My name's been called. I knew it was going to be me. Shit. Shit. What if people throw tomato ketchup on me? I hate tomato ketchup.

9.02 p.m.
The doors won't open. My heart has never been pounding this fast. There's so much noise outside!

9.03 p.m.
Oh my God. They're cheering me! I can hear a couple of boos but that's OK. I'm liked! There's a person dressed as a pig! Hang about, there are loads of people dressed as

pigs. Why is that banner saying, 'We are all the way from East Angular?' Where's East Angular?

9.04 p.m.

I am so happy. I've never seen so many photographers. They're all calling my name. Hang on, how does everyone know my name? Davina has just hugged me. She whispered, 'Look after your money, Jade – you're going to be rich.' What is she on about? I haven't won *Big Brother* – I came fourth! I can't stop smiling. I'm waving at the crowd. I don't know why but I'm holding one hand in the air like the Queen. Someone's just thrown a pair of pants at me! I hope they're clean. I have never felt *anything* like this. The adrenaline is unbelievable.

9.05 p.m.

People keep grabbing me and kissing me. I'm standing in the middle of the stage now. The cheers are so loud. 'You're all chipsticks!' Why did I just shout that? Oops, my boobs are about to pop out of this dress. In fact the whole of me's about to pop out of this dress. This big, ridiculous, pink satin dress. No wonder people are dressed up as Miss Piggy.

9.06 p.m.

Fuck. Does this mean I'm famous?!

Daddy's Little Girl ...?

I've been thinking about my dad's death a lot lately. I don't really know how to deal with it. For the best part of my life I've tried to pretend he didn't exist, or at least that he wasn't the heroin addict I knew him to be. As a young girl I'd sit and daydream about him taking me to playgrounds and fairs and on nice family holidays, but the reality was quite different. OK, so he'd come and visit me once or twice a year, but that would be on the rare occasion he was out of prison. He was behind bars his whole life: 54 convictions, or something like that, I think he had. He wasn't just a drug addict you see, he was a thief. I guess the two things go hand in hand – you steal to pay for your next hit.

I've only ever received two gifts from my dad in my whole life. One was an Armani denim jacket that he'd bought with a stolen credit card. The other one was a picnic box. I'll never forget it. It was white and red with a see—through lid. He'd nicked that from someone's bag. He only gave them to me because he felt guilty for hardly ever seeing me. Otherwise he would've sold them.

He didn't even try to hide his thieving from me – I was often a pretty useful accessory. For a time he had a girlfriend called Vicky who was a heroin addict as well. When he was out of prison they would both come to visit me and take me out to one of the local pubs. Then they'd swipe people's handbags right in front of me. Once, when I was about 7, we were chased down a high street because someone saw him do it. It was horrible.

Dad wasn't a drug addict when he first met my mum, though. He was just a robber then. Oh, and a pimp apparently. I've only just found out how my parents got together. My mum said they first set eyes on each other when she was picking up her social security cheque in the benefit office. Dad was in there with a mate of his and thought she was a bit of all right, so he asked her out. When Mum told me what he did I said, 'A pimp? Please don't tell me you became one of his hookers?!' She looked at me and laughed. 'Nah! I was into all that way before I met him!'

She's joking, luckily. Well, semi-joking. Back in the day, my mum was what was known as a 'clipper'. A clipper is someone who pretends to sort people out with prostitutes but runs off with their money instead. Mum explained it to me the other night. What would happen would be this: she'd stand on the street, looking to any normal member of the public like a prostitute – God knows what she was wearing – my mum's a colourful dresser at the best of times. Then, when a bloke came over asking 'How much?', she'd tell him to give her £100, promising that she'd sort him out with one of her girls. After that she'd disappear round the corner to this local cab office – who were in on the scam because Mum was mates with the owner – then she'd leave the money there and either do a runner or hide upstairs. She laughs about it now. My nan has still got the newspaper cutting from when Mum got arrested. She keeps it like it's a souvenir or something. There's a proper word for what she did – 'soliciting' I think it's called. So as you can see, the fact that my dad was working the game too wasn't a big deal for Mum. Gave them something in common. Romantic, eh?

Dad was only 17 years old when he got together with Mum. He lied, though, and told her he was 21. She was 23 at the time and she gave birth to me nine months later. I wasn't planned. Dad also told Mum he was called Cyrus (his real name's Andrew). God knows why he told her he was called that, but Mum clearly believed him because she went and had a tattoo on her arm saying 'Cyrus' in black ink. Oops. Mind you, my mum has funny ideas about tattoos. Her latest venture is to get one on her la la. I didn't know anything about the fact she was planning to do this until she announced it on national TV. There was a Granada camera crew following me around for my TV series of *Jade's Salon* last year, and she decided to tell them. She'd booked in to our salon to have what is known as a 'Hollywood' (where someone waxes your privates completely bald) and was telling the camera crew about it. I think her exact words were: 'Jade doesn't know but I'm going to have a full tattoo done down there. It's a butterfly and has 16 colours on it. Jade isn't allowed to know until

I've finished it. Once I've had my Hollywood I can have my tattoo done because hair doesn't grow back on tattoos – and when I'm an old lady I can say I've got a pretty fanny.' I was mortified. I would say I've never been so embarrassed in my life, but that would be a lie. My life is full of embarrassing moments.

* * *

I don't really remember Dad being around much when I was a baby. He first went into prison for stealing when I was 6 weeks old. The next time he was put away was just after my first birthday – then he was in and out of there forever.

When I think about my childhood, the first clear memory I've got is of McDonald's. Typical, eh? At least it's not a kebab shop. I had my first birthday party at Macky D's in Peckham. My mum was really friendly with this man called Kelly who worked there. There wasn't anything romantic between them, they were just mates. My mum's got loads of male friends – more than girls, really (yes, I know what you're thinking – *and* she's a lesbian!). Every morning Kelly would come past our house and drop off a breakfast for me and my mum. I used to love it. It was the Big Breakfast, the one with sausage and bacon and scrambled egg. Dad wasn't around for my birthday party. I don't actually know where he was. Mum was there, though, and my dad's sister, Aunty Ingrid. Oh, and Ronald McDonald came out and let us have a look around the kitchen.

Mum and Dad split up when I was about one and a half. My mum chucked him out because she found him hiding guns under my cot. I don't know what he was planning to do with them – rob a bank, probably, or sell them for drug money. Once he started on the drugs, that was it for him, a downward spiral of addiction. He couldn't see what he was doing to himself or his family and he couldn't care less.

Have you seen the film *Trainspotting*? Most people think it's an amazing film. Some think it's quite funny. I sobbed my eyes out when I saw it at the cinema. The scene where Ewan McGregor's character first injects himself made me physically sick. I threw up when it came onto the screen. Properly physically puked. Those faces that he pulls are the same faces I've seen my dad pull, you see. My belly churns whenever I even think about it. I don't want to remember my dad in that way, and I've spent the best part of my life trying to blank it out.

I first saw my dad doing drugs when I was 3 or 4. It was one of those times when he was out of prison for a bit. During those periods he would live with Jackie – his mum, my nan – and sometimes I'd go and stay there with him for the night. On this occasion I woke up in bed to see him stood in the corner of the room putting a needle into his arm. I'll never forget the look on his face. His eyes were rolling into the back of his head and he was shaking. I was scared stiff in case he could see that I'd been watching him. I think I thought he'd tell me off, so I only dared to look a tiny bit. Then I closed my eyes so tightly I thought I'd never be able to blink again. All that was going through my head was, *Why is he sticking needles in his arms? What is he doing that for?* It was his facial expression that scared me the most. That's why I can't watch *Trainspotting*. When I think about it now, I still don't understand it. I know that drug addicts can't help themselves, but surely there's a line

5

you just don't cross? If your four-year-old daughter is lying in your bed, how can you jack up in front of her?

Surprisingly enough, Mum says I was a daddy's girl when I was born. He was constantly checking my breathing in the night, just in case it stopped, and he'd always make sure I fell asleep cuddling one of his socks in my cot, so I had a little part of him there. Ironic how things turn out, eh? Then, when he was in prison, he used to write me letters and draw me pictures. At least he did for a while. The letters got less frequent as I grew up and as his habit got worse.

Even though she didn't agree with what he was doing to himself, it was my mum who'd make sure I saw my dad as often as possible when I was younger. That mostly meant taking me to visit him in prison. I think I've been to nearly every prison in England visiting my dad. I remember going to a prison on the Isle of Wight once and having to speak to him on a telephone while watching him through the glass. I didn't say much. He used to try and talk to me but the whole thing frightened me a bit. Whenever he said something to me it just made me want to crawl all over my mum and cuddle her. I never remember feeling any warmth towards him.

Because my dad was a drug addict, the security guards used to treat me and my mum differently to other visitors. They'd always check inside Mum's mouth in case she was hiding drugs for my dad that she could pass over when she kissed him. On one visit, when I was about 5, the guards did a body search on me and I got really scared. They were patting me up and down all over. I just kept thinking, *Oh my God, am I going to be put in a cell like my dad?*

Daddy's Little Girl ...?

My mum never really sat me down and explained about my dad's situation, that he was hooked on drugs, I just kind of knew. I might not be the sharpest tool in the sandwich box (if that's the right saying) but I'll bet I'm more streetwise than most people my age.

My dad was a scag-head, or a smack-head, which means he was addicted to heroin. You can tell the difference between someone who smokes crack (a stronger form of cocaine) and a scag-head because crack makes you all scatty, but a heroin addict will be really fussy, not with it, and they won't be able to get their words out properly. I used to have lots of conversations with my dad where he'd look at me and pull all these faces like he was really out of it, and it frightened the life out of me. Some times he'd be better than others. The thing is, if you looked at my dad you'd never think he was a heroin addict because he always took care of his appearance. He'd wear designer labels like Hugo Boss and Armani and his shoes would always be immaculate. (Obviously he didn't pay for them, though – they would have been stolen goods, or, at the very least, bought with a dodgy credit card.) It was when you looked into his eyes that you'd know he wasn't normal. He'd have a glazed expression and his pupils would be like pinpricks. And, of course, even if he wasn't high it would only be a matter of minutes before he'd be frantically searching for his next hit.

My dad's side of the family is confusing to me. I don't really know that much about him. I know he was mixed race – which is why I've got such big lips – but I've never even met my dad's dad, my granddad. All I know is that he was a black man who went by the name of Wizard.

Jade: How It All Began

One of my dad's sisters was called Aunty Ingrid. She was such a glamorous woman, always immaculately dressed. My nan, Jackie, was always very well groomed too. She had silvery-white hair and would walk around the house wearing silk shawls. But I think she got her money through suspect means. Mum told me Dad's mum was a madam in a whorehouse for a while. You'll soon realise this is the case for most of my family – they're either plain dodgy or drug addicts. My dad's other sister, Aunty Clare, used to really love me and look after me. But she committed suicide when I was about 12. Took an overdose. Her son, Adam, found her in her bed before he was about to leave for school.

Clare and Adam had lived in North London with my nan and Aunty Ingrid before Aunty Clare died. For a while, when I was really young, I used to go there every Sunday for dinner, but it wasn't like a normal family dinner because half of them were high on drugs. When I'd sit down to eat with my aunties, I knew instinctively that something wasn't quite right about them. I don't know if it was the atmosphere or just the glazed look on their faces. I found out after I came out of *Big Brother* that my nan was a crack-head. That was a nice surprise. My Aunty Clare was no different. She was always either high on something or drunk. She'd stink of alcohol all the time. I remember feeling really confused because on the one hand I loved her so much and wanted nothing more than to be close to her, but at the same time, whenever she came near me I'd think, *Oooh! Aunty Clare, you smell!* She used to have a thing about twisting her hair until she pulled it out. Every now and then I do it too. If I'm in a tricky situation or I'm feeling nervous about something, I'll start fiddling with my hair. I can't help it.

I remember Dad saying to me that he'd had a really hard life. But that wasn't exactly an excuse for doing crack and heroin, was it? At the end of the day there are people out there who've had much harder lives than he ever had and ended up better people for it.

When I was about 6 my dad was dating a woman called Maria. She was really rich. Her daughter, Mandy, who was a lot older than me, had a horse and she was brilliant at showjumping. She also had a Shetland pony and used to let me go down on weekends and groom it. Maria saw how good I was with horses and said she'd buy me my own to ride. I couldn't believe it. It was called Inker because it was black. I'd go to their house and ride Inker every weekend. I wouldn't even see my dad sometimes. It sounds really corny, but riding him made me feel so free. Mandy taught me how to showjump and I entered a few competitions and won some rosettes. Then my dad split up with Maria and he was back in prison soon after. I later found out that not only had Inker been shot because he had a broken leg, but also that my dad had had a relationship with Mandy.

I've got two brothers. One – an older brother – on my mum's side, and one – younger – on my dad's. My mum had her son, Brett, when she was 21, and he's got a different dad to me. Brett got put into foster care when he was 2 because he was found in the house on his own. It wasn't actually my mum's fault, to be fair. She'd left him in the care of his dad while she went to work in the drycleaners that my nan owned down the road. But Brett's dad went out and left him. Mum didn't know anything about it and came home to find a note through the door saying her son had been taken into care. Apparently a neighbour had called to report it after seeing him out of her window. He was walking down the street naked with one red wellington boot on.

Mum was allowed to visit him unsupervised for a while. Then one day something flipped inside her and she tried to kidnap him. She got caught and reprimanded, then lost all contact with him for years after that. I can understand why she did it, though: she just wanted her son back.

The first time I met Brett properly was when I was about 15. He was 18 and came looking for Mum. She was over the moon to see him again because she'd had to sign an agreement that she wouldn't make any contact with him until he was at least that age. We went to meet him in a bar in Bromley, in South London. I can remember thinking, *What's he going to be like? Will he be good-looking? Will he wear cool clothes?* Then when I actually saw him I just thought, *You're a bit of an egg.* It was weird. He looks a lot like my mum, but I just thought he was a geek (my actual words were a bit stronger than that – 'a knob', I think I called him). He was wearing a pair of big, black horrible jeans, battered old Nike running trainers – which you could never even run in, let alone meet your mum in – and he had tattoos all over him. Nasty ones. I just thought, *Look at the state of him!* I have to admit, he annoyed me a bit. We started chatting about what we'd done and I told him what hobbies I was into – then he made out that he'd done them too: I said I did kickboxing, and he reckoned he'd done it too; I said I did modelling, so he said he'd done modelling. It was as if he was trying to be better than me at everything.

After that meeting, Mum invited him to stay with us for a bit. But instead of feeling glad that my brother had come to live with us, I just kept feeling angry at the way he seemed to be treating my mum. She didn't have much money and from what I could see he was really taking the mick out of her. He was constantly on the phone to all his mates and ran up a massive bill, and he was always asking her for money, which she gave him because he's her son. She was so pleased to see him that she couldn't see what he was doing, but to me he was just taking the piss and I didn't like it one bit. I had quite a few arguments with Mum because of him. I used to say, 'He's dirty, he doesn't wash, he makes me feel sick, he's not one of us.' And he was such a know-it-all. I remember sitting watching an episode of *Only Fools and Horses* once – in my own front room – and telling him, 'I love this programme, it's mad to think it's been going for ages, isn't it?' Then he piped up in this really snooty voice: 'Actually, it's been on since 1981.' He always had to go one better than me and it drove me nuts. Another time we sat down to eat our tea, but instead of asking my mum to pass the salt and pepper like any other straightforward normal human being, he had to say, 'Jackiey, have you got any of the condiments please?' (Of course, I couldn't even say that myself, I thought they were called 'continents' for ages.)

I didn't say anything behind his back that I wouldn't say to his face, though. That's not my style. I told Brett exactly what I thought of him on more than one occasion. It might sound to you as if I'm being unnecessarily cruel, but I'm convinced he knew what he was doing. I was a mummy's girl and she was my main concern and I was always looking out for her. Once he tried to suck up to me by giving me money to start a course at beauty college – but I spent it on a flight to visit my nan and granddad who were on holiday in Spain. To his credit, he did take me to an East 17 concert once. But no matter how much I loved Brian Harvey, the experience was soured because I was with my big smelly brother. He lives in Australia now and has a baby. When I came out of the *Big Brother* house, the *Sun* newspaper set up this whole big reunion thing for us. At that time they couldn't have known that we really didn't get on, and with anyone else it would've been a really nice thing to have done for them. My mum was all excited about meeting up again, but I just thought it was bullshit, to be honest. I think everyone thought I'd run into his arms and say 'I love you'. But inside I just thought, *I don't even like you*. Please don't think I'm being nasty, though: I'm just not keen on him.

I've got another brother too. His name is Miles, but I doubt he even knows that's his name. He certainly doesn't know his sister is Jade Goody, that's for sure. When I was about 13 my dad had a kid with his girlfriend Vicky – the one who was a drug addict. Thing is, they were both on smack, and Vicky never stopped using drugs while she was pregnant. So when Miles was born he would cluck; 'clucking' is what an addict does when they need another hit. So Miles wouldn't cry for food, he would cluck because his body was screaming out for drugs. He was born a heroin addict. It was horrific. Social services knew this and told my dad he needed to prove he was off the heroin before they'd let him keep the baby. So he begged me to do a urine sample for him – he wanted to pass it off as his own. What did I know? I was only a teenager. All I wanted was for my dad to be happy, and he looked so scared that he might lose his son. So I did it. They didn't believe him in the end, though, they knew he'd tried to pull a fast one, so Miles was taken into care. As to whether the heroin addiction he was born with has affected him in later life, I don't know because I don't know where he is or how to get hold of him. One day I hope I'll be able to track him down though and tell him he's got a sister. I'd like to let him know he had some family who would have loved him.

2
Cops and Robbers

Mum never owned her own house when I was younger – we always lived in council flats. Our first place was in Queens Road in Peckham, and in the lounge we had this nasty wallpaper with black thistles all over it. We also had beanbags, which were black with gold trim. Ugh. Minging.

It's mostly always been just me and my mum, but the house was often full because she'd have friends round. I liked them, though: they were never threatening to me and I was always the centre of attention. Every night – and most days, come to think of it – my mum would hold puffing sessions. She was always stoned.

I rolled my first joint when I was 4. I used to skin up for my mum, even before she lost the use of her left arm. And I had my first puff when I was 5. It was sitting in the ashtray so I picked it up and took a big long drag, just like I'd seen her and her mates do. She didn't tell me off either

– she took a picture! I've still got it somewhere: there's me in a little white vest dragging on this joint like a pro. It's pretty bizarre.

Mum's not like my dad, though; she'd never get involved in hard drugs. Her only vice was weed, and she smoked it because it kept her mellow. Otherwise I think she might've gone mad (well, madder than she already was, anyway). I used to love rolling joints for her and her pals, it felt like I was part of the group. For the whole of my childhood I was always surrounded by adults having grown-up conversations and I lapped it up. As a consequence, I was taught at a very early age to speak my mind. If I wanted something I had to ask for it, otherwise I'd never get it. So I wasn't exactly polite. I went round to other people's houses and would say things like, 'I'm hungry. Can I have a sandwich?' Once I went with Mum to visit a friend she hadn't seen for ages, and as soon as we got inside her house I shouted, 'Mum, it stinks in here, I can't stay!' But I was only telling the truth like my mum had always told me to. I wasn't really a rude kid.

Most of Mum's friends were male and most of them were black. One was called Paul, and I thought he was *soooo* handsome. He was a big black man who used to come round to our house and sit and have a puff with Mum. He was probably my first ever crush. Whenever he came over I'd manoeuvre it so I always sat next to him. If he sat on the settee I'd hardly give him any space at all; I think there's even a picture of me somewhere, virtually sitting on top of him, poor guy. So it made sense that I had an imaginary friend (or boyfriend) called Paul too. I had a Wendy House where me and 'Paul' would sit for hours, discussing our future family. Then when I was given a Cabbage Patch Kid for my birthday, I naturally told everyone his dad was called Paul.

Mum had a fair few boyfriends when I was young, but most of them treated her well. I did see one of them smack a phone over her face once. I can't remember what his name was. Another tried to chuck a hot kettle of water over my nan too. I used to hate it because I was too scared to intervene, but I'd feel really sad and disappointed with myself afterwards. I felt like I hadn't done anything to protect my mum, so I'd sob and sob. I always used to tell myself I was never going to let myself be treated by a man the way she was treated (how wrong I was). Of course, Mum doesn't have any boyfriends now. She bats for the other side. 'JADE'S MUM – THE ONE-ARMED LESBIAN', isn't that how the papers referred to her when I first came out of *Big Brother?* They must've loved it when they dug that one up. Mum's never really made a big song and dance about the fact that she now likes women rather than men, and for some reason I've never felt the need to ask her. She was always attracted to women anyway, even when she had boyfriends. The way I see it, she just got fed up with men so it was obvious she'd turn to the ladies!

I can't remember when I got told about mum being bisexual. I think I just knew from an early age. I've never seen her properly kiss a woman full-on, though. In fact, the whole lesbian thing seems to make my mum cringe. She's very funny like that. When I was about 16 years old I remember saying to her, 'Do you go down on a woman then? Because it makes me feel ill.' She recoiled in horror as if I'd said the most disgusting thing in the world. 'Ugh, oooh no!' she shrieked.

I got really confused at that point. 'What do you mean, "oooh no"? How can you be a lesbian then?'

Mum says she doesn't mind it the other way round, if they do things to her – it's all about her getting all the pleasure, she couldn't care less about the other person! She reckons she's never gone down on a man in her life, either. I discovered this when I first tried talking to her about blow jobs. 'It makes me feel ill,' were her words to me. She told me I had to try it, though, just to see what it was like for myself. But all that comes later – I'm still only 4 years old at the moment, and I haven't even told you about my mum's accident yet.

I enjoyed my little life at home with Mum. She was heavily involved in a scam called 'kiting' back then. For most people 'kiting' would probably mean flying a bit of material in the air on a string, but to me it was a way of getting a nice new pair of shoes or food for our tea. It's the word used for people who 'borrow' somebody else's cheque book and bank card. One person would nick the cheque book and card, then they'd sell them on to people like my mum and her mate Sharon for £20. Then Mum would just have a field day, rinsing the life out of them in whatever shop she chose. She had a right old racket going on, but it was just a normal, everyday part of life for me. When Mum got a new cheque book and card in the post she'd sit there for hours practising the signature. Sometimes I'd practise doing it too. Needless to say, mine weren't particularly convincing. This would mean that one day when we went shopping she'd be called 'Mrs Smith', and the next she'd be 'Mrs Rogers', 'Mrs Farquar' or whatever. I think I knew it was illegal but I didn't really understand it, and it definitely didn't scare me. What did scare me was the thought of my mum getting sent to prison like my dad. That would have cut me up inside. She was the most important thing in my life, and I was in hers. Then we got caught once when I was about 4 years old, and I very nearly lost her.

We were in Lewisham, me, Mum, Sharon and her daughter Sam (my best mate at the time). We were in a supermarket – I don't even remember what its name was. Mum went to pay for the stuff she'd put in her basket and the shop assistant was taking ages to put it through. This was when we knew something was wrong, or 'on top' as we called it. Mum said you always knew when it had come 'on top' because there would be lots of waiting around once you'd tried to pay for the goods, and the shopkeeper would always look awkward and uncomfortable. And on that day the shop assistant was definitely looking both those things. Mum looked at Sharon and whispered, 'On top! On top!' In other words, 'They've caught us out.' The ridiculous thing was, they hadn't actually got caught for having a stolen cheque book and card. The CCTV camera had spotted Sharon nicking something on her way round the aisles and putting it in her pocket. Stupid woman. What exactly was the point of that? They weren't even paying with their own money! Some people just can't help themselves.

As soon as I realised my mum was in trouble my heart started beating like a wild thing. I kept thinking, *Oh my God, Oh my God*. The strange thing was, I was a little bit excited as well. It was a buzz. The next thing we knew, a security guard had come over. He said, 'Come with me please' in a really deep voice, and we were all marched to a room at the back of the shop. I just kept looking round, saying, 'Where are we going?' with a cheeky grin on my face. Sam, on the other hand, was sobbing her eyes out. I don't think she had a clue what was going on. There was a desk in the room covered in tapes, they were piled everywhere – from the CCTV cameras, I suppose. Sam and I were told to sit at the back of the room while my mum and Sharon were interrogated. One of the security guys kept asking us to tell him what had happened. I just sat there pretending I couldn't speak, like I was dumb or something. I pointed to my mouth and shook my head. It didn't occur to me that merely a few seconds earlier I'd been shouting my mouth off and asking where we were going. I think I fancied myself as a bit of an actress, so I was getting quite a kick out of it. It was just a shame Sam wasn't on the same wavelength as me. As soon as they asked her a question she blurted out, 'My mum's called Sharon,' then started spelling out her surname and address. I was elbowing her in the ribs, trying to get her to shut up. She'd blown our cover: according to the cheque book she'd been using that day, 'Sharon' was meant to be called 'Linda'. So we were sussed immediately and the police were called.

That was when it started getting scary. The police said they wanted to do a raid on our house, and I knew that if they did then my mum would definitely be sent down. I could not let that happen. Mum was dating a guy called Arthur at the time and I thought he was at home. I knew that if the police got inside and Arthur hadn't been warned, they'd have plenty of grounds to lock Mum up for good. She didn't just have one cheque book and card, she had loads of them – and right now they were sprawled all over the lounge in our house. Not only that, but there were half-smoked spliffs in the ashtrays and bags of weed on the table. I might've only been young, but I knew instantly what I needed to do. The thought of my mum ever going to prison would've killed me, so I had to protect her.

We were escorted from the shop and told to get into the police car. As we drove nearer to our house, I started saying to the driver, 'I'm dying to go for a wee!', to which he just nodded and said we'd be there soon. 'I need a wee badly!' I begged. In the end, by the time we started to pull up outside the house, I'd opened the door of the police car and pegged it towards the front door before anyone could follow me. I didn't need a wee at all, of course. As soon as I got to the door, I yelled for Arthur through the letterbox: 'Arthur, Arthur! On top! On top!' There was no reply. He wasn't there after all.

My heart was pounding so much I thought it might fly out of my mouth and land on the doorstep. But luckily, when I turned the handle the door was open. I didn't even think twice. I rushed into the house and grabbed all the cheque books, cards and puff that I could see. I must've looked like that cartoon character that flies about with a whirlwind behind him – the Tasmanian Devil. I was on a mission and speed was essential. I knew the police must've parked up by now and were about to come in the door behind me. I also knew the officers didn't suspect a thing, because to them I was just a normal four-year-old who needed the loo.

I headed for the kitchen and opened the freezer drawer, picking up a bag of oven chips. Without stopping for a second, I emptied half the chips out and put everything – all the cards, chequebooks, everything – into the bottom of the chip bag. Don't ask me why. I don't know how the hell I even thought to do it. It was like I was on automatic pilot or something. This burning desire to protect my mum just took over me.

As soon as I'd put the chips back on the top and shoved the bag back into the bottom of the freezer drawer, the police came in. My mum was terrified. You could see on her face she was just thinking, This is it. But, thanks to me, the police couldn't find anything. I'd hidden it all. As they looked around the lounge I watched my mum's facial expression change from fear to complete bewilderment. She was just utterly puzzled. Where had it all gone? It wasn't until a couple of hours after the police had left, and Sharon and Sam had gone home too, that I took her to the freezer to show her what I'd done. I had this proud look on my face as I led her down the hallway and exclaimed, 'Mum! Look what I did!' When she saw inside the chip bag she broke down in tears and gave me the biggest cuddle ever. She kept saying, 'Oh my God, my baby, my baby!' I was so pleased with myself that I'd managed to save my mum. I knew I'd been dishonest, but I had such a sense of achievement. All I kept thinking was, *I've just helped you, Mum*. I went to bed a very happy girl that night.

Cops and Robbers

My nan and granddad have always lived near us for as long as I can remember. Mum seems to have followed them wherever they went. Whenever they moved, she moved straight afterwards, and pretty much next door. My granddad John wasn't my mum's real dad, though – my nan had left my real granddad because he used to beat her up when my mum was young. I always loved going to Nan and Granddad John's. They would spoil me rotten. I think my mum felt a bit of animosity towards Granddad John, although to this day she admits she doesn't know why, because my granddad has always treated my nan like a princess. It's probably because he used to tell her off when she was at school. You can't blame him, really. Mum was a very naughty kid. She chopped someone's ponytail off in school once because they didn't give her the fiver she'd told them to nick out of their mum's purse. Oh, and she pierced someone's bum with a drawing pin because they were picking on her mate. She was quite mental – and still is.

It's difficult asking my mum to remember things because of her accident. When she lost the use of her left arm she also lost some of her memory. She didn't even know who I was for about two months.

My mum's life changed forever on 31 August 1986. I was five years old. It was about 6 p.m. and we were in our house with Tony, her boyfriend at the time. Mum was cooking dinner: chicken, rice and peas – my favourite. There was a knock at the door; it was my Uncle Budgie. (God knows why we called him that, his real name was Martin.) He was the loveliest man ever. Uncle Budgie lived with my nan and granddad John down the road. He was their first child together (which made him my mum's half-brother) and was really precious to them. He was all excited because his mate had lent him a motorbike for a few days, and he told Mum he was going out to get my nan some fags, then asked if she wanted anything. I remember Mum answering, 'No, but I definitely want to come with you if you're going on that bike.' So she told Tony to keep an eye on me and the dinner.

Over an hour passed and I knew something was wrong. I heard my nan at the door talking to Tony and she was saying, 'Jackiey and Martin are in hospital' in a really shaky voice. Tony was panicking, telling me to get in the car. It all happened so fast, it's a bit of a blur now. I can picture myself at the hospital and the doctors telling my nan and granddad that my Uncle Budgie was dead. He had died instantly from internal bleeding. They were sobbing and sobbing. I just stood there in the corner, staring at them. Then my nan took me aside and told me not to tell my mum that my uncle had died. But I didn't understand what being dead meant. I knew it was bad, but I couldn't register what it was. I just felt numb and kept looking at them all, wondering why they were behaving like that.

On the way to the shop, Uncle Budgie's bike had hit a kerb. It was later discovered that this kerb had been built too far out in the road, which meant the council were at fault. On impact, my mum and the bike had flown up in the air and hit a tree. You can still see the scars on the tree now (Mum always points it out when we walk past; it's near an area in Bermondsey called 'The Blue'). My mum's left arm was dislocated, there was something wrong with her neck, she had broken her collarbone and her eye had fallen under her cheekbone (so now she's got one really tiny pupil, which makes people think she's on drugs all the time). She's got a big scar down her leg too, and she's lost all feeling in her left arm.

I was taken into the room where my mum was and there were tubes sticking out everywhere. I could barely recognise her, her face was covered in bruises. Immediately I said, 'Mum, Mum! Uncle Budgie's died!' I soon realised why I'd been told not to tell her. She tried to rip her tubes out and the heart–rate monitor started to make funny beeping noises. Those words very nearly killed my mum. Everyone was in chaos trying to calm her down and keep me away at the same time. I didn't know what had happened – the doctors were rushing in with all these silver machines. My nan told me off but she didn't shout. I think I'd have throttled me if I was her, but she just said I was naughty and shouldn't have done it.

My mum lost her memory for a while after that. It came back slowly after Nan and Granddad John showed her pictures to see if she could remember any of her previous life. She got there in the end, but it certainly took a while – she was all over the place and getting everyone's names wrong for months.

I remember visiting her once in Stanmore Orthopedics, where they were trying to make her better. I went with Granddad John and we bought fish and chips and a gherkin on the way. All I could think about was what this gherkin was. For the entire visit I asked questions like, 'Why is it green?', 'Why does it smell of vinegar?', 'How does it grow?' and 'What's it made of?' You'd never think I hadn't seen my mother for a few months.

Mum was in hospital for two years, on and off. I'd stay

with my nan when she was in there, and Mum and I would live back in our house when she was out. Which was hard, for both of us.

My mum looked awful. She was so, so thin, and she had her paralysed arm in a sling for ages. The doctors wanted to amputate it but she said no. They tried her out with a false hand for a bit; it had a funny gadget on the end to pick things up, but she hated it. So she decided to keep both her arms, but the left one is pretty much dead and she always places her left hand in a pocket so as not to draw too much attention to it. The thing is, Mum was left-handed, so she had to learn to do everything like writing, cooking and brushing her hair all over again. That's why she got so frustrated.

Losing the use of her arm was infuriating for my mum, and as a result she often beat me. She felt helpless. I had to do all the chores around the house because she couldn't pick anything up. I was five years old and I did it all – the cooking, cleaning, ironing (I don't even do this now but I did then!). She had dreadlocks for a time, so I had to do her hair. I remember having to split it into sections so I could wash it. It took hours. I'd stay up until some stupid o'clock in the morning and then fall asleep at my desk at school the next day. Of course, I didn't always get it right, and if I burnt the dinner or one of the shirts I was ironing, Mum would get annoyed and she'd lash out. She hit out from pure frustration more than anything, and I never once held it against her. I didn't ever think, *I hate my mum*, no matter what she did to me. I just took it on the chin because I wanted to protect her. My mum was the only person I'd ever had in my life, and I was determined to do everything to make sure no one took her away from me.

But then it happened. One night she beat me with a belt and my bum was so, so sore it was bruised all over. It was only over something silly, but to her it was a massive deal because she felt so annoyed and helpless. I still didn't ever blame my mother, though, and I'd hate for someone to say I did. I truly believe that my mum made me the person I am today, and I think I'm a great mum. But this time she'd lost control and she knew it. I went to school the next day and the teachers knew something was up straight away. I couldn't sit on the carpet during reading time because it hurt too much. I was aching all over. I tried to sit down and ended up yelping 'Ooh, ooh!', so of course the teacher noticed. She immediately took me to the nurse, who asked what had happened, and I said I'd fallen off my bike. But they weren't stupid, and Social Services were called.

To be fair to my mum, she called Social Services herself before that incident. After hitting me with a belt one night, she rang them and said, 'I'm scared of what I might do to my daughter.' You might think that's strange because she was at risk of someone taking me away, but she honestly didn't want anything bad to happen to me. She might beat me on the bum or smack me in the face, but immediately afterwards she'd feel remorse and break down in tears saying, 'I'm so sorry.' I never tried to hit her back, though. I've only ever hit her once, when I was 18, and we'd had a huge argument. And she gave me a bloody black eye in return!

The night before Social Services came round to take me away, I just lay in my bed, sobbing. They came on a

Monday and I knew it was going to happen. As they entered the house, I begged, 'Please don't do this to me. Don't take me away from my mum.' I was pleading with my mum not to let me go, but she kept saying, 'It won't be for long. You have to go for your own good. It'll be OK.' I screamed, 'Please, Mum! I don't want to go.' Both of us were clinging on to each other in desperation, crying and crying. Then they drove me away in this white car and I looked out the back window to see my mum getting smaller and smaller as she stood at the front door, watching us drive away, tears streaming down her face.

Nothing was said to me that whole journey except, 'You're going to a new family. You're going to have a sister and a brother.' I was thinking, *No, no, please, no.* I didn't want a new family, I wanted my old one.

I was sent to stay with a foster family who lived far away in the countryside somewhere. I don't know what the place was called, I just know it was a long way from where my mum lived because the journey took ages. And I hated it. I *hated* it. It honestly still makes the tears well up when I think about it now. It was the worst time of my life. My mum was told it would be a three-week break so she could sort herself out. What did they tell me? Nothing. I had absolutely no idea how long I was going to be there, and for all I knew I was never going to see my mum again.

It was a big house and they had one of those dogs with loads of hair, like in the Dulux adverts. I had a little old suitcase with me. When I got there, I was greeted by the mum and the dad and there was a girl and a younger boy playing in the driveway. It all seemed very posh. I can't even remember their names because I hated it so much I've tried to erase it from my memory. They were trying to be nice to me at first and when I arrived they gave me a glass of milk to drink. I don't like milk, it makes me feel sick. Even now just the smell of it makes me want to vomit and it brings back visions of that family and them forcing me to do things I didn't want to do. I had a permanently queasy feeling in the pit of my stomach when I was there.

They had a big garden with swings and a pond. I played in the garden some of the time, but I just wanted to go home. I felt like an outcast. As time wore on the mum and dad started treating me noticeably differently to their real kids. Their daughter, the girl, was a bit older than me – I think she was about 11 – and the boy was about five. I must've been about six. At mealtimes I was convinced I'd get given less food than them. We often had chicken nuggets and baked beans and they were always given a huge plateful. I wasn't used to eating food like that, because my mum would insist on making me proper meals like chicken, rice and peas. The stuff they were serving up was what my mum called 'rubbish food', and I felt like I was betraying her by eating it. I didn't really like their kind of food either, but I was scared that if I said anything and they thought I was being naughty, they'd keep me there for longer. But I wanted to go home so much, I'd have done anything not to make a fuss or give them a reason to keep me there. They'd give me about three chicken nuggets and a spoonful of beans. Then I'd look at the others' plates and they were piled high. All that went through my head was, *They don't like me as much as their own kids.* But then I suppose I didn't like them as much as my own mum, I just had to get on with it.

Jade: How It All Began

It wasn't until I'd been there for at least two weeks that I was told I wasn't staying forever, I was going home eventually. I think I was there for about a month in total. A woman from Social Services came round to check up on me a few times and she would ask how I was getting on. She would take me to my own room so no one could influence what I was saying, but it didn't seem to make a difference. When I told her about them forcing me to drink milk and said that I felt like they were picking on me, she didn't believe me. She just thought I was being a stupid little girl. She told me the milk was 'good for me' and didn't seem to understand that I hated it and that drinking it was like the worst form of punishment.

The family made me wear long socks too. I think the social worker found it funny that I thought this was such a bad thing, but she just didn't understand – it was messing with my head. I *hated* long socks. My mum would always let me push socks down when I wore them at school, but this lady made me pull them right up and wear them with sandals and shorts. To me that was a fashion *crime*. I just couldn't do it, so I'd push them down whenever the lady wasn't looking. Every time I did, I got into deep trouble. She would make me go and stand on my own in the middle of the garden. Once she wrenched them back up and leant right into my face, shouting, 'Keep them up!'

They weren't so strict with their own children. I don't know why people like that are allowed to take kids on. I spent most of the time crying in my room, but, of course, then they'd tell me off for crying. I wasn't even allowed to talk to my mum on the phone, apart from maybe once. It was horrible. I would tell the social worker I wasn't allowed to talk to her, then, when confronted with this, the family would say I was lying and that of course they'd never *dream* of stopping me talking to my mum. That would just make me all confused and I'd start to question whether I had actually spoken to Mum or not in the first place. It was like mental torture. I'd also lie awake worrying myself stupid that Mum wasn't being looked after. I was so used to caring for her myself. Was she even still alive?

When I finally returned home to my mum and told her what I'd been through she got so angry – just not with me this time. The hitting stopped. I can't remember any more bad times after that. She'd still get stressed for having to get used to a whole new way of living, but she'd never take it out on me.

We had a home help for a while, but Mum couldn't handle it. She didn't like someone else cleaning her house or doing her work, so we got rid of her after about a week. Then it was down to me to do all the chores and errands; I was like a proper little Cinderella. But we were struggling for money. Mum's accident left her unable to work, which meant sometimes we'd find ourselves sitting in the house without any electricity. She wasn't getting on with Nan and Granddad either. I think they blamed her for Uncle Budgie's death. It must've been really hard for them to lose their only son. Still, they were never bad to me, and they'd never let me see or hear them talk about it. The main bone of contention was that they'd got compensation for Uncle Budgie's accident – I'm not sure how much, but it was a lot – and Mum would have steaming rows with them because they wouldn't give any to her. Eventually she got what she was owed from the council, but it took a long while.

In the meantime she'd be having rows with my granddad because she needed money to top up our electricity key and he refused to lend it to her. So we made do with candles instead. Mum had a dresser/wardrobe thing with a mirror in the middle and two ledges with candle holders on either side. We'd light the candles and sit in her bedroom playing games like snakes and ladders, hangman or noughts and crosses. One evening, we were playing snakes and ladders and we both dozed off. When I woke up the place was on fire. Flames were licking through the wardrobe and all that kept ringing through my head was, *We're going to die*. I didn't know what to do. It was really hard trying to wake Mum up because she was on all these painkillers for her arm – the more I tried to rouse her, the more I knew I was wasting time because the fire was burning even more. Mum was still struggling to cope with using one arm, so I knew that when she did eventually stir she wouldn't be capable of doing much.

When she opened her eyes drowsily it took a good few minutes for her to comprehend what was going on. I dragged her out of the house with all my might and ran like a maniac to my nan and granddad's round the corner. I drummed on the door and howled for them to call the firemen. Once the fire had been put out, Mum went ape at Nan and Granddad. 'It's your fault,' she yelled. 'You couldn't even give me a tenner to pay for the electric!' They stopped talking for ages after that. I still went to visit them, but Mum was having none of it. I couldn't understand why she was so angry with them myself – they spoilt me rotten and I loved them to bits. Mum used to say they bought my love, but I couldn't see it. They told me I was their little angel.

Sometimes we didn't even have enough money for loo roll, until one day a cheque landed on the doormat. It was from the council: Mum's compensation from the accident. I never knew quite how much it was for, but from the way Mum subsequently started splashing the cash, I figured it was a pretty hefty amount.

Not long after that, Mum and I went on a family holiday to Jersey with my nan and granddad. They were on speaking terms since Mum's windfall, but there was still a bit of tension. I must've been about seven years old. I remember having tea and scones with my granddad outside a house made of pearls, and the tea tasted awful. One night I got up on stage in this holiday camp and sang 'Papa Don't Preach' by Madonna. I was wearing a green dress and afterwards I refused to get off the stage, so when the can-can dancers came on for their performance I just joined in.

I adored performing. After school I did tap dancing, jazz, ballet, the lot. My Madonna album was my favourite and I would alternate between playing that and Bros on my white plastic record player. I was in love with Bros. I would've married all three of them at the same time if I could. I reckon I was one of the first Brosettes to wear those ridiculous Grolsch bottle tops on my shoes. I was always singing songs around the house, which made Mum and her mates crack up laughing. I had great ambitions to be a singer for a while. I would hole myself up in my bedroom for hours on end, then emerge, all dolled up like a dickhead, and perform for whoever was in the house at the time.

My speciality was 'The Greatest Love of All' by Whitney Houston, and I honestly thought I was her for a time. Mum would video me and take tons of photos. I took it so seriously that once I came home and said to her, really poker-faced, 'Don't call me Jade, please, call me Whitney.'

Mum's compensation money meant we could move to a slightly bigger house in Bermondsey. It's the same place Mum still lives in today. Now I could have my own room – I was sharing with Mum before that – and I had it decorated with wallpaper that was pink with purple bows on it. It was still a bit of a grotty council house, though; we never really lived in a lovely place with a nice interior. Mum bought a black leather sofa with some of the money she got. The rest of it she lent to people, most of whom never paid her back. She'd always do anything for anyone. She never saved any of that money at all. We got a few holidays out of it, though. Mum's a bit of a free spirit and she wanted to travel all over the world.

We went to Spain first, and I had a whale of a time for two weeks, sunbathing on the terrace in my pants. Next we went to Egypt, where we stayed for over a month. It wasn't planned, though; Mum wasn't the type to go to Thomas Cook and book a package holiday weeks in advance. She'd just say, 'Right, we're going to Egypt tomorrow.' She never bought return tickets either; her theory was, 'We'll go out there, stay as long as we want, then come home.'

I remember getting to Cairo and thinking, *Eww! This place is dirty!* It was boiling hot and dusty. I liked seeing the Pyramids though. They were stunning. We stayed in a five-star hotel, which was so posh we felt like someone was going to chuck us out any second for not fitting in. We were there for so long that the manager used to invite us round to his house for dinner with his family all the time. I think he must've felt sorry for us. I remember sitting on the floor to eat and his wife put paper down, then laid all the dishes out and said, 'You eat with your hands.' I picked up this thing that I'd spotted on the floor next to me and said, 'What's that?' It was all fluffy, like the inside of a mattress. Turns out it was a dead rat that had mummified because it had been there for so many years! I threw it across the room, wailed 'I'm never eating here again', and stormed out.

Believe it or not, I'm a surprisingly unfussy eater and I don't mind trying unusual things. Mum and I ordered this thing called 'escalope' every night from room service. Because we were practically living there, the hotel cooked for us more or less whenever we wanted. These escalopes were the best thing ever and I thought it was chicken with breadcrumbs all over it. I later found out that these Egyptian escalopes were made of camel. Oh my God! We had our own cab driver while we were there, and it was he who told us. I called him 'Lucky Seven' because he had dice hanging in his window and we felt lucky when we were with him because he drove us everywhere we wanted. One day I saw a lorry packed to the rafters with these poor, tired-looking animals. I said to him, 'Where are all those camels going?' and he replied, 'To get slaughtered.' I was appalled. 'What? You eat camel out here?!' 'Yes,' came the answer, 'it's called escalope.' Mum and I both went white as a sheet and my legs went all funny and goosepimply. I thought I was going to throw up. I couldn't believe I'd eaten such a nice animal. We ate it again that night, though. It was far too tasty.

We were in Egypt for such a long time that Mum decided she should put me in a school over there. It was very weird. I had to try and read in Arabic and learn their special alphabet. And they read their books backwards. I just sat at the back of the class, looking confused and scratching my head most of the time. I wasn't allowed to wear shorts either, because you had to cover your body up. I would sit there thinking, *What am I doing here? This is odd. And why am I reading backwards?* I think Mum soon recognised that it was a waste of time because she let me stop going after about a week. Anyway, I'd thought it was meant to be a holiday.

Mum spent most of her days smoking those fancy pipes in the cafés. They're called Shelia or Sheesha pipes or something, and they come with different flavours of tobacco like apple and orange and things. Mum used to put her puff in there, though, and just sit around with a big fat grin on her face, chatting up the locals. Then, one day, without a flicker of warning, she announced, 'We're going home now.' So that was that. When I got back to school in Bermondsey the other kids called me brown girl in the ring and clapped their hands. I loved having a suntan. Mum and I are both sun-worshippers; in the summer we would cover ourselves in cooking oil and lie in the garden on a sheet of silver paper.

We'd go off on holiday all the time after that, for literally weeks in a row, and once again I'd never know until the day before. After Egypt we went to Lagos in Nigeria. I remember getting in the hotel pool because Mum wanted to take my picture, and all these kids started grabbing me. I think I was the only white person there. I made friends with three boys – one was really rich and the other two were really poor. They all got on so well. It was like there was no class divide and no prejudice out there. You'd never get that in Bermondsey. We stayed in Africa for about three or four weeks.

Mum liked to do things on a whim. As I got slightly older, it was perfectly normal for me to come home from school to an empty house. I'd think, *Where the hell is my mum?* and my mind would be racing because I'd worry that something had happened to her. Then I'd go to the kitchen and see a note stuck on the fridge saying something like, *'The food is in the freezer. The electricity key is on the side. I've gone to Scotland for the weekend.'* I'd read it and think, *Oh, OK then.* Most of the time it didn't bother me as long as I knew where she was but, looking back, it's not the way I would have done things. Occasionally, when she left notes like this, I'd phone her up and tell her off for being so irresponsible, then she'd whinge at me as if she were *my* daughter: 'Oh, sorry, Jade! But my mates were all going to this party and you weren't there to tell! I didn't want to miss out!' I was more like her mum than the other way round. You'd think I'd at least see an empty house as an opportunity to invite all my mates round and have a wild party, wouldn't you? It never even crossed my mind. I was proud, you see; I didn't want people coming over to my place, because I was embarrassed. Our house was never properly decorated because Mum would always start things and not finish them. All our rooms were half decorated – except my bedroom. So I just didn't bother. Instead, I'd get home from school, watch telly, have my tea, then go to bed.

Jade: How It All Began

I sold my bed once. I was about seven years old. I used to hang out with a girl called Zoe who lived across the road. We would play in my bedroom for hours. Mum often left us there while she went to visit one of the neighbours. I had this red metal cabin bed with stairs down the side, and Zoe loved it. She'd always come round and say, 'I want that bed!' So one day I decided to sell it to her. I said, 'It's yours for £50.' Zoe looked at me as if I'd gone mad, and said, 'How do I get that much money?' So I thought about it for a while and realised she had a point, so in the end I said I'd sell it to her for £25. Zoe ran home and got the cash off her mum, who obviously thought it was a bargain or that we were just playing a game. But we were deadly serious. The bed was put together with those screws that you need a flat screwdriver for, and I couldn't find any of them, so we took it apart with kitchen knives. We didn't have a clue what we were doing but it came apart all the same. I was quite handy with a tool: I'd already had to learn to change a plug after Mum's accident. Zoe went over the road and told her mum that we needed her help to move it, and that was that, bed sold. When my mum came home she just looked at me in disbelief. She didn't have a go at me because I think a part of her actually found it quite funny. The downside was, I had to sleep with her for ages after that until we had enough money for a new bed. I bought some wicked new shoes with the money Zoe gave me, though.

Mum bought a caravan with some of her cash from the council. She kept it on a site in Canvey Island in Essex and we'd stay there at weekends and school holidays. They used to hold karaoke competitions in the nearby pub and, when I was about 10 or 11, I would insist on being the first up there, lording it about in my baggy MC Hammer trousers. I'd started to turn into a bit of a tearaway by then, though, and got us kicked out of the caravan site for terrorising the neighbours. I was mates with the fairground people who used to set up the fair nearby, and we played tricks on people we didn't like. We'd stand and shake their caravans, then light pieces of paper and leave it outside their front door. The thing is, we'd put dog poo on the paper first, which meant that when they came outside and stamped out the fire they were treading in poo.

3

'Goody – See the Headmaster Now!'

It was normal for me not to be at school much when I was younger. I was off loads after Mum's accident because I stayed up doing chores until God knows what time, so I often overslept. Then there were the extended holidays and modelling assignments. Yes, you did hear me right: Jade Goody was a model in her youth, believe it or not. When I was two, Mum sent my picture to a model agency called Scallywags in Essex. I did quite a few TV adverts as a result, until the age of seven when I started caring for Mum. Even though I didn't get the job, my favourite audition was for a Starlight Barbie commercial. I was playing the main girl and I had to skate about on rollerskates, then all of a sudden I got turned into a Barbie doll. I think the directors liked me because I wasn't one of those precocious kids who turned up smothered in make-up thinking they were it. I was also in the Milky Bar advert. I was part of the crowd of kids who shouted, 'Look! It's the

Milky Bar kid!' We didn't get free Milky Bars though. Not that Mum would have let me eat them anyway.

That was the only real thing that Mum was strict about – my teeth. At school all my friends would be allowed bags of sweets at breaktime and I'd have to make do with an apple and some crisps. Whenever I asked her for chocolate she'd just shake her head and say 'No'. Even when I was a teenager she watched me like a hawk to make sure my teeth were brushed before I went to bed. She used to get up in the night and feel my toothbrush, and if it wasn't wet she'd wake me up and march me to the bathroom. I remember coming in drunk from a nightclub when I was 16, staggering into bed, then hearing this banging on my bedroom wall. Mum was half-asleep in the next room shouting, 'Oi! Brush your teeth!'

I modelled for quite a few catalogues too. Back then I wasn't self-conscious at all, I was always pretty sure of myself. I'd try and keep the modelling thing quiet when I was at school, though, in case some of the kids got a bit jealous. Of course, my mum wanted the whole world to know what her Jade was up to, she so wasn't good at keeping her mouth shut. This caused a few fights in the playground, but it was nothing I couldn't handle. There was a girl called Nicola Walker who used to give me the most shit. We were both in the same class at St James's Primary School. But then I got her back because I went to her house once and saw her eating cat food. So I told everyone.

My mates and I spent most of the time hanging around a stone in the playground because we thought it was haunted and had convinced ourselves there were people buried underneath it. It was just a little square block of concrete! We'd stand there, holding hands and chanting 'spirits of St James's, come out!' The teachers must have wondered what the hell we were doing. I don't know what I would have done if any spirits really had decided to come out. I've never even done Ouija board because I'm too much of a wimp.

I took kickboxing lessons when I was about seven, as Mum knew a lady who taught it. I got really into it for a while and she told me I was good enough to be in the England youth team, but training was such hard work that in the end I got bored. Next thing on my list was the Brownies but I didn't like the uniform. I did, however, find myself with an affection for Girl Guides. I felt it was more 'adult' than Brownies and I could get a badge for lighting fires, which I thought was cool. Mum was a helper at Girl Guides: a nightmare more like.

I had my first boyfriend at St James's. His name was Charlie Gallagher and he was plump and ginger with freckles. God knows why I went out with him. We had a lot in common, though, because his mum was a lesbian and he used to get picked on, so I used to stick up for him because my mum was bisexual. I had my first kiss with him when I was about 10. I was going out with Charlie and my mate Katie was with his friend Ryan. We all went and stood against a wall and they started kissing too. Ryan kept looking over at us and saying, 'You're not doing it right', so Charlie tried to put his tongue in my mouth, which I didn't like very much. We were boyfriend and girlfriend all the rest of the way through my primary school years. Nicola started going out with him after me, so we had a huge fight in the playground. Well, we kneed each other for a bit.

We used to play kiss-chase sometimes. There was also another game we'd play – about seven of us – called 'Cat's Got the Measles'. We'd stand in a circle and sing 'Cat's got the measles, the measles, the measles, cat's got the measles, the measles got the cats...' while crossing and uncrossing our feet. As you got to the end of the rhyme, whatever position your feet were in would decide whether or not you had to take any clothes off. If they were crossed you could put an item on, but if they were uncrossed you had to take it off. The most I took off was both my socks, shoes and my tie. I never did a striptease in public (I was clearly saving that for the *Big Brother* house!).

Apart from that, I didn't have much involvement with boys until I was about 14. And I certainly never let any boy touch me down there until I was 16. I'm proud to say I was quite a clean girl.

Bermondsey was quite a racist place to grow up, but I was fair-skinned so you couldn't really tell I was mixed race. I'd always tell people my dad's origin if they asked, though: I can't lie if someone asks me a question. My mum got into fights with a lot of women who lived in our block because she thought they were prejudiced. She's fiercely protective of me, and I am of her. I think the neighbours were scared of Mum so they left us both alone after a while.

I went to a few different schools as a result of my mum's temper. I got kicked out of one because she punched a teacher. This particular school – whose name I won't mention for obvious reasons – already had a reputation for being racist. When the teachers found out where my dad came from they refused to let me join in with one of the lessons – cooking, I think it was. I was fairly young at the time, but I can clearly remember one of them explaining that I wasn't allowed to join in because I was a 'brown girl'. Naturally, when I went home and told my mum that evening, she was fuming. She didn't actually say much to me there and then, she just went a bit quiet. Then, when we got to school the next day, she told me to wait outside the classroom. I heard shouting, then that was it: I never went back to that school again. Mum's always been defensive over me: if you say I'm wrong, she'll say I'm right.

I got kicked out of another school because of her too. This time it was because she hit another pupil's mum. I was six years old and a girl called Danielle touched me in the school toilets. She said we were playing doctors and nurses. Then she pointed down to my la la and said, 'What's that down there?'

You can imagine my mum's reaction when I arrived home and told her (even if she is a lesbian!). After school the next day she stormed over to Danielle's mum, Sue, shouting all the expletives under the sun. Then Sue started accusing *me* of touching *Danielle*. Well, Mum didn't like that. Danielle was stood at one side of the playground and I was stood at the other, and we both looked at each other sheepishly. Our mums were in the middle having a massive row. Then my mum threw a punch (she's not very good at arguing with words), so I had to leave the school.

There was a supply teacher at one school who had fuzzy grey hair. He used to touch the girls in a not-very-appropriate way and pat their bums. He patted me on the tush once and I scoffed, 'Get your fucking hands off me!' I was having none of it. I was starting to become a bit of a ringleader. When he was covering one of my next classes I whispered to everyone not to do any work and they sat there with their arms folded for the entire lesson while I pinged pieces of paper at him. I was quite naughty. He sent me to the headmistress's office and I told her he was a pervert. Then they discovered that he'd received complaints at the private school he was teaching at before us. So he got kicked out.

I used to have the longest hair ever. It was beautiful. I was born with one streak of pure white at the front, near my fringe. My mum treated it like it was some precious jewel or something, so I was never allowed to get it cut. When I was about eight, I decided I wanted a change. I went to the hairdresser's and told them my mum had said they had to cut it into a bob. It was called Spinlo's Hairdresser's in Bermondsey. But I'd been going there with my mum for years, and they knew full well I was only allowed a trim, so it took a lot of convincing on my part. I sat down in the chair and said to the woman cutting my hair, 'If you don't cut it how I've asked, I'll move my head from side to side so it'll go wonky. Then Mum will see what you've done and hit you.' Then I shrugged my shoulders and said, 'It's up to you.' So the hairdresser cut my hair level with my chin. After she'd done it I just sat staring at myself in the mirror. I had dripping-wet hair and it stuck to my head like a helmet. I thought, *What have I done? I look disgusting*. But as she started to blowdry it, it started to look better and a smile began to creep across my face. I could see the reflection of the hairdresser's window behind me through the mirror, and I was gazing outside thinking about how gutted the girls at school were going to be when they saw how good my new hairdo was, when, out of nowhere, my mum appeared.

She stood for what seemed like an eternity, staring at me through the glass. I shat myself. Then she burst through the doors, turned on the poor hairdresser and shouted, 'What have you done?' before looking at me and whispering, 'You look like a pig.' Then she walked out. So, you see, it was actually my mum who started this 'Jade is a pig' malarkey, way before Graham Norton ever cottoned on.

Mum didn't talk to me after that for about four weeks. I'm not even kidding. She was like a sulky child. I tried everything I could to make conversation but she wasn't having a bar of it. And I hated silences. It wouldn't have actually bothered me if she'd said I was grounded, because I'd just go to sleep in my room quite happily, but she knew that the worst thing she could do was not talk to me. I hated the thought of being cut off from my mum in any way at all. I begged her to have even a tiny bit of dialogue with me, but she just blanked me. I still liked my hair, though.

I dyed it once. I put a load of bleach in the front, but I left it on too long and it went bright white and started to fall out when I brushed it. My best mates at secondary school were three boys – Danny Williams, Ricky Rowe and Robert Radford – and as soon as they saw me they called me 'birdshit head' and pissed themselves laughing for about an hour. That became my nickname after that. Birdshit Head. You could see me coming a mile off. Apart from that little hiccup, I'd say I was quite trendy at school. And I had this genius pair of flat blue loafers.

I had a passion for shoes and still do. They're my pride and joy. Every single pair has to be kept in its correct box, or else. My mum's got a picture of me with about eight boxes in my hand, all tied up with strings. I don't stick photos of them on the front or anything, though, like you see in films, I just know which are which from looking at the boxes. And if anybody ever touched them, that was it! Once, when I was about 13, I came home from school and Mum had tidied up my bedroom. I looked in my wardrobe and to my horror she'd written in black marker all over my shoe boxes: 'pink ones', 'black ones', 'blue ones'. I went mad. 'You've written on my boxes!' I cried. 'You've ruined them!' I sobbed about it for days. Even now, if she comes to my house and starts having a clean, I'll say, 'Don't go in my shoe cupboard!' But I don't think she'd dare.

Mum used to always let me keep my child benefit – it amounted to about £65 a month – and I'd use it to buy shoes and a nice coat. I made damn sure I had a nice designer jacket, swanky trainers and shoes. Even in primary school I'd always have the best shoes. I refused to get them from Ravel because it would mean I'd have the same ones as everyone else, so I'd go to Shelleys in Deptford and I'd be in that shop for hours. There was a black man with dreadlocks who worked there and he always looked after me because I was in there so much. I'd waltz in after school and say, 'All right, Winston! Can I have some shoes?' Mum tried to make me wear a pair of sensible proper things once – they were like grey dolly shoes from Clarks. They had a hologram of a key thing on the bottom of one of the soles and a castle on the other. Everyone else at school wanted them for some reason, but I hated them. I didn't like the idea that you turned your shoe upside down and there was some weird picture underneath. The very first pair of shoes that I loved were black patent with a two-inch heel and a thick gold chain across them. I had buck teeth at the time but it didn't matter because I had the best shoes. I thought I was the nuts.

I went through a phase of wearing a different type of trainer on each foot when I was at primary school. That way people would know I owned both pairs. I had two pairs of Fila trainers – one in pink leather and the other in baby-blue suede – so I wore one of each. We weren't really allowed to wear trainers to school – it was quite a strict uniform – but I told the teachers I'd hurt my ankle. Mum couldn't get her head round why I wanted to wear odd shoes, but she didn't argue. Nobody else said anything either, they just thought I was cool. I actually think I started a trend, because I went to the playground a few weeks later and there was a group of younger girls with odd shoes on.

We used to go on school trips at St James's. Once we went to this place called Nethercot Farm. God knows where it was: Nethercot, I suppose. I know it was a fair way away because we had to write letters home to our parents. But for me, if I was off somewhere enjoying myself, I didn't really have my mum on my mind. So the letter she received was from a girl of very few sentimental words. All it said was, 'Hi Mum, having a nice time, love you, bye.' She's still got it now because she found it amusing.

Jade: How It All Began

We were there for about two weeks. I loved the social aspect of it but hated doing the farming. We had to get up at the crack of dawn and muck out all the animals. At 6 a.m. we'd be forced out of bed by the teachers to get the eggs from the chicken hut, then we'd wash them and take them back to the farmhouse so the farmer's wife could cook them for our breakfast. After that we'd muck out the stables and feed the sheep. There was a big pond in the middle of one of the fields and one day I stood at the edge, messing about in front of the others, wobbling about, pretending I was going to topple over. Then I fell in. I had my best skirt on, I got weeds in my hair and all these tadpoles got in my knickers. They were wriggling all over the place. I wasn't happy.

My mum stitched me up massively on this school trip. Knowing how much I loved my footwear and that there was no way I'd agree to wear wellies like everyone else, she bought me some new trainers. She also knew I would never be seen dead in anything that wasn't Reebok, Princess or Nike. No way! So the day before we were leaving, she gave them to me in a Reebok box. I was so excited. I didn't want to open it until I got there because I wanted it to be a surprise (I also wanted to make everyone else jealous). So we got to our dormitory: there I was, sitting on my bunk bed with four of my mates, and I opened the box in anticipation. Inside, to my disgust, were the worst trainers in the entire world. They were white plastic things with a sticky bit of fabric across them, 'Top' written along the side, and a giant '3' on the sole. 'Top 3' they were called, and they'd cost her £3 at the market. I was a laughing stock. I refused to wear them, of course, and wore my best shoes instead, which got muddy and ruined. Then I got home and Mum saw I hadn't touched them so she forced me to wear them to school as a punishment. I cried so much it hurt. I hated them.

All my mates loved my mum. They thought she was so cool. They always told me they wished theirs were more like her. They loved the fact that she came with us to the cinema and smoked joints in the house. I wished she was more like their mums. It's not that I didn't love her – I did, with all my heart – I just wanted her to be like a normal mum. That way I might not have to come home to find my house being raided by the police.

We got raided all the time – it was nothing unusual for me. Most kids would arrive home to the sight of their mum hanging out the washing or putting the dinner on. I'd come round the corner from school with my face in my hands, hoping I wouldn't be faced with another police car outside my house. I'd get off the bus from school and my heart would sink: *What's she done now?* Then I'd go into a cold sweat and panic with the fear that they could take her away from me. I was always worrying. I'd often walk in to see policemen ripping up the carpet and pulling things apart in my bedroom. I'd shout, 'Put that back! It's in my room! I've just tidied up!' Still, they never used to find anything. Mum puffed and occasionally she sold Tamazepam to get a bit of money, but that was about it. Nothing worth locking her away for.

Mum could be quite strict, though. She had values, my mum. I've already mentioned the teeth thing – *obsessed*, she was, with me having nice clean teeth. That's probably why I ended up being a dental nurse. She made me wear braces for a while because I had quite widely spaced teeth. There was such a gap that whenever I blew my nose my lip would get stuck in between my teeth and I had to flick it out. I didn't actually mind having a brace, though. I even wanted glasses to go with it at one point. I had both types of brace – the train-tracks and the ones you take in and out – but I choked once when I was eating a sandwich because it got stuck on the roof of my mouth. So I threw the brace in the bin – I thought it was dangerous.

Mum's other fixation was swearing. OK, so she'd curse herself, but she'd never let me utter a bad word. Once, when I did, she poured washing-up liquid down my throat. I was about eight at the time, and I'd come out with the word 'tar-arse', which is a really rude word that black people use. It's like the equivalent of motherfucker or something. I remember saying it and then leaping round the lounge kissing my teeth. She went mental. I protested, 'I only learnt it from you and your friends!' So she put my head back and squeezed all this washing-up liquid into my mouth. I had bubbles coming out when I spoke for days after that.

Mum used to keep a Bible by her bed too, even though she wasn't particularly religious or anything. I think she just thought it was a nice thing to have. I've still got it somewhere. She had it for keepsakes – letters from me, stuff from my Uncle Budgie, all sorts. Mum would always leave the Bible on the pillow of her bed and I'd try and read it sometimes, just to look intelligent. I didn't ever actually understand a word of it, mind you. She would always tell me I had to pray before or after food – give thanks and praise and all that. I wasn't allowed to get down from the table before I'd done it. I used to pray at night-time before I went to bed; I still do it now sometimes. If I've had a bad week I'll always start with, 'Our father who art in heaven…', then I'll add loads of my own things on the end like '…let my mum sleep well tonight, and my cousins, even though I hardly ever talk to them – oh, and I hope Mum gets me that nice top I saw…'

Mum would never let me sleep at other people's houses either. She used to question my friends all the time, it was so embarrassing. Even when I was as old as 16. Once I came home from school with my mate Kelly and said I was going round to hers to stay. The Spanish Inquisition instantly followed:

'Have you got a dad, Kel?'

'Yes.'

'Have you got a brother?'

'Yeah.'

'How far's your dad's and brother's rooms from your room?'

'Er . . .'

I was such a heavy sleeper that Mum was worried one of the men in Kelly's house might do something to me while I was in bed. I never slept with nightwear on when I was at home; she couldn't seem to get her head around the idea that if I was staying at someone else's house I'd wear pyjamas. She was convinced that because I wasn't used to wearing them I'd subconsciously take them off in the night and then someone would creep into bed with me. I could never really get angry with Mum, though, because I was

53

allowed to have anyone I liked round to ours. I could have twelve mates there at the same time if I wanted, and she wouldn't mind.

4

'That's It, I'm Done'

I remember when I first got pubes. I was about 11 or 12 and I was in the bath, washing. I left the door open as I usually did when it was just me and Mum in the house, so Mum came in to ask me something. When she clocked them she leant over with the razor and shaved them into a heart shape. I was crushed. 'What have you done? It's never going to grow back! You've taken it away!' I'd been so proud of them too. Mum laughed her head off and walked out.

I never could get to grips with the grooming routine at that age. I tried putting Immac under my armpits once because I was too nervous about shaving them, but I left it too long and stained my armpits yellow. And it smelt funny.

I started to get boobs around that time and I was pretty self-conscious. I had a mate called Nicola who I hung around with all the time (this was a different person to the Nicola who ate cat food in primary school). Nicola was

55

one of my best mates but was a real tomboy and totally different to me (for a start she wore shellsuits all the time). We were walking along the road once, just after we'd watched *Home and Away* at her house, and it was about six o'clock. As we went past this alleyway, a man suddenly appeared from nowhere and grabbed me. It was so frightening. I'm convinced he would have raped me if Nicola hadn't been there. Without thinking, she booted him as hard as she could, then we just ran and ran as fast as our legs would take us. As I looked behind, the man was taking his coat off, as if it was slowing him down or something, then he sped after us. We reached my house and I started banging frantically on the door for my mum. The problem was, I'd cried wolf so many times before – knocking on the door screaming 'Aaarghh! Someone's trying to get me!' – that this time she was thinking, *Oh, here we go again*. I was hollering at her to let us in but she just ambled along the corridor, taking her time. When she did finally open it, I collapsed through the doorway onto the mat while Nicola breathlessly explained what had happened. Without flinching, Mum went back into the house and grabbed a hatchet that used to belong to my Uncle Budgie. She ran straight outside looking for this man, until she saw him, two houses down from us, talking to our neighbour Sylvie as if he'd done nothing wrong. He was even asking Sylvie if she'd seen me. My mum went over to her and said, 'Do you know this guy?' Sylvie replied, 'No, but he's just described your daughter, Jade.' That was enough explanation for Mum. She launched at him with the hatchet and he shot off round the corner to this cab office. But she didn't let him out of her sight and managed to whack him on the shoulder, cut through his shirt and draw blood. Then the police got called and I had to go down to the station and give a statement. When the police did a check on him, it turned out that he had two children of his own who were both put into care because he'd molested them. It was so chilling. I wouldn't go out for ages after that. I feel like Nicola saved my life that day.

My secondary school was called Bacon's College (quite an apt name for someone they call a pig, eh?). I'd put my name down to three schools and was accepted by each of them. Mum wanted me to go to Greycoat's, which was an all-girls school, but everyone I knew was going to Bacon's, and me and my mates had grown up watching the older kids walk past in their uniform, dreaming we'd be there one day. I loved the uniform at Bacon's too; it was a kilt, a white shirt and a blue and gold tie. I liked the summer dresses best, though. They were all checked like the ones they wore in *Home and Away*.

The first day was like an open day and we were allowed to go in our normal clothes. Most people I knew were forever worrying about their appearance, but I was really confident with the way I looked back then. So when I fronted up to the school gates in my latest gear I thought I was the business. And the fact that I knew a lot of people who were going there meant I was as cocky as you like. I remember sitting down at my desk and this girl called Lucy borrowed a pen off my table and I just sat there pulling faces and giving her attitude all morning. I wasn't exactly the friendly type. But we became really good mates after that, and the way I'd spoken to her became our little joke: 'What are you doing? They're *my* pens!' I haven't seen her for years, but if I saw her now I'm pretty certain that would still be the first thing she'd say to me.

The following day, when we had to wear uniform, I turned up wearing long white socks all scrunched down round my ankles and the fattest, shortest bad-boy tie you've ever seen. I had a fight on the second day – with a boy called Stacey. He told everyone he was going out with me and when I found this out I marched up to him and screamed, 'How dare you tell people you're going out with me? You'll ruin my reputation! You're a boy and you've got a girl's name.' Fancy being called Stacey. I couldn't understand why anyone would give their son that name. He wasn't exactly the best-looking boy in the world either. He had bleached-blond hair with black roots coming through and was as skinny as you like. To top it all, he had a girl's name. So I bashed his head against a table.

I don't think people were exactly scared of me at school, but they knew I could handle myself. If someone confronted me I would never back down. For example, there was a girl who was two years above me; a big black girl she was, called Toni. Everyone was shit-scared of her because she was about six foot tall. She became my mate for a while and asked if I wanted to go out one night, but I told her I didn't have enough money, so she said she'd pay. She arrived at my house that evening, then, while I was rushing about getting ready, she nicked a charm bracelet and a ring that were lying on the table in my bedroom. Unbeknownst to me, she sold them to some dodgy guy down the road to get enough cash to take us out. I got wind of this the next day and challenged her at school. Toni stood there squaring up to me, giving it all the attitude, and denied everything. When I said I didn't believe her she got all aggro and said to her mates, 'Hold me back!' as if she was going to thump me. I wasn't budging. I stood about an inch from her face and threatened, 'What do you mean, hold you back? Come on then!' Then I paused before adding, 'If it's not back in my house in two days, my mum will knock you out. So I suggest you sort it.' Toni soon backed down. If people weren't scared of me, they sure as hell were scared of my mum.

I didn't have a bad attitude towards people though: I wasn't snobby about who I mixed with. I'd speak to absolutely everybody, whether they were the school boffin, the local tramp or Fishy Anna. Fishy Anna was a girl in our school who no one else spoke to because she had ginger hair and she stank. I'd never be nasty to her or pick on her. She couldn't help what she looked like.

I was always quite good at maths but I *hated* English. I never knew where to put a full stop or an apostrophe or anything. I'd hand in my homework and when I got it back there'd be about 80 million spelling mistakes with all these corrections and full stops sprawled across in red writing. At the bottom of the page it would always say 'See me', 'Stay behind' or 'Need to discuss'. Still, it didn't really bother me. I never had that sense of fear about going home in case Mum got angry that I wasn't doing well at school, as she wasn't the type. And even though my writing wasn't very good, my reading was. I could read so well that the teachers thought I might be dyslexic for a while. Sometimes I'd read so fast that I'd actually add my own words in. What an oddball.

My school reports either said I talked too much, never

concentrated or I was 'dominating'. This was the teachers' way of saying I was a bully. But I wasn't a bully, I hated that kind of thing. I was just, shall we say, a bit bossy. Most of the time this just translated into me making my friends do certain dances with me in the playground. I danced after school, you see, so I obviously just wanted to share my moves with them.

Jazz was my favourite. I went twice a week in a little hall and I won loads of trophies. I had a yellow costume with ribbons on. We did loads of competitions and I would have to perform in front of the judges. I never got nervous. I just loved being the centre of attention. I've always got a kick out of people watching me, whether I'm falling into a pond, doing a dance or romping under the sheets in the *Big Brother* house. (OK, I lied about that last one. I wish that could be erased from all your memories forever!)

Most of my friends at school were boys. Danny, Ricky and Robert, my best mates, would let me copy their work. Ricky and Robert would help me with maths and Danny would help me with geography work because I didn't understand it. Geography was one of my worst subjects. I never turned up to lessons. I just thought, *What's the point?* I never wanted to be a weathergirl, so why did I need to know what direction the water went in or where it came from in the sky? When I did occasionally rock up, I used to sit there and talk while everyone else worked. I might just about have managed to write a paragraph before I got chucked out. Being sat outside the classroom is actually a stronger memory for me than being sat inside it. That's where I spent most of my days.

'That's It, I'm Done'

I had my first proper crush on a boy – let's call him Danny Smith. All the girls fancied him – *adored* him – me included. He was in the year above us and we'd write his name over all our school planners (our timetables). There was one particular group of us who were like his fan club. We'd walk about the school deliberately timing it to make sure we bumped into him. I'll never forget the day I actually did. I was so embarrassed, as we'd just finished PE and I was wearing a little polo shirt and blue skirt with cycling shorts underneath. I'd just come on my period at the time and I was running down the corridor to the toilet because I was late for class. Who should I bump into but Danny Smith and all the boys. I careered right into them and they looked at me and Danny said, 'All right, Jade?' I was so chuffed that he knew my name that I dropped the Tampax I'd been hiding in my hand and it landed right at his feet. I went bright red. Then they started shouting, 'Whaaeey! Look at the lady!' I was so embarrassed, I wanted the ground to swallow me up. I tried to laugh and mumbled, 'See what you made me do, boys!' and scuttled off as fast as I could. Then Danny started calling after me, 'Jade, you sausage!' and I couldn't stop smiling. You see, in my school, if a boy thought a girl was sexy and had something about her, he'd say to his mates, 'Yeah, she's a right sausage', and if a girl liked a boy she'd call him a 'sort'. So I was well pleased. This meant he liked me. After that, I always plucked up the courage to go and talk to him and his mates. The rest of my friends were too embarrassed to say a word in case they made a fool of themselves, but I'd sit down and have lunch with them. My mates would be on another table nibbling daintily on a sandwich and I'd plonk myself next to the boys and stuff my face with a burger and chips. I think they found it refreshing. Danny knew I fancied him rotten – it was written all over my school books, after all – but that didn't make me stop talking to him. I was always quite popular at school and I definitely made myself known. There's no way no one noticed me, that's for sure.

Then things, er, developed between me and Danny. I can't believe I'm about to write this (but I guess it is part of my growing up), so close your eyes and skim this bit if you'd rather not know what I'm about to say next. Danny was the first boy I wanked off. He was never really what you would call my 'boyfriend', though, because he had another girlfriend at the same time as he was seeing me. But that just made it more of a challenge for me. He used to live by the River Thames and all the girls would loiter around there after school – that way we'd know it was inevitable we'd see him. We must've been about 14 or 15. It was all pretty innocent; there was no alcohol involved or anything. We'd just sit around on the bench in our big coats, chatting rubbish for the best part of the evening. It was later, when we were 16, that we started introducing alcohol to the proceedings and would spin ourselves around the park with a bottle in our mouths, seeing who could get drunk the quickest.

Anyway, one day I was sitting by the river next to Danny and he started kissing me. It was very nice, much nicer than the last boy I'd kissed (he was called Peter and kissed like a washing machine on speed). After a while, Danny got up and walked over to where his house was and started beckoning me towards him. 'Jade, come over here,' he said.

'That's It, I'm Done'

I knew he wanted me to go inside with him, and I also knew what that might lead to, so I crapped myself and said, 'No way, I'm not coming inside.' I didn't even try to be cool. I was scared because anything more than kissing and I didn't have a clue what to do. He was older and more experienced than me, and I was still 'untouched' (as I liked to call it).

We'd meet for kissing sessions most nights after that, and he'd try things like putting his hand up my skirt, but I wouldn't let him. Then, when I'd eventually plucked up the courage to actually go inside his house and we were kissing, he grabbed my hand and whispered, 'Jade, wank us off.' I remember thinking *Help!* but I just mumbled, 'No, Danny, I can't. I've got to go...I'm late.' As soon as I left his house I ran home and immediately called my mate Kelly. I said, 'Kel, he's asked me to wank him off. What do I do?' She couldn't believe it and screeched, 'Didn't you do it?' I replied, 'I didn't know HOW TO!' So Kelly told me to go over to hers after school and she'd show me.

The next day we sat on her bed and she asked me what happened. I told her how he'd grabbed my hand and put it on his willy and I'd freaked, to which she kindly informed me he was probably going to think I was a 'right frigid'. But as far I was concerned, I didn't know what to do, so I wasn't doing it. That night, Kelly took it upon herself to give me a lesson in how to pleasure a boy. She was very matter-of-fact about it all. She picked up one of her hairbrushes – it was one of those round ones for curling your hair underneath – and she sat there, straight-faced, moving her hand up and down the brush. I was going bright red just watching her. She tried to make me have a go on the hairbrush after that, but I refused.

The next time I saw Danny and it came to the crunch, all I kept seeing was this big round brush looming in my face, so I still couldn't bring myself to do it and muttered something about having to be home early. It was the time after that that I finally plucked up the courage. I didn't have a great deal of choice, to be honest, because he undid his trousers before I could do a disappearing act and just put my hand there. I just did what Kelly had told me and hoped for the best. Immediately afterwards I stood bolt upright and told Danny I had to go home. Then I ran back to my house and headed straight for the bathroom. I washed my hands so much they nearly came off my arms. But although there was a part of me that thought it was a tiny bit disgusting (all this stuff on my hands afterwards? Yuk!), there was another part that felt very pleased with myself. I'd finally done it. I still never let him do anything to me, though. I never let a boy touch me until I had my first proper boyfriend at 16. I soon ended it with Danny anyway. I don't remember exactly why. I think he just started getting fat and ugly.

Another man I was in love with, of course, was Brian Harvey from East 17. I was *obsessed* with him. All my mates were into Take That, but I'd just scribble Brian's name over their pencil cases. I thought Take That were a bunch of poofs who wore girly pink T-shirts with 'baby' written across the top. East 17 were my band. I camped outside Tony Mortimer's house with my mate Joanne once. We thought he'd take pity on us and invite us in for tea, and then maybe take us out for a nice romantic meal (after he'd called Brian and asked him to join us, of course). But when we got there, there were loads of other groupies already camped up. We all sat there shivering outside his drive until about 7 a.m., when he appeared at the front door and we screamed our heads off as he got in his car. After that we went home. I only did it once. My mum thought I was staying at Joanne's house. She'd never have let me sleep on the street: she would've thought it was ridiculous. I thought it was brilliant.

Then I went out with another Danny, Danny Jarman. He was good at football and a very good-looking boy. He was the person I lost my virginity to when I was 16, but it didn't seem like a scary thing with him because I'd known him since I was at primary school. We were very serious – he was my boyfriend until I was about 19. He'd had sex with one other person before me and we always talked about doing it, but I was convinced it would hurt. He was a bit of a charmer, though, and one night it kind of happened. Thing is, I'd worked myself up so much thinking it was going to be painful (it didn't help that my mate told me that when she did it for the first time she bled all over the bed) that rather than it being a lovely romantic experience, I shrieked the whole way through. I kept saying 'I'm gonna bleed! I'm gonna bleed' at the top of my voice (and you can imagine what that sounded like). When we'd finished I was convinced I could see blood on poor old Danny until he told me it was just the colour of the condom.

But the next morning I thought I was really grown up. I felt like a proper woman. My mum noticed instantly. The first thing she said to me at the breakfast table was, 'Jade, have you had sex?' I couldn't understand how she possibly knew and I kept going to the hall and looking in the mirror to check I didn't look any different. The thought of telling Mum I'd done it was daunting. Would she think I'd waited the right amount of time? Was I too forward? But there's not much you can get past my mum, and when she asked again I just answered, 'Why do say that? What do you mean?'

She looked at me with a smirk. 'Ha! You have.'

'Um, yeah, OK – but how d'you know? Do I look different? Do *I smell*?'

Around that time, just before I left school, there was an 'incident' in which I was meant to have bitten a 'huge' chunk out of a girl's ear. She was called Julie Websdale, and she sold her story to one of the papers while I was in *Big Brother*. She went to Bacon's College, she was a twin, she was ugly and she smelt. I was going out with Danny Jarman at the time and I heard on the grapevine that Julie had said something to him about me (which wasn't very nice, by all accounts). I'd been told that she'd called me a slag and said that he shouldn't be with me (although she claimed it was because she had grassed on me for apparently bullying a pupil). As you know, I've always had a bit of a temper, so when Danny and I were at our mate Richard's house one day and I heard Julie's voice at the door, I leapt up. Danny tried to stop me – 'Jade, don't go out there' – which was like a red rag to a bull. When I saw Julie standing there I punched her in the face, then she grabbed my hair and bit my finger. But she was gripping it so firmly in her teeth – clamping my little finger so hard – that I thought it was going to come off! So when I noticed her ear peeping through her hair I thought, 'Bite it!' Problem was, I bit it too hard, so when I pulled my head back a chunk of her ear came off. It wasn't a huge part of her earlobe or anything, just the tip, but I spat it right out all the same. I felt suddenly very sick and ran inside crying. You can imagine what my mum had to say when I went home and told her I'd bitten someone's ear off. I was convinced I had some kind of deadly disease for weeks after that.

By this time I was dressing like Queen Burberry. Burberry bag, Burberry coat, Burberry scarf – you name it, I had it, and it was probably Burberry. Or maybe Moschino. I did own this white Moschino outfit that I thought was the nuts. It consisted of a white skirt and a white shirt with little black stick-men and women all over it. I wore it everywhere. What the hell was I thinking? We used to go to this club called The Gin Palace on the Old Kent Road. We'd go every Thursday, Friday and Saturday, regardless of school. I didn't seem to get a hangover in those days. If I wasn't wearing my Moschino or Burberry outfits it would be some other kind of matching suit, probably from Karen Millen. Me and all my mates would rock up at the club at about 10 p.m. and do the Bermondsey Two-Step all night – one step forward, two steps to the side then one step back and two steps to the other side. All the girls used to stand there and do it in a row. The Bermondsey boys had a different dance: theirs was called 'Head, Shoulders, Knees and Toes', which I realise sounds like something you'd teach your kids at playgroup, but we all thought we were well cool at the time. The Gin Palace was a proper full-on nightclub and you were meant to be 18 to go there, but I never got asked for ID until I actually turned 18. Typical.

The first time I got really drunk was at The Gin Palace. Bacardi and Coke; that was my drink. I was too scared to mix in case I did anything stupid. The first time my mum let me go there she told me I had to be home by 11 p.m. I moaned and said, 'But it doesn't shut till about three or four!' When I came in, I was so pissed I fell out of the cab and rolled all over the pavement outside our house. I couldn't see a thing – I thought I'd gone blind. I can't remember anything except waking up in the morning with her shouting in my ear, 'I told you to be in on time and you showed up at half past one. I was up all night thinking about you and worrying.' The next time I went, I got so hammered that I fell asleep in my neighbour's garden. I still never got a hangover, though. I could easily get up the next day and go straight to school.

I never smoked at school. Well, not cigarettes anyway. I puffed weed instead. I used to roll a joint on the hills with the older girls. Anyone who was anyone would be found on the hill behind school in their lunchbreak, puffing away. The first time I got stoned was with my mates Jemma and Stacy. We'd bunked off school and Stacy had bought us a bit of skunk from someone she knew. She was mixed race and knew all the rastas. We rolled a joint and my head went all funny and I just couldn't stop giggling for what seemed like about a day. We started having this random conversation that didn't make sense at all – it was all about aliens or something. The grins on our faces went from ear to ear. It was hilarious. Then we went back to school for another lesson (our deputy head was taking it so we knew we had no choice, otherwise we'd probably have skived that one too). It felt like it took us about eight hours to get to class, when in reality it only took five minutes. We sat at the back and laughed for the whole lesson. Stacy fell asleep, and me and Jemma nearly wet ourselves. We reeked of marijuana, so why the teacher didn't say anything I still don't know. It blew our heads off.

Me and three of my friends turned ourselves into the Spice Girls for a few weeks. We were rehearsing for a performance at school. I wanted to be Ginger Spice so I put all these red bits in my hair – it looked disgusting. There was another group of girls who'd decided they were going to be the Spice Girls too, so in effect we were competing. I was determined we were going to be the best. I had my outfit all planned. It was a tight black rubber dress with fishnets – I looked like I was wearing a wetsuit. But I got caught puffing on the hill a week before we were meant to be performing, so we were banned from doing it and had to stay behind after school for a week, picking up litter instead.

I knew my GCSE results were going to be crap, and so did my mum. And I really didn't care how well I did, if I'm honest: I slept through my maths GCSE. It was in two parts – I went to the first one but my alarm didn't go off for the second part. I got an E. I did try to revise. I would read all the stuff I was meant to but it just wouldn't stay in my head. I didn't know how to revise anyway. When the teachers said 'revise', I just thought 'What?' I didn't know what it meant. If you didn't know what the questions were going to be on the exam paper, how could you revise the answers? Still, the teachers tried to make me stay behind at school every Wednesday until six o'clock to do revision lessons. We did a bit of English and a bit of science, but I didn't see the point so I didn't go after the first one. I had a few Saturday detentions too. You couldn't skive them, otherwise you'd get expelled. I'd get on the bus at a weekend, and the same old ladies used to say, 'Ooh, Jade, you know it's Saturday, don't you?' I'd shrug and say I'd been naughty. They just smiled.

When the GCSE results came through my friend Hebba called me up and said she got three A's, two A stars and two B's. Then she said she was worried about what her dad would say. I said, 'You're joking, aren't you?!' I'd have given anything to get that – my results were mostly E's and U's. I did get one A star, though, for drama. I was good at drama; I think it's because I had a lot of attitude. I always wanted to be an actress and I loved performing arts. Mind you, I don't think I ever seriously thought I'd be on TV or anything.

One of my best mates at school was called Robert Radford. I was still close to him when we all left and got jobs, but he was killed when we were 17. It was the first time I'd experienced death and really understood its consequence. I was too young to really register what it meant when Uncle Budgie had died, but when Robert died it was like a chill going right through my core. Robert was such a cool guy, he'd always make everyone laugh and was the one person you'd always want to sit next to at school because you knew there'd be no chance of you getting bored. While we were at Bacon's, Robert was going out with a girl called

Carly. They were still together when he left school. Her ex-boyfriend was a boxer and was notoriously jealous, and one morning he waited round the corner from Robert's house. Then, when Robert left for work, this guy just beat him up. And beat him up. And beat him up. Until he was dead. The first I heard about it was on the radio. I remember waking up and hearing the news – 'Robert Radford from Old Kent Road has died.' I thought it was part of my dream at first. I kept thinking, *I know that name.* Then I got the phone call and I've never felt such a flat, empty, hollow feeling in my whole life. How could someone do that? I couldn't get my head round it. All our friends got together for the wake (despite the fact that I kept thinking it was called 'the warning', for some reason) but it was just awful. I find it so hard to deal with things like that. It's like with my dad: my instinct is just to try and block it all out so I don't have to think about it any more. I'm terrified, knowing that death is something that's going to happen to my mum one day, and she's going to leave me forever. So I'd rather not be part of it, or confront it.

I went for loads of different jobs when I left school. The first I applied for was as a receptionist. In the interview I was told I had to type at the speed of light. I just looked at the guy and said, 'Where am I s'posed to learn that? I've just come out of school, for God's sake.' Funnily enough, I didn't get it.

Then I got a job at Saatchi & Saatchi, the advertising company. Posh, eh? Before you choke on your tea in amazement, I wasn't an account manager with my own office or anything – I used to set up the coffees and biscuits for the boardroom meetings. It was good money, though: £6 an hour. They liked me there because I always looked after my appearance.

I'm such a tog sometimes. Naïve, some might call it. Once I saw an advert in the paper saying '£250 an hour to work in a massage parlour' and when I read it I literally gasped with delight. *Wicked!* I thought. I trekked all the way to the interview – which was miles away at the end of the tube line – and I was grinning to myself for the whole journey, thinking my luck was in. What a cracking job. I'd always wanted to work in the beauty industry, and massage classed as 'beauty', didn't it? It should've dawned on me that something wasn't quite right when I looked at the address and it said the street number was 69. But no, not me. I couldn't find it for ages, either. I even asked these two old dears for directions. Needless to say, they gave me a funny look.

When I eventually did find it, it had blacked-out windows, and as soon as I walked through the door I immediately realised it was one of those dodgy places where you're required to do much more than a simple 'massage' for your money. I was so embarrassed. I didn't know where to look. But once I'd got inside I was too polite to just turn around and leave. It was dark inside, with purple suede seats. The receptionist had earrings all up one ear and was wearing a white uniform. She motioned for me to take a seat on the sofa and I just sat there, gobsmacked. A man and a woman came out and asked me to go into the back room with them. They then proceeded to show me around the 'massage parlour' and the man pointed to a bath and said, 'You'll be expected to get into the bath with your client.' I just looked at the floor and mumbled, 'Oh, I got the wrong idea. I'm really sorry but I thought it was different. I don't think I'm old enough to do this. I'm only 16.' (I was 17.) They told me not to worry, they were really nice about it in fact. Then the woman added, 'It's OK, you can do reception. All you need to do is keep them on the phone and give them a bit of naughty chatting.' I was so tongue-tied, I couldn't bring myself to tell them I didn't want to do it, so I said I'd take it. Then, once I got outside, I ran to that train station as fast as my legs would take me. I called my mum on the way home and said, 'You'll never guess where I just had an interview. I got offered a job in one of them dirty massage parlours!' She could not believe it. But we both had to laugh. I'd been so puffed up about the idea that I was going to earn all this money, spent 20 quid getting to this God-awful place, only to find out it was a sleazy old sex shop.

I managed to bag a job as the manager (yes, that's right, I was in charge!) of Dune, a shoe shop on South Molton Street in London. It was like all my Christmases had come at once because every single week I got a new pair of shoes. Perks of the job, they called it. We used to send shoes to Posh (Victoria Beckham) too; I had to arrange for a cab to take them over to her house. We'd have to box up all the new stock and send them to her as a gift. Annoyingly, I never got to meet her myself. I did offer to hand-deliver them personally, but for some reason I wasn't allowed.

Although I loved that job, I became a bit restless and bored so I left there to work in Marks & Spencer for a while. I was on knitwear and lingerie. I was a bit naughty, though: I used to give the old ladies free things. As far as I was concerned, M&S was quite expensive, because to get two bras would cost you 50 quid or something. That's a lot of money. So when these old ladies used to come in I felt terrible. I'd think, *That's their entire pension.* So I'd override some of the cost on the till. They'd always know what I'd done and say, 'Ooh! Cheers, gal.' It would make me feel all nice. Problem is, when I wasn't working they'd go up to my supervisor and ask, 'Where's that young girl Jade gone?', which very nearly blew my cover.

I was caught for shoplifting, myself, once. I didn't do it on purpose – it just kind of materialised from nowhere. I was in Selfridges with my mate Jolene and I 'accidentally' walked out of the shop with a Moschino umbrella. When we got outside I realised what I'd done and turned to her and stuttered, 'Oh my God. I've just got away with this umbrella!' We looked at each other for a few seconds, and then, almost simultaneously, a mischievous glint appeared in both our eyes. So we decided to go back inside and nick as much as we possibly could. It's as if we thought we were invincible or something. I managed to clear £1575 worth of stuff by myself alone. Jolene had just under two thousand quid's worth. I was already carrying a big Burberry bag anyway, so I just filled it up. It's not exactly cheap in that shop, so I didn't have to have many items to add up to that amount. I think I had at least four pairs of jeans when I realised enough was enough and I said, 'Walk out, Jolene. Walk out.' There was all this adrenaline pumping through us because we thought we'd got away with it. It was such a rush.

We headed for the exit and got out onto the street. At that point we should've just got into a cab straight away, but we didn't. It was pouring with rain outside, so numbnuts here decided we needed a carrier bag to put our stuff in. Without thinking, I marched back into the store and fronted up to the cashier. 'I'm so sorry,' I said, 'but I've just bought a load of stuff, my bag's broken and it's raining outside. Can I have another one please?' The assistant told me they didn't normally give out bags but she gave me one anyway. I said 'thank you' and went back outside. Next thing I knew, someone was tapping me on the shoulder. (I actually thought they had stopped me to tell me they liked my shoes!) I turned around to see a man and a woman behind us. All I heard was, 'We work for Selfridges. We're undercover. Can you come with us please?' My heart dropped to my feet. *Oh my God. My mum is going to beat me*. That's all that went through my head at first.

We went back to the store, through to the back, and got taken to a small room. I sat there with my head in my hands. Then they started taking our photos, and for some stupid reason we sat there smiling and posing as if someone was taking our holiday snaps! I think I'd gone a bit hysterical. The woman who was interrogating us was pregnant, so I started trying to make conversation as if I'd just met her in the park or something. 'Is it your first? How far gone are you?' She wasn't amused and kept giving me filthy looks. She spread all our stuff out on the table and stared at us.

I don't think it properly hit us until the police arrived. We got escorted to the police station and had to have our fingerprints taken. We had swabs taken out of our mouths too, and a hair follicle removed. Then we were put in a cell. We thought it'd be fine, but it was the worst thing in the world. We made up a lie saying that we had to nick the stuff because we were being threatened by people and we needed the money. Where all the lies came from, I don't know. But we couldn't exactly tell the truth: 'Oh, we got away with it once so we thought we'd have another go.' We said there were these people who were going to kneecap us if we didn't give them any cash. They didn't buy it. I think one of the policemen quite liked me, though, because he kept smiling when I asked him questions: 'So what's my fingerprint look like then? So why are you taking my picture? Is that because I'm going to go to prison?' There was another girl in the cell next door to us. She was about 18, and as soon as we got inside we could hear her gobbing all over the walls. The next thing we heard was this high-pitched East End voice: 'All right, gals, what you in 'ere for?' It was like being in an episode of *Prisoner Cell Block H*. I felt so pathetic replying, 'We were nicking things in Selfridges.' She was probably a murderer or something. Then Jolene piped up, 'What you in here for then?' She took great pleasure in telling us that her and her boyfriend were a team who stole things in stores across London and took it in turns taking the blame. 'I've been here loads,' she said. 'I've been caught about five times. Nothing much happens. You'll get a caution and that'll be it.' That made me feel a bit better because by now I'd started thinking we were going to be in jail for the rest of our lives, and I was resigned to the fact that I was going to end up like my dad. But this was the first time we'd ever done anything like this, and I vowed there and then *never* to do it again.

We got let out of the cell and sent home. On the way we concocted a lie to tell our mums. We'd tell them that we were in Selfridges and we came across these two black girls on the escalator who started having a go at the orange nail varnish on Jolene's toenails. We couldn't think of anything else. Then we'd say we had a fight and all the black security guards came over and accused us of being racists because we were picking on the black girls, then all of a sudden all this stuff – stolen stuff that the *other* girls had pinched from the store – fell on the floor, and we'd say we were framed for it. Well, you can imagine my mum's face after that lot came tumbling out of my mouth. She just took one look at me and said sarcastically, 'Uh huh. Now tell me the truth.' I was pleading, 'Mum, that is the truth!' But she wasn't having a bar of it. 'Well, you'd better say now because otherwise I'll come to court and then I'll hear the truth.' So I confessed. She didn't hit me or anything but she left me in no doubt that she was angry. I felt shit too. I thought, *What am I doing? I've got a good job. I didn't need to do it.* And the buzz I got in the store soon wore off once I'd been to court.

We were summoned to court but our case kept getting adjourned, so every time we turned up at the courtroom we kept getting sent home again. We were starting to get worried now, because one of my mates (who'd been in trouble with the law before) said that normally by this stage it would've just got dropped. The day finally came. A prostitute went up before us and she had to pay a fine. Then it was our turn to take the stand and the judge read our story out in this booming, disapproving voice. As she came to the end of it she stared straight at me – the fiercest look in her eyes – and said really slowly and loudly, 'And Jade Goody had the audacity to go back in and ask for a BAG! Is this true?' I just stood there. I'd been told not to answer back because you're not meant to talk in court. She kept her eyes fixed firmly on my face, like they could see right through me. 'Do you have *anything* to say?'

After a pause I eventually said, 'Yeah, er, what happens now?'

Well, that did it. 'WHAT HAPPENS NOW?' she bellowed. I thought the whole courtroom was going to fall down around us, it was so loud. The judge then proceeded to read out how much we'd stolen and we looked down at our feet, both shamefaced. She kept repeating herself: 'And you have the cheek to ask what happens *now*?' Then she shouted, 'You shouldn't be going to court. YOU should be going to prison.'

I've never been so scared in my life. *Shit!* I thought, *I'm going to get raped by a big fat dyke.* I didn't think I'd survive if I went to prison.

The judge surveyed the court and said, 'These two girls need serious punishment.' We were told in no uncertain terms that if we got caught fighting or stepping out of line in any way in the next two years we'd go straight to prison. The judge's parting words were, 'I hope to never see either of you before me again. NOW GET OUT OF MY COURTROOM!'

You've never seen two girls run so fast in all your life.

After that I got myself a proper career – as a dental nurse. It wasn't like it was my destiny or anything, or even that I had any real dream of looking in people's mouths for a living. I was just flicking through the paper one day and saw an advert for a trainee dental nurse, so I thought, *£3.50 an hour. OK, I'll try that.*

I really liked being a dental nurse: I felt like I'd found something I was good at. I knew all the lingo (or 'lingwo', as I call it) and had no problem learning what all the different utensils did. I liked wearing the uniform too. It made me feel all clean. I was a dental nurse in loads of different practices. I worked in orthodontics in Guy's Hospital for a while, dealing with people who wore braces. I was a dental nurse for three years, on and off, and it was my last ever job before going into *Big Brother*.

Amanda Barrie (Alma from *Coronation Street*) was a dental patient in one of the places I worked. I only met her twice, though. When I came out of *Big Brother* one newspaper made out we were best mates. Another even said she was the one who'd made me my eviction dress. That's rubbish. The person who made it was a lady called Tina who wanted to be a fashion designer, and I promised I'd wear it to give her some publicity. Although when I look at pictures of myself in that eviction outfit now, I actually think I did her more harm than good. Sorry, Tina.

When I was about 19, Danny Jarman and I split up. There wasn't any major fall-out, we just grew apart really. I'd started wanting to hang around with my mates more than be with him, and I was also puffing a lot, which probably had something to do with my laziness in relationships! I used to go round and smoke at my friend Carrie-Ann's. Her house was awful; she had no carpet or anything, so we'd just sit on the floor. There were about eight of us, a mixture of boys and girls, and for about six months solid we'd puff every night – more than you could possibly imagine. Carrie-Ann's mum was a bit mental – a nutter in fact. Whenever we walked through the front door she'd shout at us, 'You fucking slags! Get out of my house!' She was properly mad: Nutty Noreen we called her. She's sorted herself out now, though, bless her. That stage in my life was all a bit of a haze, if I'm honest. Very funny, though. I don't think I've ever laughed so much.

Once we had a competition to see who could smoke the most. We bought a stupid amount of puff each – I think we spent about 50 quid – and we tried to see who could smoke the most in the quickest time. Me and my mate Lee were in a team together and we won. I have never been so out of it; I must've been green. Then we all put our heads under a blanket, smoked another whole spliff, and breathed it all in. When we popped our heads out my mascara was running all over my face. What mugs we were.

Once I'd got over my stoner phase I was back into the idea of having a boyfriend again. Or boyfriends, I should say. There was a period of time when I actually had four men on the go! One of them was called Matthew and I'd known him from school. Matthew was about three years older than me and I always felt like he looked after me. He was a charmer and he lived in a wicked apartment. I think he was a bit of a mini gangster because he was quite rich. Then there was another guy, also called Matthew, who was a painter and decorator. I met him when he was on community service with his mate John outside one of my mate's houses. We used to think they were 'well fit', and every time we passed them we'd all flirt loads. It wasn't long before me and this Matthew started doing more than flirting and we ended up dating for a bit. At the same time as this I was seeing my ex, Danny Jarman, again for a little while, and then I met the guy who was to be my next serious boyfriend, Danny Benstead. (Have I lost you yet?) So there were two Matthews and two Dannys, which could only happen to someone like me. But I couldn't handle all four for long. It was too complicated for my head. One minute I'd be on the phone to one Matthew, then the other would ring, then I'd be supposed to be meeting Danny. Oh God. It was all catching up on me. I only had two names to learn but I still very nearly called Danny 'Matthew' (and vice versa) a few times. There was no way I could keep it up. At the end of the day I wasn't a very good player. So I sat there one night and worked out who I should end it with. First I finished with Danny Jarman (because that was old news anyway), then it was a choice between Danny Benstead and the two Matthews. In the end I chucked both Matthews and opted for Danny B, which turned out to be the worst mistake I ever made.

I met Danny Benstead when he nearly ran me over. I was with my mate Sam, who he already knew from seeing her about, and after skidding in front of us in his car he got out and asked for her number. She really fancied him and we both thought he was keen on her. But he ended up calling her and asking her for my number instead!

When I first clapped eyes on Danny, he was wearing the biggest thick gold bracelet and the fattest gold necklace you've ever seen. Not only that, but he had on white Moschino trousers with black writing all over them. Obviously, going by my taste in fashion at the time, I thought he was the man. Yuk! The first time I went round his house I was dressed in a pair of red hotpants (to be fair,

I did have quite a good figure when I was younger), black shoes and a black top. He was living with his parents at the time and I heard him whisper, 'She's the bird I want to be with.' His dad replied, 'She's fucking fit, Dan.' I was so chuffed, although of course I pretended I didn't hear. Danny had a girfriend when I first met him, but he got rid of her once I agreed to go out with him. She was a nutter called Vicky. After they broke up she used to drive past his house in her car, singing that song 'The Boy is Mine' by Brandy and Monica at the top of her voice. Mentalist.

Danny worked as a tyre-changer for ATS. I thought it was quite a good job. He always had a bit of money and would treat me to meals and buy me lots of presents. Then he started working as a postman. It was around this time that he began to turn nasty. He started getting into cocaine and he'd do it nearly every night. Once I was walking down the street with him and he disappeared down an alley. When I looked over, he'd pulled a street sign off the wall and was doing a line off it. I didn't ever do it, though, I didn't want to. I was always in fear that if I tried it I might like it and be tempted to move on to something else, like my dad had. The thought of getting hooked and turning out like my dad has always stopped me doing class-A drugs. I've always believed that if someone in your family's got an addictive personality then it's got to live somewhere in you too. It must be hereditary, surely? I could stop myself from puffing – which I did, because I knew I couldn't carry on like a zombie forever – but the hard stuff was different. My only addiction is buying shoes, and I'd rather keep it that way.

Danny really changed whenever he took coke, and he'd

be really aggressive. I remember being in The Gin Palace one evening on a girls' night out, and he came storming in to find me. I was really humiliated because we'd planned it, he'd agreed to let me go out without him, and he wasn't meant to be there. He just stood in the corner giving me dirty looks and drinking and sniffing. Then, all of a sudden, he walked over, grabbed my hair and tried to drag me out. The thing is, this was a place I'd been going to ever since I was at school, so it was a stupid move on his part. All the blokes in there knew me from way back, and when they saw this guy pulling me by the hair they immediately jumped in and started beating him up. They could see he was hurting me. I tried to tell them he was my boyfriend and to stop it, but to them, being Bermondsey boys, you just don't hit a girl. So they carried on.

I lost a little bit of respect for myself that night, because even after the way Danny had treated me, I still went back home with him. We got back to his house, closed the front door, and he just turned on me in the corridor like a wild animal. He started punching my face and my head. My lip started pouring with blood. The worst thing was, his dad was in the lounge throughout the whole thing. He just sat there staring at the TV. I was petrified. Somehow I managed to open the door and run out. I could hear Danny's footsteps behind me, chasing me as he shouted, 'Don't think I'm not going to get you!' God knows how I got away in the end. My heart was racing so fast.

The next day he bought me a watch to say sorry. I don't know why I forgave him but I did. If this had been happening to someone else I'd be the first to tell them to leave, but when you're in that situation yourself, it's so hard. You devalue yourself; they make you think you'll never get another boyfriend, that you're ugly and worthless. I found myself lying to my mum about the cuts and bruises – I'd say I'd banged my head or fallen over – all the usual clichés. I was simply scared of him. He was nasty. That was one of the main reasons I wanted to go on *Big Brother*: to get away from Danny. I couldn't see another way out.

My relationship with Mum was starting to deteriorate too. She began hanging around with some really dodgy people: crack addicts, to be precise. There was one in particular who'd always come round to our house. She'd come to the front door, look at me with this glazed expression and say, 'Is your mum in?' I'd reply, 'Fuck off, get out of my house.' Mel, her name was. She was absolutely vile, dirty and disgusting. I used to argue with Mum about her all the time. Why did she want to see this woman? How could she walk along the streets with someone who looked like that? They went everywhere together and she used to lean on my mum like a limpet.

I had a fight with Mel once. I hated her. She lived in the same block of flats as my nan and granddad, and one day she walked past them on the landing and muttered under her breath, 'You bastard' to my granddad. When I heard she'd said that I pulled her out of her house and started laying into her. I was so het-up and angry with the way she'd been behaving and what she was doing to my family. I screamed, 'Come near my door again and I will fucking fuck you up!' Then Mum started sticking up for her! For some reason she had it in her head that this Mel was a great person. She wasn't, she was a parasite.

'That's It, I'm Done'

The thing is, my mum's quite vulnerable and weak-minded, and that's always scared me. I worried about her then like I worry about my kids now. She was easily influenced, and for some awful reason that I just couldn't fathom for the life of me, she'd started befriending these crack addicts. My biggest fear was that she'd start taking drugs herself and that she'd turn out like my dad. After all we'd been through with him, I just couldn't work out why she'd want to be friends with people like that. Although I believed her when she said she hadn't tried crack herself, I still couldn't settle. I'd go to work and I'd worry all day. When I came home I'd have this empty feeling in my stomach, not knowing what I was going to find. Would she be on crack? Would she be alive? I used to argue and argue with her and was forever telling her she'd got in with the wrong crowd. I hated it; we were fighting like cat and dog. It got so bad I actually ended up raising my hand to her. That's when I felt shittest. I let myself down by hitting my own mother. Mind you, I came off worse; I had a big black eye and cuts all over my face. But we properly laid into each other as if we were from rival gangs on the street. It wasn't nice. But I felt like I couldn't get through to her, she didn't understand how I felt. It was like a knife going through my heart and shattering all my good thoughts about her. I could handle her puffing but not anything harder. That was my dad's territory, not hers. I just kept thinking, *what's next?* That's another reason why I wanted to go into the *Big Brother* house – I couldn't bear being at home.

I hated being in my mum's house. I hated being with my boyfriend. I felt like I just had nowhere to go. I hated living. I had to get out. So I tried moving out of Mum's and getting my own flat. I forged a letter and took it to the council. (Mum refused to write me one herself because she said it was 'immoral and irresponsible' to let her daughter move out. Huh!) The council found me a room in a hostel in the Oval (I can't say it properly, though, so to me it's 'the Overall'). It was the worst hovel I've ever seen, it was so filthy. Outside the building there was every single nationality of flag hanging from the windows and off the balconies, except the English one. The entire place stank of piss and was so grubby you could barely see the surface when you wiped your finger across it. My mate Jolene came with me because she was having trouble at home too, but when it came to it neither of us could live there. On the first night, two men came and knocked at our door. They had no tops on and just looked at us with sly grins on their faces and said 'Hellooooo'. There was no way we were going to sleep there after that, but we had to pretend we did, otherwise we'd never be placed in anything better, so we'd sign in every morning and night, then go and sleep at one of our mates' houses, or wherever we could. Sometimes I'd go back to Mum's, but only when she wasn't there. I'd lost my job at the dental practice as I was always coming in late and had eventually stopped turning up because I was feeling so down. I'd lost the will to do anything. I just thought, *Fuck it*. For a few days I went to this place on Jamaica Road called the Bosco Centre – which was where little kids went if they were naughty – and I did a few courses like typing and stuff. After that I lived off the Jobseeker's Allowance. Occasionally I'd do the odd shift on a sweet and cake stall owned by another mate's dad because he gave me cash in hand.

Then I was finally allocated a proper flat. Jolene got one too. It was a nice little place but I wanted everything to be just right – I was proud, remember? – and in the end I had hardly any furniture, because I'd only want it if it was expensive designer stuff. I had a mattress on my front room floor, which I slept on, and in the corner was a shiny silver fridge worth £500 and a kettle worth £70! I loved that fridge, even if I couldn't afford to buy anything to put in it. But although I was starting to get houseproud and feel positive about myself, there was always something, or someone, to bring me back down to earth. Namely, my mum and Danny. I would lie on my mattress thinking, *I don't really want to be here, I want to be with Mum,* but I couldn't bear to go home to Mum and see what she was doing to herself. Whenever Danny came round he would smash up walls or hit me, and afterwards I would sit alone in the dark, nursing my bruises and rocking back and forth. I thought I'd be better off dead. I seriously wanted to take my life, I felt that low. But the thing with me is, I don't like the sight of blood on myself. I don't mind it on other people but, even to this day, if I get a cut or graze I panic. So there was no way I could have slit my wrists or anything. I didn't have the brain to realise that if you mixed tablets with alcohol you could kill yourself that way. So I would just lie there in the dark for nights on end, wallowing in my own sorrow. But I hated living. I fucking hated it.

I'd hit rock bottom. And I was feeling so low that I didn't have any respect for my body either. You might remember the newspaper report saying: 'JADE: THE SECRET PORN STAR' that appeared in the *Sunday Sport* while I was in the *Big Brother* house? Well, I wouldn't go quite that far, but I did come close.

I was walking across Tower Bridge on my way home from work one day, mulling over the vicious fight I'd had with Danny the night before, and a man came up to me and said, 'I don't mean this in a horrible way but you've got a great set of boobs. I think you could make a lot of money out of them.' I looked at him in shock and said, 'Oh, no, no. It's OK, thanks.' But he gave me his card anyway and tried to persuade me to 'Go away and think about it.' I walked off. I'd never have thought I'd be one of those girls who'd get their kit off or behave in a sleazy manner, but as I was walking, I have to admit a grin appeared on my face. Someone had just told me I had great boobs!

I went home and told Danny, who, unsurprisingly, wasn't too pleased about it and started ranting about pervs on the street. It was case closed as far as he was concerned.

Then, one morning, after we'd had another row, I just thought, *Why not?* This guy had said I could get up to £500 for a set of topless photos. With that kind of money I could buy some more shoes or something else for my flat – a table, maybe. So that was what I was going to do. I didn't tell *anyone,* not even my closest mates. I just drew out some money, got on a train and went. I was scared because I knew anything could happen to me. I knew I was being silly not telling people my whereabouts, but I was so down I thought, *Fuck it, what have I got to lose? I've got nothing else. If someone kills me, so what?*

The train journey took ages. I can't remember exactly

where it was, but it was far. I got to the street and there was a building with just one solitary door and virtually no windows. I walked inside and there was a receptionist who could hardly speak English, and she pointed towards the staircase. I went up the stairs, which were creaking like they were about to collapse any second, then I got to the top and walked into a room. I was greeted by a fat, sweaty-looking foreign man. 'Hello, how are you?' he said creepily. I was under the impression I was going to be met by the guy who'd approached me on the street, but he was clearly just the middleman. I was so nervous. This man kept prodding his chest and saying 'Me photographer!' and gesturing for me to take my top off. I didn't have a clue what I was doing and my heart was pounding. I took my top off and leant against this white background with my bra on, stiff as board I was. 'You can do nude, no?' he nodded. I shook my head. I don't recall what he said to me after that but he was obviously very persuasive, because the next second I was stood there with no bra on. I'd never ever thought I'd do anything like that. If you saw the pictures now you'd see how uncomfortable I was. I was biting my lip, looking nervously around me, as if I thought someone might be watching. It was so degrading. I remember thinking, *What the fuck are you doing, Jade? Why are you doing this?* The fat man kept telling me to wink and look sexy, but I just couldn't. I wanted to die. Even now, just thinking about it, I feel disgusting and dirty. It was one of the most embarrassing, horrible things I've ever done.

As I walked out of the building to the train station I thought, *I can't do this.* So I turned and I ran back to the building. I flew up the creaky stairs and said breathlessly, 'I'm so sorry. I didn't mean to waste your time or anything but I don't want you to sell those pictures. I don't want to be in magazines.' He was surprisingly fine about it. I ripped up my contract and he told me he would never develop the film. I trusted him and he said, 'No problem, no problem.' Little did I know he'd kept the film just in case he could make money from it one day. Which he did. He must've nearly wet his fat pants when he clocked me on *Big Brother*.

The main thing that made me turn back that day was the thought of my grandparents. I just kept thinking, *What if my granddad sees this?* That's what I couldn't stand. How would he cope with seeing his granddaughter in a porno mag? (I know he shouldn't be looking at it in the first place, but that's not the point.) My nan and granddad are so special to me. I always feel the need to protect them. No matter how shit I feel, I never let them see that I'm suffering. I never have. I always go round to their house with a beaming smile on my face. As far as they've known, I've never had a crap day in my life, everything's always been brilliant.

I told my mum about the photo shoot when I got back. I couldn't keep it to myself any longer; I'm not very good at secrets. Mum was more annoyed about the fact that I'd gone on my own and not said anything to anyone about where I'd gone. She just kept shouting at me, 'Anything could've happened!' So we had another argument.

One day, I was watching the telly and an advert came on asking for contestants for *Big Brother 3*. I just thought, *I'd love to go on that show.* I'd never applied for anything in my life, but I was desperate. I often wonder what would have happened to me if I hadn't been chosen. How would my life be now? I'd probably be in a mental institution by now (or visiting my mum in one, ha ha!). I think that's the reason I behaved the way I did when I was on the show. I just needed to act like a kid because it felt like I'd never been one before. At the age of five I was washing, cleaning, cooking and changing plugs, because my mum couldn't do it. But for once in my life, within the walls of the *Big Brother* house, I had no weight on my shoulders. I could do what I wanted: I was free.

One of the nicest things about being in *Big Brother* was not having to think about coming home and what I might find when I got there. Once I entered that house, it was like a load had been lifted from my body. It might sound strange, but it was as if my brain said, 'You must shut off everything from your past life and start afresh.' So I didn't think about Danny, my mum or even my nan very much. I know it sounds selfish but I needed to be me and not to have to think about other people for a change. I'd been running around after others for my whole life. This was my chance to start again and let people look after *me* instead.

Mum and I patched things up before I went into the house. She finally stopped seeing Mel and co. so I agreed to move back in with her (OK, the real reason is actually because I couldn't keep up the rental payments on the flat). I took my fridge and went back home. Mum did come to her senses about the people she was hanging round with, though. She told me she was sorry and she didn't know what had got into her. And we got on really well again. I never could rid myself of that nagging fear about what I might find her doing when I came home from work, though. I was often paranoid that she was meeting them behind my back, and sometimes I got that familiar sick, scared feeling in my stomach whenever I was around her, just in case I didn't know the full truth. But I had to believe her. If I couldn't trust her, who could I trust? I love my mum.

5

'What? They Want Me?'

I never watched the first *Big Brother* on TV, I just knew the person who won it gave their winnings to charity. I started watching the second one when Helen and Paul were getting all cosy in the love shack. Even then it was never my ambition to get on the show myself. But when the number appeared at the bottom of my TV screen asking for applicants for next year, I thought, *Why not?*

I remember calling the number and trying to leave my message. I was working in Guy's Hospital at the time (you know, with people who had braces). I had to go outside to a phone box, but the phone kept cutting off because I hadn't put enough money in, so every time I got halfway through a sentence I'd have to ring back again. I must've done it about three or four times in total. 'Hello, this is Jade Goody. I've just rung you...'

'It's only me again! Remember? Jade Goody. I called a minute ago...'

'Er, I just got cut off again but it's Jade Goody here, I work in a dental surgery, I'm meant to be in there now actually but...'

'Sorry, Jade Goody, aged 20, you've probably had about three messages from me already. I'd like to apply for the next series of *Big Brother*, please...'

Finally I got my words out and the application form was sent to my house. It was massive. At first I thought I'd never get through it, but one evening after work I sat there and just wrote *everything*. It all seemed to come flooding out. I told them about my mum, my dad, the whole lot. When they asked if I had a criminal record I confessed that I'd stolen from Selfridges and that I'd smoked puff. I kept drawing little smiley faces or sad faces by each answer, depending on whether I thought I'd said a good thing or a bad thing. I was never thinking for one minute I'd get through.

The next thing I had to do was make a video, so I went round to my mate Clem's house because she had a video camera. There was no planning involved, or any reason why I did what I did – and I think you could tell. I sang a song, it was to the tune of Rod Stewart's song 'Maggie May', but I made up my own words: 'Wake up, *Big Brother*, I think I've got something to say to you. Get me out of Bermondsey and put me on TV, Davina and all your friends pick me.' Ha ha ha. Then I started going into some random rant about my boobs, and said my nickname was Pamela Anderson because of these two things. I didn't know what was coming out of my mouth. After that, for some bizarre reason, I decided to put my body through an elastic band.

'What? They Want Me?'

Looking back, it was obvious they'd never forget me. For a start, I was the bird who'd rung up for a form and got cut off three times. Lo and behold, I got called to an open day, where the producers give you all these different tasks to do to see how you bond with other people. I had on a black and white stripey jumper, black trousers and a black and white pair of pointy shoes. I turned up late – I got lost on the way there. My heel came off too because I was running up this escalator and my shoe got caught in one of the grooves. When I walked into the place where I thought it was, it turned out I'd actually gone into a law school. And because the whole *Big Brother* thing is shrouded in so much secrecy I wasn't allowed to say, 'I'm here to audition for *Big Brother*'. When I walked into the room full of all these lawyer types, all I could say was, 'I'm here...for an audition.' A stern-faced man looked at me and said, 'You're in the wrong place.' I went into nearly every room saying the same thing until I realised I was in the wrong building.

When I finally tracked the place down, I ran up the stairs with my shoes in my hands, burst into the room and said, 'All right! Sorry, it's Jade Goody.' Kate Lawler was at my audition. We didn't really talk though – it was one of those instinctive things when you meet someone and know you won't get on. I didn't like her and she didn't like me. There were quite a few people in there who didn't like me actually. We had to play loads of games and afterwards we were told to nominate someone from the group to leave. The producers said that the person who got the most nominations would have to walk out of the room and wouldn't get a chance to come in again. Guess who got the most nominations? That's right, me. Everyone had to write down a name and a reason why. It was all, 'Jade – she's too loud', 'Jade – not my cup of tea'. I thought *Great,* but I held my head up, said 'See you later' and walked out.

However, once I left the room I discovered it was a trick, and that in actual fact I was through to the next round. I got to the bottom of the stairs and there was a camera crew and I was asked to talk for a couple of minutes about myself. Easy. Then I was sent back up to the room. It was like they were playing mind games with us. The people who'd nominated me were looking at me as if to say, *What the hell are you doing back up here?* I just grinned and said, 'Ha! You thought I was gone, didn't you? Well, I've got through to the next round, so nar nar na nar nar!!' Then half the group were sent away and told they hadn't got through, so the rest of us had to stay and play more games. At the end of the day we were given another – even more gigantic – application form. It was full of questions about how we thought we'd cope inside the house and stuff like that.

The next stage was being invited to meet with the psychotherapist – Brett Kahr his name was – and if he decided you were strong enough to survive in that kind of environment, you were asked to meet Phil Edgar-Jones, the head honcho.

So, off I went to meet Phil. I wasn't nervous, I just thought I'd be myself and have a chat. I was told to wait for someone to meet me outside Kentucky Fried Chicken somewhere in North London at some weird o'clock in the morning – it was all very cloak and dagger. Then someone in dark glasses arrived to pick me up, like something out of a spy movie, and took me to meet Phil and two other producers on the show. The meeting seemed to go OK and after that I had another chat with the psychotherapist. Brett sat me down and held his hands a few inches apart. He said, 'Imagine this is a bench full of people.' Then he moved his fingers so they were almost touching. 'Now this is the amount of people who are left. And you're one of them.' Oh my God. Now I knew how close I was to getting in. I thought, *Shit, this is serious. I could actually be on this programme.* I was excited. I was frightened. I was peeing my pants.

Then I was assigned a chaperone – he was called Paul – and I was told he was to join me and my mates for a night out. I think the idea was to see how I behaved in a normal environment and what I'd be like if I'd had a drink. But I had to introduce him to them as if he was someone I'd known for years. I think I said he was my cousin (although at one point I nearly forgot and started referring to him as my chaperone). We went for something to eat, then he came back to the house so he could meet my mum. After that he left and went back to report his findings to Phil Edgar-Jones. He probably said, 'Just as we thought, she's mental – and what's more, her mum is too.'

I'll never forget what happened next. I was at home with Mum and Danny and my phone rang. It was Phil Edgar-Jones. He said, 'Jade, I'm pleased to tell you you're one of the contestants we want for *Big Brother*.' I was shaking, I couldn't breathe, then I think I started screaming. I might've even dropped the phone at one point. He kept saying, 'Now, Jade, remember, you're not allowed to tell anyone.' That was the one thing I'd been told all along: 'It is of utmost importance that you don't say anything about this to a soul.' But I couldn't keep my mouth shut. *Of course* I told people. As soon as I went in to work (I was working at a dental practice in Covent Garden at this point) I told everyone that I was going to be on *Big Brother*.

I soon realised there was a very good reason why I'd been told to be quiet. In a matter of days the press got wind of it and rang up my work asking questions about me. I thought I'd blown my chance. Phil Edgar-Jones had warned me that if the public found out my identity I'd lose my place in the house. There were press outside my granddad's house, outside my mum's place – it was amazing how quickly it got out. But they never got a picture of me, and that was my saving grace in the end. They knew my name but what they didn't know was what I looked like. Ironically, in the same week that I got told I was through to *Big Brother*, I received a call from my model agency telling me I'd got the part in a music video. They'd sent my picture off to a director who was making the debut video for a new band called Busted. He wanted me to play the part of the teacher, Miss McKenzie, in 'That's What I Go to School For'. Just think, I could've had the lead singer Charlie Simpson running after me through a field in his underpants!

Because of my blabbermouth, Phil Edgar-Jones sent my chaperone Paul to come and get me early. He met me from the dental practice, then we got on a bus and went straight to my house. It was two days earlier than I thought I was leaving but he told me I had to pack there and then. I had to gather all my belongings and say my goodbyes within the space of about 30 minutes. I didn't know what was going on. I didn't know what I was and wasn't allowed to take, so I just threw everything in. I said bye to Mum – it wasn't a long, lovey-dovey goodbye or anything, just 'I'll see you later, good luck', that kind of thing. I wasn't registering the fact that I might not see her again for ages. I wasn't really with it at all, it was all going so fast. I thought I'd have an extra day or two to prepare myself but because I'd opened my big mouth I didn't. I called Phil Edgar-Jones and kept saying, 'Phil, I swear I haven't said anything. It wasn't me, honest.' He must've known I was fibbing, but he was very good about it. It's a good job I was taken away when I was, though. That night I was planning to have a farewell party in this club called Bon Sonnies and I found out later that Kate Lawler was going there too. If we'd seen each other you can guarantee we would've started showing off that we'd got in and blown it all. What a mad day!

I was taken to a hotel in Elstree near the studio, and from the moment I walked into the room I was not allowed out again. I wasn't told how long I was going to be there, all I knew was that I wasn't leaving until they said so. It was a box room with a bed and a telly. Of course, I wasn't allowed to watch the telly in case I saw something I shouldn't. Because information was being leaked, I was banned from having any contact with the outside world in case I accidentally learnt something about any of the other housemates. I was barred from all newspapers, radio, TV and phones. The only visitor I was allowed to see was my boyfriend Danny. He came to stay with me for my second-to-last night in the hotel. I didn't really want him there but I thought it was best to smooth things over before I went into the house. He kept telling me he didn't want me to go on the show and he said, 'You will be there for me when you get out, won't you? Don't do anything to embarrass me, will you? We're going to be together forever...' But no matter what he said to me, I knew that as soon as I got through that door he was not going to be my boyfriend any more, because *Big Brother* was going to be my escape. Then Danny gave me a kiss on the forehead and said, 'You'll be out soon anyway – you won't last that long.' Nice, eh? I just thought, *I cannot wait for you to get out of this room and out of my life*. We ordered room service. I had a Diet Coke, crisps and a steak sandwich – it was the toughest steak I'd ever tasted – and my belly felt so heavy afterwards.

Danny was told to leave really early the next morning. After he'd gone, one of the producers came to check my suitcase. She was called Clare and I thought she was wicked because she was really nice to me and always laughing and joking. She looked inside my case, then went away. Then another producer came in and this big discussion ensued. I didn't have the foggiest idea what was going on. They counted how many knickers I had, how many bras, what colour...It turned out I hadn't put any socks in, so that was another talking point. I'd put in three bras and six pairs of knickers. I think I thought I was going on a week's holiday. Well, when I was packing, I didn't think, did I? It was all such a rush. They went and got me some extra pants and some toothpaste and a bottle of wine for my luxury items (I hadn't thought of that either). I had planned to take toilet roll as my luxury item but I forgot.

'What? They Want Me?'

I'm very particular about toilet roll – if I have a number two I like it to be quilted. But when I asked if they could get me a pack of twelve, they said no.

I'd packed loads of bags too for some reason. I had four handbags: a Gucci bag, a Fendi bag, a Burberry bag and a sequinned black bag. Why, I don't know. What was I going to do? Walk around the *Big Brother* garden with them over my shoulder? I also didn't know you weren't allowed designer labels on TV. Most of my things were Gucci and they had big fat G's all over them. All my sandals were Gucci and I was told I wasn't allowed to bring them in. In the end, they let me take two of the more subtle pairs because I moaned that I wouldn't have anything to put on my feet otherwise. As I watched all the producers rummaging through my case I started panicking – all my clothes were being taken off me! I was saying, 'What am I going to do?' The whole thing caused a right kerfuffle. In the end, about four different people had to come and have a look in my case to decide what I could and couldn't take in. I lost about seven T-shirts and three pairs of shoes in total.

I was allowed one phone call to my mum, the extent of which was literally, 'Mum, my bags have been checked, I'm going in tomorrow, I'm really excited.' And we had a chuckle about the fact I only had six pairs of knickers. Then it was time to have my picture taken. I had a pink top on and I had to stand against a white wall. I had to do a happy face, a sad face, a straight face – all these different expressions. I was so excited I didn't care. Neither did I realise that these photographs were being sent to the press. They were the only professional pictures that the entire nation would see of me for the duration of my time in the house. If I'd known that I would've made more of an effort.

Then the day arrived. I was woken up at the crack of dawn (well, seven o'clock anyway). I had a full English breakfast, but the sausages were rock hard and burnt so I left them. My suitcase was checked a final time. Then they got rid of my tatty old thing and replaced it with a shiny silver case and took it into storage. I was left with a smaller version of the same case, which I was told to fill with my luxury items, so I put in a bottle of wine, make-up, deodorant, that sort of thing. It had a sticker on it of the big *Big Brother* eye. It was when I saw that staring up at me that it suddenly became much more real: I just kept thinking, *Oh my God. I can't believe this...*

I was put in a car and driven to another place. I didn't know where because the windows of the car were all blacked out so I couldn't look outside. I had no clue where I was going. We arrived at this stark-looking building and I was led inside to a white make-up room. I knew it was a make-up room because there were lights all round the mirror. The only piece of furniture was a chair. I was sat on that chair from about 9 a.m. to the minute I walked into the *Big Brother* doors, about twelve hours later. All the other housemates were there too, but no one was allowed to see each other. We were all locked away separately, all sat in a different room, all with a different chaperone, all shit-scared. But I could hear them being talked about on the walkie-talkie my chaperone had with him in the room. I heard things like: 'Girl One wants to go to the toilet, make sure Girl Four is out of there in two minutes.' 'Can Boy Three have a sandwich?' 'Boy Two wants a can of

Coke:' It was so exhilarating, so secret and so undercover. One chaperone slipped up, though. I heard my name mentioned, quickly followed by a 'shit', because the person who said it knew they'd made a mistake.

Every time I needed the toilet I had to ask and wait ages to be escorted out. All day I was desperately trying to get information about the other housemates out of my chaperone but he wouldn't budge. It wasn't Paul this time – I think Paul was doing some proper work because he was one of the producers. This time it was a gay man. I can't remember his name, but he was hilarious. He kept my mind off the reality of the situation and helped me relax by making me laugh. I remember him telling me that he once thought the phrase 'If your name's not down, you're not coming in' was 'If your name's not Dan, you're not coming in'. I cried with laughter when he said that.

At about 4 p.m. I had my make-up done and a camera crew came in and filmed it. I had to talk about how I was feeling – a 'final thoughts' sort of thing. Then someone took a Polaroid of me, which I think was for the producers to put up on the wall of their office. I think it was also for the cameramen so that when I first got into the house they would know what I looked like if the director said, 'Zoom in on Jade' or whatever. By this point I was really tired. It was dark outside, and my old chaperones Clare and Paul came back in to see me and to check I was OK. I felt like I had literally run out of all my energy. Clare gave me a vitamin tablet you put in your drink called Berocca. It was the first time I'd ever had such a thing and it worked a treat. I have never ever felt so lifted in my life. I swear by Berocca now, I drink it all the time when I'm flagging, even though it makes your wee a funny orange colour.

I was starting to get really, really nervous by now. I kept asking, 'What's the time? What's the time?' over and over again. I knew it was near, but I had no idea what to expect. I'd never seen the beginning of any of the *Big Brother* shows, and in actual fact, I don't think they'd ever had a grand entrance with a crowd before, so this was the first year there was such a dramatic build-up. I could hear the crowd whooping outside and there was a man telling stupid jokes on the microphone, warming them up. It was so scary. There was an amazing feeling surging through my body. Clare was great and just kept telling me, 'You're going to be all right, just be yourself, you're a brilliant person. I'll be here when you get out...'

Just thinking about that night still sends shivers down my spine. I remember waiting to get in the car – even though it was only driving me a few yards – and I was craning to see who was in the car in front of me. Then I was sitting in the car, waiting. I could just see the stage in front and a big screen. I caught the end clip of another housemate's video – I think it was Sunita's – then, suddenly, I saw my face appear on the big screen! It was my audition tape and I was wriggling in and out of the elastic band. Clare tried to shield my eyes and said, 'You're not meant to see that', but it was too late. I could hear my voice booming out like a banshee and the audience just watching and cheering. Then I was told to get out of the car and smile. After that it just turned into a blur. A sea of faces; noise; I remember seeing my mum; Davina saying, 'Your family's over there, go and say your final goodbyes,' and then I saw Danny in the crowd too. I thought, *Oh God, not him again,* and kissed him really quickly. My mum was in bits, upset, excited, or something. I found out afterwards she even had an asthma attack because she got into such a panic. She was stood in the crowd outside the studio and eventually they had to call an ambulance for her because out of nowhere she shouted, 'I'm a lesbian! I love Davina!' and fainted. The whole experience was as intense for her as it was for me.

The next thing I can recall is walking through the doors to the *Big Brother* house and saying 'Oh my God! The bedcovers have got stones on!' There were two orange sofas in L-shapes and a heated swimming pool in the garden. Wicked! I think Spencer was the first one to jump in. There was a vegetable patch too. I remember having a conversation with Spencer and him telling me there was a vegetable called asparagus, which I thought was very weird. I liked the chickens, though.

I wasn't allowed into the diary room straight away, but the first thing I asked when I got in was, 'Is my mum all right?', which luckily she was. Although you're not allowed to be given any information about the outside world, on your application form you are granted one request. So I'd written, 'If anything happens to my mum I want to know about it.' I didn't care about anything else.

6

'Do You Think the Cameras Saw Us?'

I didn't think about the cameras once. The boys were the first ones to go into the house, so by the time I walked down those stairs they were already there. I was the third girl in, straight after Alison, who I immediately warmed to because she was just so much larger than life. I remember thinking she might overshadow me though because she was very loud. Mind you, I wasn't exactly a wallflower. I fancied Alex when I first saw him, I thought he was gorgeous. Then I got a closer look and decided he had big teeth and looked a bit like a Bee Gee. I didn't take to Jonny at all, I just thought he was an irritating git and he had really sweaty armpits. Sandy was dressed in his trademark kilt and I thought 'you could be interesting' – wasn't wrong there was I? Spencer was clearly in there as the heartthrob of the bunch, but I didn't really notice him to start with. He was so laid back he nearly fell over. When I looked at Lee I thought 'black boy with big muscles' and PJ 'bald, short

Brummie'. Kate was the only one of the housemates I'd met before, because she was at the same audition as me. We probably both thought the same as each other when we met again in the house: 'Fucking hell, it's you!' I can't remember having any opinion about Adele, which was strange considering she was the one I ended up hanging out with most. Lynne was just Scottish and loud, but she's slipped from my mind because as things transpired she only ended up in there for about five minutes. I didn't really get to know Sunita that much either. I didn't mind her but on the first night I had an argument with her because she started preaching about drugs. She looked at me and said, 'You don't know much because of your age,' and I remember getting really annoyed. I said, 'Don't talk to me about my age. I probably know more about drugs than you lot put together.' Me, Spencer and Sunita were the last up and decided to play hide and seek. I hid in a drawer (it was a big one).

At the end of the first week Davina's voice came through on the loudspeaker. She told us the phone lines had been open all week and that the public had already nominated the two people they most wanted to go for eviction. There was a nervous hush from all the housemates. Then she said, 'They are Jade and Lynne.' I thought, *Fucking hell, I've only been in here about ten minutes*. I felt gutted. I was so upset. I sat on the bed thinking, *Why do they want me out? What have I done wrong? I've just been myself. OK, I was a bit overexcited, but that's it*. I was so scared of going back out there, mainly because of Danny.

The rest of the housemates were told they had to choose between us, and Lynne and I were sent to the bedroom.

'Do You Think the Cameras Saw Us?'

When they picked me to stay I was so bloody relieved, but I still felt bad because of Lynne. She got really annoyed about it and ended up giving her opinion about everybody in the house, which wasn't very nice. I can't remember exactly what she said, but Spencer knows the full conversation as he still recites it all the time. He thought it was hilarious.

I thought Lynne was a bit irritating anyway, so I'm glad she went. I know I wound a few people up in there but I think she would have been more annoying than me if she'd stayed.

I really liked Spencer from the moment I met him. I didn't fancy him, he was just cool. On that first evening, while the rest of us were running around him like loons and over-excitedly chatting rubbish, he just slumped on the sofa as if he couldn't give a shit. People probably looked at him and thought, *You miserable bastard,* but I thought he was great. He wasn't a show-off. He was himself throughout. If he couldn't be bothered to talk, he wouldn't; if he had an opinion, he'd voice it; if he wanted to sleep, he'd sleep (which was quite a lot!). I had some good chats with him; I felt like he listened to me and didn't mind me asking him questions all the time. I knew he found me quite endearing because he'd smile a lot when I said things. I didn't understand at the time that he was laughing because I was being such an idiot. When I was asking him all those questions about East Angular (OK, East *Anglia*) I didn't have a clue it would make me so famous. I also didn't have a clue I sounded quite so thick. I was sitting on the end of his bed and asking him where he lived and what he did. He said he was a punter or something. People still come up to

109

me now and say, 'Have you found out where East Angular is yet, Jade?' And I have, for the record.

I thought Adele and I were really good mates in the house, but it wasn't the case. She was extremely two-faced. People have said since that she'd wind me up to the point that I'd go and slag people off, almost as if I was doing her dirty work for her. She was the gun and I was the bullet. She would use me to do things. I didn't speak to her after I came out, once I'd seen how she'd behaved.

I couldn't work Kate out to start with. I think we both knew we were never going to be the best of mates so we just tried to get on with it as best we could. Spencer really liked Kate, but I think she led him on. She kissed him between the bars once when we had the rich and the poor side, but that was as far as things went between them in the house. She was the one who initiated things, but I think she was just playing a game the whole time. She used her sex appeal to get what she wanted – she's got a great figure and she knew it. Spencer told me how he felt about her but I didn't like what she was doing and warned him off. He found out for himself when they got out of the house anyway, when they did an *OK!* photo shoot together. They were sent off on holiday as a couple, but when they got back she ditched him. He said to me afterwards that he'd felt really hurt by her because when the cameras were clicking away she was all lovey-dovey, but as soon as they stopped she didn't want to know. According to Spencer, they definitely shagged though.

Kate's affections in the house went from being all over Alex, then to Spencer, then back to Alex again once

Spencer had left. And the whole time she had a secret boyfriend called Charlie! I found this out later because Jeff knows him and told me about Charlie when we first met. Once Spencer had gone, Kate started playing 'Follow the Van' with Alex. That 'Follow the Van' shit pissed me off. I was always sat there thinking, *Why aren't I playing it? Why am I being left out?* I didn't like it! Alex told me once, 'You won't want to play, believe me.' We were cleaning out the chickens and I said to him, 'What is "Follow the Van"?' and he replied, 'Basically, the van goes around parts of your body, and when the van stops, the person who's got the van has to kiss, suck or lick the part of the other person's body.' I thought, *No way!* I know I did what I did with PJ, but to me this was much more seedy.

There was worse stuff going on too. Kate had a snog with Adele, Alex had a snog with Kate and Adele, Kate sucked Adele's nipples, Adele did the same to her. Alex told me all this after we'd come out of the house, because he got so frustrated that Kate had played him for such a mug on the show. He also told me that when Kate played 'Follow the Van' with him, she'd kissed his willy, played with his balls, let him kiss her tits *and* down there on her la la too. The reason he was so angry afterwards was that she could do all that and then still go into the diary room and nominate him. He couldn't believe it. He hates her now, or so he tells me.

I thought Alex was gay to start with, but there's no way he is. OK, he's in touch with his feminine side and likes his hygiene and wears little Y-fronts and prances around like a fairy, but I can assure you he's definitely not gay. Adele and Alex had a snog just before she got evicted and we really thought something might happen between them. Then, after she left, he ended up getting it on with Kate under the duvet. Things moved on quickly in that house!

Alex has got the biggest willy I have ever seen. Right at the end of the series, when there were only four of us left, we all had a shower together. I'd heard rumours from the others about the size of it, but I hadn't ever seen it for myself. When I saw him naked I was gobsmacked. I couldn't speak. I shouted, 'That is the biggest willy ever' Alex just pulled this coy face and said, 'I know, I can't help it.'

Then Jonny, who clearly felt left out, decided to show us this trick he could do with his balls. He had the biggest balls ever. They were disgusting. He could twist them around about eight times. I nearly threw up. Jonny was OK, he did make me laugh sometimes, but I could only take him in small portions. PJ always said that his humour was a bit repetitive. Jonny could be quite aggravating at times too – everything he did was 'showbizzy'. Both he and Kate were the worst for that. It was as if they were on a holiday camp all the time. They would get together and do the same dance, and I'd think, *Oh my God, I feel like I'm in Butlins*. It was too much.

Alison was also part of their gang, but I liked her. She broke so much furniture in that house, it was hilarious. Bless her. On the first day she broke the settee, then she broke one of the sunloungers, then a chair that was made to look like a stone. The garden table was probably the most memorable thing she demolished, though. She was jumping up and down on it like a right doughnut. What did she think it was going to do?

'Do You Think the Cameras Saw Us?'

Sometimes she would shovel food into her mouth, turn to me really deadpan and say, 'I can't eat any more. This really isn't good for my figure,' then she'd turn back and keep shoving it right in. She'd always make a joke out of herself, which I admired.

When the bars went up for the 'heaven and hell' divide in week three it was such a shock. I was only even on the poor side for a week and I was cracking up. To be fair to Kate, whatever I thought of her, she was over there for most of the time and she was quite a good sport about it. I was moaning so much when I was in there. I kept saying, 'I can't eat chickpeas and lentils all the time!' I don't think I even knew what a chickpea was. I thought there was chicken in chickpeas at least. In one of his finer moments, Spencer taught me how to cook on a barbeque and light it. I remember standing outside in the rain one day with an umbrella over my head, trying desperately to get the bloody firefighters to work. It was shit. And the showers were freezing. That was Spencer's excuse for not washing, though. One night I was lying in the bed next to him and he properly stank. He had chicken poo on his socks and hadn't washed for days. I said, 'You've got to have a shower – you stink!' So I got him up at about two o'clock in the morning and forced him outside to have one. We used a colander thing to wash him, from what I can remember. No matter how much I liked Spencer, he did smell. And his feet were awful.

When I was on the poor side all the housemates on the rich side really pissed me off, and I didn't mind saying so. Lee in particular did my head in for a while, especially when he was fawning all over Sophie. When I talked to

113

Spencer about it he'd try to wind me up and say I was jealous. I'd say, 'Sophie is a mug, I'm not jealous!'

When Sophie came into the house I have to admit I wasn't very nice to her. I'm not usually a bully, but I did bully her. But when she walked in on day whatever (like I remember now!) and started saying, 'Yeah, we're all going to Ibiza!', I thought, *Fucking hell, are you some sort of beg-a-friend or something?* She was trying too hard and I didn't like it one bit. After that I kept picking on faults in her. She had an amazing figure but I'd say things behind her back like, 'How fat is her fanny? It's like a camel's hoof,' which wasn't very nice really. I used to say to the boys, 'Has she got something down her knickers, boys?' It did look like something massive to me, though.

I got drunk most of the time when I was on the rich side. I just thought, *I'm with boring people so I might as well get pissed*. The producers called me into the diary room once and said, 'Are you aware how much alcohol you're consuming, Jade? We're here for your safety and think you should cut down.' I said, 'I can look after myself!' They'd say things like, 'But you're falling over,' and I'd argue, 'Well, I'm clumsy.'

I got told off quite a lot actually, and should've really got more strikes or punishments than I did. I think *Big Brother* liked me actually. Once I passed toothpaste through the bars and got called into the diary room and they told me I had an instant strike. I said, 'I'm not being funny but I'm a dental nurse and stuff like that is disgusting. They're in the poor side and plaque will build up on their teeth. I have to give them toothpaste, I'm sorry.' In the end I got away with it. I reasoned, 'It's not

114

like I'm giving them a bit of chocolate. It's like someone bleeding to death over there and me not giving them a plaster.' Good argument, I thought.

I had a huge row with Adele halfway through the show which really affected our friendship. I found a verruca on my foot, which Sophie and Adele proceeded to tell me was a 'fungal disease' and started laughing about it. I'd never had a verruca before; I didn't know what it was. And, typically, I was drunk and couldn't handle it. Adele told me not to sleep anywhere near her bed and that I should wear flip flops in the shower. I was so upset, I felt like they were saying I was unclean or dirty ('minging', I think I called it at the time). Admittedly I was pretty pissed, but I was in the rich side and we had wine virtually on tap. I remember just bawling my eyes out, and running to the bedroom and crying to Alex. Then all of a sudden Adele walked in, and for some reason just turned really nasty. She said, 'You've got fungus on your skin, get over it.' I felt so hurt and embarrassed because everyone was laughing at me. Then Adele started accusing me of lying to Alex about what she'd said to me, and told me she was going to deck me! I think I said, 'Come on then!' But we never did actually fight. It all calmed down after a while, but I never felt the same about Adele after that. I remember hearing shouts over the fence, people saying stuff about Adele, like 'You two-faced bitch! Don't trust Adele!' and I couldn't work out why they'd be saying it.

Despite what happened between us (hold your horses, I *will* get to that bit in a minute) I didn't particularly fancy PJ. I think what went on under the covers was born out of cabin fever more than anything else. I don't mean anything horrible against him, but PJ's not exactly the sort of person I'd notice in a club or want to pull. He's not my type of bloke. But I got on really well with both him and Spencer and, because of the environment, we used to flirt loads. That's one thing about me – I love to flirt. It doesn't mean I'll go and sleep with loads of people or anything, I just like to have a bit of banter. It's just like when I was at school, back-chatting the boys in the year above – I enjoy the cheekiness of it all. PJ would often tickle my feet and we'd mess about and have a joke. It was all quite sweet really. He told me at one point that I reminded him of someone he used to go out with. He said, 'You don't give a shit what people think of you, you're quite outspoken, which is a good thing, I suppose.'

PJ used to say he was worried that he would be the first one in the house to 'have a wank'. He thought that if he did do it, it would have a negative effect on his law career once he left the house. Ha. He didn't bank on being in bed with me, then, did he? We talked about sex a lot in that house. PJ would announce things like, 'I've had five erections today.' Once, he started comparing himself to a volcano before it erupts. Nice.

In the lead-up to that night there was a bit of sexual tension building up between me and PJ. It just wasn't in an overwhelming oh-my-God-I-can't-wait-to-get-into-bed-with-you kind of way. But I would never do something like that with someone just out of the blue. There was definitely a bit of the old chemistry floating about; and when a guy's showing you that sort of attention, it's hard not to notice.

If you're expecting me to remember every gory detail of that night, then I'm sorry because I'm going to disappoint.

Oh God! I don't get embarrassed easily, but that incident makes me go redder than anything. I can remember certain *bits* though, which I will tell you, of course.

I had no master plan to do anything like that on national TV, but I'd honestly forgotten about the cameras from the minute I walked in there right up until the minute I walked out. The night it happened we all got extremely drunk because Sandy had announced he wanted to leave, so I think we were allowed alcohol as a kind of 'farewell to Sandy' thing. I know we definitely had a lot to drink anyway, whoever we were drinking it for. I remember me and PJ both going to bed because we were so bladdered. At first I was in the bed next to his and we were holding hands and talking for a bit. The next minute, I got into his bed with him and I was only wearing a G-string, nothing else. People have asked me since, 'Did he have a big willy?' but I literally cannot tell you whether it was big, skinny, long or small. I was *that* pissed.

I have since had the displeasure of watching the tape of that night, though, and, yes, I've seen my head bobbing up and down. Put it this way, things got very heated between us. I do remember thinking, *There's no way I want to have sex in the* Big Brother *house,* which is probably why I opted for the next best thing. I just can't believe I did it, that's all. I don't *do* blow jobs, you see. Danny, my most recent ex-boyfriend at the time, had never had one from me in his life. So it's not like I thought, *I'm really good at this, let me show you how it's done.* I don't like them! That's why, when I watched the footage, I found it so hard to believe. I know it sounds stupid, but I think I felt like that was the only thing I could do to stop things going any further. To

117

be in bed with someone, with no bra on and just a thong – well, I was giving poor PJ the impression that sex might actually happen, wasn't I? So I thought, *Shit, what can I do here? I know, I'll help him out and that way he'll go to sleep and forget about it.* I'm not a strong enough person to have just said 'Stop' and got out of bed. So I thought if I went down on him he wouldn't be sexually frustrated any more and I wouldn't be able to get pregnant either.

The only time I was aware of the cameras was the next morning when I went into the diary room. God, I felt awful. I'd woken up and my first thought was *Shit.* Luckily, Sandy had decided to escape over the roof, so I thought that might gloss over the whole thing. But oh no: all day the other housemates were asking if anything had happened, which we both denied. Then PJ started to get quite rude about it. He began saying stuff like, 'No, I'd never touch *her.*' He kept worrying about my ex, Danny, too. Even though I hadn't made a big deal about having a boyfriend, a few people – including PJ and Spencer – knew about him. Personally, I couldn't have cared less what Danny thought, but PJ did. He kept going on about the fact that he was lawyer and saying, 'How can I represent someone in a divorce court if I've been the cause of infidelity myself?' I guess he was right, and I did see his point. He just made that point *a lot,* that's all. It didn't bother me that he denied it, though. It's not like I loved him or anything. I just felt very disappointed with myself. Yes, I admit, I did want to feel a bit closer to him afterwards, but that's just so I didn't feel like a slag. I wanted a cuddle. I wanted him to make me feel better about why I did it. If he'd given me a bit of warmth and affection I would've thought, *You know what? It's all right,* but he didn't. He couldn't stand to look at me. So I felt pretty shit about myself.

I went to the diary room and started crying and asking if it was going out on air and if there was anything I could do to stop it. The producer ended up getting Brett, the psychotherapist, in to see if I was OK. I spoke to him but none of it was on camera. He asked if I remembered doing anything and I said, 'Not really,' but that I knew something had happened. He told me what had gone out on the live E4 streaming. I don't think he was meant to, but I was so distraught. He said, 'I will tell you that it does look like things have been performed. You're in the bed and the covers are going up and down.' I remember saying, 'Was everything hanging out? Were the covers off? Could you actually see anything at all?' He replied, 'No,' but said that's not what the viewers would think. I breathed a sigh of relief that you couldn't see anything, but at the same time I thought, *Fucking hell, I know it's definitely gone out now.*

Brett was so comforting, though. He said, 'Jade, you have to promise me you will not let this ruin your *Big Brother* experience. You have to not let it get to you. It's just stuff that happens in life. You're not going to be viewed badly from this.' So I went back out into the house and I brushed it off. Kate didn't really like me so she was muttering things about it to some of the others, saying that it was making her feel sick that PJ had done something with me. But she didn't want to risk winding PJ up, so she didn't talk about it too much. Spencer sang 'Jade gave PJ a blow job' under his breath in a jokey way a couple of times, and I told him to fuck off. But I did laugh. I was more worried about PJ's job and the consequences of our actions than what he thought of me after that. I wasn't too bothered about my mum because I knew she'd stick by me forever and nothing I did would affect that. It didn't bother me what the public thought either. It still doesn't.

I used to look up to Sandy. A lot of people afterwards told me they thought he was a miserable bastard who did nothing but swim in the pool, but I liked Sandy; I felt comfortable with him. I know that he and Alex kept themselves apart from the rest of the group quite a bit, but because I didn't really belong to any one group I could easily flit about. If anyone said anything bad about Sandy – Jonny thought he was boring, for example – I'd always stick up for him. So what if he mowed the grass five times a day? He was such a straight-talker, he was funny, and he pissed in the bin before he left.

The night before he escaped he told us all about his plan. He'd worked out his whole route, scarpering across the roof and everything. He said, 'It's so easy. It's like they planned for somebody to do it.' Although I didn't want him to leave, I was glad he chose the night after my fumble with PJ to do it because it was a welcome diversion. I had a stinking hangover but I remember Alex shouting, 'Don't hurt yourself, Sandy!' in a really posh voice, which made me laugh. I got out of bed and ran outside with a blue sheet wrapped round me hollering, 'Go on, Sandy! Go on!' We all cheered him on as he got this plant pot to get himself up, then he clambered up the wall and sprinted off.

That day we had to do a task so we could watch an

England football match. All the jammy rich housemates sat on comfy sofas, wrapped in duvets, and could see the plasma screen perfectly. I was in the poor side and we had to watch all the action from a distance, standing up behind the bars. Alex shouted, 'Look at those fuckers go!' because the other side were really fast. I remember screaming, 'GO ON OWEN!' PJ was nearly in tears the whole way, biting his nails because he was so nervous. We were only allowed to watch some of the game, though, about 25 minutes I think it was. Then the screen went blank. England hadn't even scored at that point, so we were gutted. I think that was worse than not being allowed to see any of it. Kate didn't seem to say anything during the match at all, which was odd considering she was meant to be really into football. After that, PJ went outside and prayed, because when England had played another team earlier, someone had a plane flown over the house telling us the result. I think he was begging it to fly past again with the results of this match too. It never came, though.

I hated it when Spencer was evicted. He was up against Alex and none of us had a clue he'd be the one to get the chop. Alex was such a moaner! Spencer gave me a little gold band as a memento, which I've still got – a little ring. He was like my brother in there and he really looked after me. He was upset when he left, but, as always, he took it in his stride. I kept running around him like a lost sheep, packing his suitcase for him.

Days and weeks all seemed to merge into one during my time in the house. I was pissed for the best part of it, too, which explains why my memory's a bit patchy. The thing I've never lived down from my whole *Big Brother* experience is stripping off to my la la, or lu lu (I call it both names depending on my mood). We were all playing a drinking game where you had to say a celeb's name and then the next person had to start the next celeb's name with the first initial of the previous one's surname, or something like that anyhow. Whatever the rules were, I didn't understand them properly, hence I ended up starkers, showing my kebab belly to the nation. Like a doughnut, I got everything wrong and had to pay the penalty. I know I shouldn't have done it but I was pissed, and when I watch that tape back now I just think, *How could the others have let me do it?* If it had been Kate, there's no way I would have let her do it, or if she did I would at least have run to the bathroom and got her something to cover herself afterwards. But on the footage you could see her encouraging me, egging me on, saying, 'Oh my God, I can't believe she's doing that.' What grates even more is that the night before, she was throwing up and I was rubbing her back and I cleaned up her sick. I was there for her. I didn't really get on with Kate but when you're in that situation and you see another girl in such a state – not really in control of herself, like I was that day – you help them out, surely? It's not as if I had a body like Elle Macpherson or anything! But I tell you, I'm the best ever at that game now. My mates get pissed off with me because I don't ever get one name wrong. I never lose any of my clothes these days.

I know I was portrayed as the drunken bird who threw herself at everyone, but there were things that happened in that house that just didn't get shown. Once we were really bladdered and me, Kate and some of the others were skinny-dipping in the pool. One of the boys took our bikinis away while we were in there, which was so mean because we had to get across to the house with nothing on. Alex gave me a towel, but Kate got out fully naked and ran right across the lawn. Kate was the first person ever to go naked on *Big Brother* but no one knows that. She ran out of the pool into the house, then slipped on the kitchen floor and her legs fell open, all akimbo. It was the most disgusting sight, but it never got shown on TV. You can bet if it was me falling all over the place like that it would've been shown in slow motion or something.

A few days before Sophie got evicted we sat down and had a bit of a heart to heart. I did feel a bit bad for how I'd been to her. We had to talk between the bars because she was in the poor side and I was in the rich one. I tried to explain to her that I'd felt a bit paranoid in the house at times because I felt like there were people in there who'd gone to law school, travelled all over the globe or gone to university, but I'd sacrificed my education to look after my mum – I'd had to – so it made me a bit insecure at times. The thing that had annoyed me about her was how into Lee she'd been from day one, and I told her she just butted into other people's conversations all the time and was a bit of a try-hard. Sophie said she thought I was too loud. Funny that.

On the night Sophie was evicted, I thought I heard someone chanting my name over the wall. I told Adele and she said I must've been imagining things, but I knew what I'd heard. 'Get Jade out,' they were shouting. PJ tried to convince me that they were saying 'Da-vin-a' but I knew he was wrong. I just thought, *I'm hated on the outside*. I tried very hard not to be bothered by it, even though it was a bit upsetting. I got used to it after that. I'd hear things like, 'Hey, Jade – Fat Pat!' and I'd just have to shrug my shoulders, think, *Oh well, bovvered*, then go inside and drink another bottle of rosé.

Someone shouted Kate's name once. They said, 'Kate's a slag and has got more orange peel than an orange.' She was gutted. I remember her walking around in these tiny denim shorts all the time, then asking, 'Why is everyone picking on me?' I said, 'Picking on you? At least you don't get called a pig! And if you weren't walking round in those denim shorts all the time while you were on your period then maybe they wouldn't.' I thought she was sick wearing hotpants while she was on her period. I mean, anything could've poked out!

I split my best pair of white jeans when I was in the house. Forget the nakedness, I think that was my most embarrassing moment ever – I ripped a pair of trousers at the bum crack on national television! They ripped right round the arse too. I just thought, *Oh my God, these are my nicest trousers from French Connection. I loved these trousers and now I've ripped them.*

I dyed my hair in there too. It was a right mess. I'd entered the house with highlights and by the middle of the show my roots just went down to my ankles. I asked *Big Brother* for some bleach and I ordered it off the shopping list. But when I got it I left it on too long. I was sitting out in the sun with it on too, which wasn't the best idea. When I washed it off I looked awful. I was really brown because I'd been using cooking oil and baking myself in the sun, and I had the yellowest hair in the world. It was revolting. Now I know why people called me Miss Piggy, especially when I was in my eviction outfit. I lived up to their standards. I left with a fucking pink dress on. What did I expect?

Talking of hair dye, then there was Tim. He came into the house to replace Sandy. My first thoughts when I met him were, *What a wanker!* But I did get to like him. People would shout things over the wall like, 'Tim the ginger'. That baffled me. I said to him, 'Tim, they're calling you ginger!' and he replied in this really plummy voice, 'Exactly. It just goes to show how intelligent the people who watch these programmes are.' Then I said, 'Yes, cos you've not got ginger hair, you've got brown hair,' and he said, 'Exactly, Jade, exactly,' and nodded. I found out later he was a ginger after all! I'll give him his dues, though: after we left the house and we'd all be at events together and crowds would boo him, he'd give as good as he got. He'd egg them on, then grab a girl and start snogging her on stage.

Our *Big Brother* was madness from beginning to end. Right up until the last day we were up till stupid o'clock in the morning, showering together in the nude and getting rat-arsed. Of course, this meant that we all had the worst hangovers ever for our final day. All four of us felt like shit. I'd been puking, I was crying, Kate was crying, and all our heads were killing.

I don't remember much of the last week because I really wasn't that clued up about my sense of time in the first place. I turned round to one of the housemates – Alex I think it was – and said, 'How far into this show are we?' and he said, 'Oh my God, Jade! We leave in a week! How can you not know *that?*' The night before everyone left the house, the final four – me, Jonny, Kate and Alex – properly lived it up. And that's why I loved our *Big Brother* so much. We got absolutely plastered and ended up getting our bikinis and shorts on and dancing in the shower together. When Alex started showering, I joked that the sight of him was turning me on. So he told me not to look then. Of course I did, and ended up seeing his huge willy. I know I drank virtually every day in that house, but this night was something else. At one point, Kate, Jonny and Alex started hiding from me – they were always doing that. They got in the pool and hid under the lilo. I told them not to be so mean because it was my last night. Bastards. You'd think we'd want to have an early night, what with it being the big final the next day and all that. You'd think we'd want to make sure we looked good for when we had to go back out in public. Oh no, not us lot. We caned it. Me and Kate got a bit closer that evening and she said, 'We're the last girls, we've got to stick together.' I think we even agreed we'd go out when it ended. That shows how drunk we were. Then we were all making bacon sandwiches at 6.30 in the morning. That night I had a dream about Kate doing some ironing. Kate had a weird one too. She dreamt that there was a tram on top of the *Big Brother* house, and that her family came to stay with her in the house.

I ended up falling asleep on the couch in the living room and waking up to those bright lights and thinking, *My head!* I've never had a headache like it (and as you know I don't usually get hangovers). Kate came out of the bedroom holding her head in her hands and Alex was moaning all day in pain. We all went into the diary room and begged for paracetamol. I was lying in bed, willing myself to feel better, with an eye mask on and a glass of flat Coke. It didn't work. Alex told me later that every time he got a headache after that he'd be reminded of me. I don't know if that was a compliment or not.

Still, it numbed the nervousness for a bit. It didn't even sink in that we were leaving, that in a few hours one of us was going to win *Big Brother*, until they put the scaffolding up outside. It started going up at about two o'clock, and from that point on there was no getting away from the fact that this huge event was about to happen and it all centred around us. That's when it really hit me. We were all saying, 'Shit, can you hear that?' We heard the crew checking the mikes, talking about where we'd all be standing, *everything*. On the previous eviction nights they drowned the sound out with fake crowd noise, but they didn't seem to bother this time. It was the last day so they probably thought, *What's the point?* We tried to climb up and see what was going on and could see lights going up. I said, 'It's getting really real now, one of us is going to win this thing! One of us is going to walk out of here a lot richer than we ever were before!'

I have to be honest, though, I was not really thinking about the money at all. If I'm being realistic, I didn't know what £70,000 was. I knew it was a lot, but I didn't know *how* much. I didn't know you could buy a house with it or anything. I didn't have a clue. I guessed it was probably a lot more than my salary as a dental nurse, but that was about it. I certainly never thought I'd win. I looked round at everyone that afternoon and was convinced the winner would be Alex or Jonny. As far as I was concerned, it was a clear race between those two. It would be me out first, then Kate, then Alex and Jonny would be in the last two. I knew I'd be out first because of the things I'd heard shouted about me over the wall. But as long as I didn't get all boos, I knew I'd be OK.

Alex gave me and Kate a pair of his clean white pants to remember him by, then started rambling about feeling like Tom Jones because he was flinging pants around. My heart started pounding. I knew the time was coming. Before I put my dress on I remember Kate showing me two outfits because she couldn't decide which to wear. The first was a black one, which I thought looked lovely on her (and she should've worn). The other one was a skirt and a top. I was all for the black number but Jonny said he liked the second one so she chose that. Looking back now, though, we both looked awful. I looked dreadful and so did she. We'd already seen Jonny's outfit because he'd worn it 20 times before because he was up for eviction virtually every night. Alex had on his red jacket and I told him he looked hot.

Kate painted my toenails and Alex tried to do up my necklace. He started complaining because it kept coming undone. He did a lot of complaining, that boy. I remember being in the toilet putting my dress on and thinking, *Oh my God, is this still going to fit me?* I had split my white trousers, after all! I didn't try my eviction outfit on during the whole time I was in there. I think I was in denial. I was about a size 10 before I went on to *Big Brother*, and when I came out I was a size 14! So when I put the dress on – this pink satin number – I was bulging out everywhere. It was my mate Tina's design, though, bless her, so there's no way I wouldn't have worn it, whatever I looked like. I knew she'd gone to a lot of trouble, so I kept it on. It was my idea to have my dress made anyway. Helen from *Big Brother 2* had had hers made, so I thought, *Right, that is wicked. I want one. I'm doing the same.* It wasn't quite as good, though. Plus, of course, I had the added extra of my famous 'glove', which basically consisted of a pink bit of material on one arm. Me and my one sleeve. What was that all about?

I kept telling myself that whatever happened I must not cry. Otherwise I'd have the biggest, ugliest eyes in the whole wide world. There we all were, washed, dressed, scared, all sitting on the sofa. Then I remember hearing Davina's voice and thinking, *Shit! Shit!* The only thing going through my head was, *What if they throw ketchup on me?* Everyone knew that I had a ketchup phobia. I thought, *What am I going to do? If they hate me and throw ketchup on me I'll definitely cry! What am I going to do, what am I going to do?*

Davina said, 'The votes have been counted and verified. It's been very close...' and I just knew I was going. Then she said my name, 'Jade', and I thought, *Aaaah!* There was just a rush of adrenaline surging through me. I wasn't gutted I hadn't won. I was really happy that I'd got that far: I was one of the last four in the *Big Brother* house! I said goodbye to everyone and started walking up the stairs. My heart was pounding. I wanted to get out there and see all the cameras! I wanted to meet Davina!

I really can't explain the emotions that were going through my body: pure excitement and anticipation. My hands were shaking, my body was jiggling. I didn't feel afraid, though, because when Davina said my name I just heard loads of cheers. I think there were a couple of boos but the cheers gave me such a boost. The thing is, two people booing is much louder than a million people cheering, so no matter how many cheers you hear, you'll always hear the boos more. As the door opened, I stood on that step and there were just loads and loads of cheers and people shouting my name. I've never heard anything like it before or since.

Davina always says that to this day she thinks I had one of the best exits ever. Without meaning to sound big-headed, I thought I did as well. It was amazing. I lapped it up. I definitely made the most of it, that's for sure! Although I was practically falling out of my dress, I didn't care. There was a banner in the shape of a ketchup bottle, and I saw these two girls with a poster saying, 'We've come all the way from East Angular'. (I didn't get it of course – I just went 'oh, thanks'.) There were loads of people with big blonde wigs on and Miss Piggy noses on their faces. I thought, *Do I need a nose job?* But even though they were dressed like that, it didn't feel horrible because they were just cheering and smiling. It was like they were slagging me off but praising me at the same time, because they were holding banners like, 'Miss Piggy, we love you'.

I thought, *Wow! This is it!*

I acted as if I owned the stage – I was waving my hand in the air like the Queen with one glove on. It was one of the most incredible experiences I have ever been through, aside from giving birth. And it just got better and better after that. I had pants thrown at me, teddy bears, flowers. I was picking them up and saying 'thank you, thank you,' and kissing everyone. Then I met Davina and she grabbed me and gave me a huge hug. In my ear she said, 'You were

brilliant, absolutely fabulous. Enjoy this, just take it all in.'
She said some really lovely things to me. She even
whispered, 'I wanted you to win,' in my ear, and I couldn't
believe it. *Davina* wanted me to win!

Another thing she said, which I found quite odd at the
time, was, 'Be wise with your money,' and I thought, *Eh?*
She was saying, 'You get that house you've always wanted'
– it was like having a celebrity financial advisor. I was
flummoxed. I didn't have any money, what was she talking
about? But I just replied, 'Oh, OK.'

I loved the fact that Davina was being so caring towards
me, but then – Oh my God! – as I walked down past the
paparazzi Graham Norton appeared! He said 'Helloooo
Jade!' in his Irish accent, and gave me a cuddle. I looked
over at Davina, gobsmacked. I felt so happy.

She took me through to the studio for the interview. The
first person I saw was Avid Merrion – I didn't know who
the hell he was. This was the first year he'd really appeared
on telly – as a *Big Brother* stalker – but of course I'd been
inside the house the whole time, so to me he was a
complete stranger, and a bit of a scary one at that. He had
a T-shirt on which read 'I love Jade', was speaking with a
strange accent and standing shoulder to shoulder with my
mum, my nan and my granddad like he was part of the
bloody family. I just thought, *Who is this weirdo? He's
freaking me out.* My mum was saying, 'This is Avid', but I
just didn't want to talk to him, he was really creepy. Now
I know him (and that his real name is Leigh Francis), it's
funny to think he scared me as much as he did back then!

My mum said, 'I'm so proud of you,' but I'd be lying
if I said we had an emotional reunion. Don't get me

wrong, I was pleased to see her, but I was so overwhelmed and excited that I couldn't think about family. There were people outside I'd never met before who were calling my name! Everyone knew who I was, and they liked me. So I think it's pretty understandable that my mind didn't have time to adapt to seeing my mum for the first time in nine weeks.

The next second I was on the stage and on the big screen there was film footage of – wow! – JOHNNY DEPP! He was saying, 'That Jade Goody should win, she's a great girl.' I was in shock. A Hollywood film star talking about me! It was mind-blowing.

I could see all the other *Big Brother* housemates looking on as I was doing my interview and I was getting cheers. It was such a lovely feeling. Then they showed a clip of all these things I'd said in the house like 'tictacticals', 'Portuganese', 'an escape goat', 'wirelephones', Tunisia being near India, and talking about 'East Angular' – which obviously I still didn't know was wrong until I found out later. They even had the bit where I was walking about with spoons on my eyes to get the swelling down. I just thought, *You're such a nugget, Jade. What were you doing?*

Davina showed a clip of me being bitchy about some of the housemates, especially Sophie. I thought. 'Everyone must think I'm awful, but I'm not.' Then she gave me this really kind look and said, 'You came across as one of the most two-faced bitches ever, but you weren't, were you, Jade?' And I'm glad she said that because I really wasn't. Davina then went on to say that she'd trawled through all the footage to check that everything I'd said behind someone's back I'd also said to their face, and she found it.

I felt like I'd been redeemed. Davina also said that she thought I was used as a puppet by Adele.

Then she asked, 'What do you think of Adele?' And before I could say, 'Well, she's my mate, the best friend I had in there really,' all I could hear was boos. The loudest boos you've ever heard. And Davina said, 'Before you say anything I think you should watch this.' I saw footage of Adele talking about me and bitching behind my back. She was saying I was sly. I was shocked. I couldn't believe it. Afterwards, Adele kept telling me she was 'so sorry' but I didn't want to know. I thought she was my mate, but it turned out she wasn't. I was disheartened, but again, I was on too much of a high to worry about it.

Then the interview turned to the subject of PJ, and we saw the clip: us 'in action'. My head was going up and down under the sheets. I wanted to cry. I felt ill. Then the questions came: 'Come on, Jade, what did you do?'

Davina had a piece of card saying 'wanking him off/giving him a blow job/sex', and she said, 'Point to which one it was.' She said she couldn't talk about it out loud because there might be children watching. *Thank God for the children,* that's what I thought. I just wanted to hide and kept pleading, 'No, no, no!' But she wasn't going to give up, so I just quickly said 'that one', and pointed to the bit on the card that said 'wanking him off'. Davina was trying to get me to say I fancied him. I think she wanted it to be this beautiful *Big Brother* romance, but I told her I didn't feel completely compatible with PJ. And anyway, it felt so weird because that incident seemed like ages ago – it was hard to believe it had only been six weeks!

The camera went to PJ at this point, I think. I couldn't

see him properly but I'm told he went red. Luckily he'd denied fancying me in his eviction interview too.

But that wasn't me done yet. Another drunken incident was shown, namely me getting naked during the drinking game. Then Davina said, 'I think you should stop drinking.'

Straight after the interview, before I could see any more of my family, I was taken to see Brett, the psychotherapist. We were in this little room, he sat me down and said, 'I've never seen so many press cuttings on a *Big Brother* contestant as I have seen on you.' He was sitting on a chair and he pointed at four huge piles of press cuttings: they were all stacked up and they were nearly as high as the chair. And they were all about me.

Brett started going through them and he read out headlines like: 'BURN THAT PIG'. The papers had called me a 'slag', talked about my mum as a 'one-armed lesbian', and everything about my life was plastered all over the front pages. Some reporter said I looked like a monster. In one paper they'd messed with a picture of my face and turned it into a pig.

Brett looked me in the eye and said, 'How do you feel?' But I was just laughing. I was on such a high, it didn't get to me, I didn't want it to spoil my night. Besides, there were a few nice bits too that had been written when the papers decided they liked me in the last week.

Meanwhile, Alex and Jonny came out, in that order. Then I was taken outside and I sat with the rest of the housemates as we waited for Kate, the winner. I wasn't upset or sad that she'd won. At the end of the day, she won it fair and square, and I thought, *Good luck to you – fair play*. We'd all been in there for the same amount of time, we'd all put up with the same amount of crap, so whoever won deserved to win. We went on stage to congratulate her, and almost immediately after that it was time for the press conference.

7

'What's a Ferret? Is It a Bird?'

The first point of contact with the outside world for all *Big Brother* housemates after they've been interviewed by Davina and met the psychotherapist, is someone from a PR company called Outside Organisation (funnily enough). They look after you until you've got your own agent, and they are there to brief you about what to expect from the press conference. The guy looking after me was called David and he told me not to be scared, and, more importantly, not to think I had to say *everything*. He told me, 'Say what you've got to say and keep it as short and sweet as possible.'

It was my first taste of the media. Suddenly all these reporters were bombarding me with questions. The most ridiculous thing was that I was sat beside Kate, the winner, and all I could hear was, 'Jade! Jade, over here!', 'Jade, what happened with PJ?', 'Jade, where's East Angular?' It was odd. All these questions were getting thrown back and forth. At me!

Then we were taken to a room in the building where there was a special VIP party being thrown for all the housemates – and celebrities! The boys from Blue were there – they'd come in support of Kate. To be honest, though, I didn't really know who they were, so I didn't feel starstruck when I met them. Duncan came over and I remember him staring at me really sternly and saying, 'Kate might be the winner, but you're the *winner*. You look after your money.'

What? Another celebrity talking to me all seriously about money! What was going on? 'Take care of yourself,' he continued. 'You're going to be very rich. Spend it wisely. Don't be fooled. You won't ever be short of cash.' I didn't have a clue what was going on. I just looked at him as if he was a bit bonkers and said, 'Yeah, all right then', and walked off thinking, *He's had too many bevvies, that boy!*

Later that evening, Spencer told me he had an agent. Then he started launching into one as well! 'You be careful. You make sure you go to the right people. You need people to look after you. You need a good agent.'

Me and my mum had to leave quite early, and Mum was really angry. I couldn't understand why until we got to the hotel. She kept saying, 'It's Clem, it's Clem.' Clem was my friend. Mum told me that Clem had done a deal with the *Daily Star*. They were going to wire her up with a microphone and she was going to get a story out of me for them, then they'd pay her for it.

Apparently there was a bidding war going on for me. David told me that all these newspapers and magazines wanted me. I didn't know what it meant. What I did know was that my life had changed completely and it was never going to be the same again. For a start, my mum looked all different. She'd had a new hairdo, was wearing Dolce & Gabbana boots – the works. I thought, *Where did you get all that?* She looked lovely and everything, but how could she afford it? Turns out it had all been bought for her by Sharon Marshall, a reporter from the *News of the World*. She'd been spending loads of money on my mum, treating her all week to sweeten her up. That way she hoped Mum would persuade me to do my first interview with their paper. I was in demand! David said, 'Jade, I don't want to scare you but you've got a lot of interest in you and tomorrow you're going to have a meeting with an agent called John Noel and his publicist called Katherine Lister'

'What? Aren't I going home?'

'You won't be going home, girl.'

'Aren't I going back to being a dental nurse?'

'No,' he laughed.

'What?'

'You'll be having a meeting tomorrow.'

I felt like I just needed to take a breath – I thought I was going to faint. Mum told me she'd recorded every minute of me on *Big Brother*. She said she used to watch me until she fell asleep at night.

Then Mum started going on about Clem again. She said, 'I'm not happy with Clem,' and told me that Clem was trying to shaft me. It seemed Clem had done some photo shoots when I was in the house, and because the *Daily Star* weren't convinced they were going to win the bidding war for me, they'd bought her as their backup plan. Mind you, knowing what I know about journalists now, I'll bet Sharon Marshall fed all this to Mum to make sure she kept her on-side.

At the end of the day, Sharon wanted me for her newspaper, the *News of the World,* and she would probably have done anything to get me. My mum is very trusting, and by now she was convinced that Sharon Marshall was her best friend. They'd spent the whole of the past week together. To be fair, Sharon was just doing her job and she was great at it. She'd been very clever about getting in with my mum in the first place. She'd found out that, in the lead-up to the final, Mum had been having to pay £3 for a cab down the road to the newsagent's because there were so many paparazzi and reporters outside our house, all asking questions about me. So Sharon had said, 'Come and talk to me, and I'll look after you and get you away from all this.' I've learnt since that tabloid journalists are never your best mates. Now I always say to my friends, 'Do not trust them. Do not get sucked in to what they tell you.' But I wasn't anywhere near as savvy at that time. Mum kept saying all these things about Clem and Sharon and my story, and it was just doing my head in and confusing me. So I got the hump. I didn't like all these people saying, 'You're going to be big' and 'You look after your money' and Mum telling me about people selling their story and me not being able to trust my friends. It was weird. I said, 'What the hell are you talking about? For fuck's sake, Mum, just leave me alone!' Then she got all upset and I had to say sorry. But it was so much to take in. Eventually we both fell asleep. And the following day, Mum was whisked away from me again and I was taken to meet the people who were to become my agents.

The first person I met from John Noel Management was John Noel himself. He was sitting there as cool as a cat. He must've been in his late thirties, with silver hair, an untucked shirt and a kind of 'who gives a fuck' attitude written all over his face. I liked that. He explained he acted as an agent, mainly for TV and radio presenters, including Davina and Dermot. I found out later that Davina calls him 'The Rottweiler' because he doesn't take any shit when it comes to his clients.

Then I met Katherine Lister. I loved Katherine from the moment I saw her and knew I could get on with her massively. She explained the whole post-*Big Brother* process and said there was a lot of press interest in me and that I'd need an agent to act on my behalf. Phil Edgar-Jones had recommended John Noel Management so I thought *Oh, OK*. Let's face it, at that point I'd probably have signed up to *The Muppet Show* if they'd asked me.

John leant back lazily in his chair and said frankly, 'There's a bidding war going on, so we need to work now. Are you happy?' I said, 'Er, yes,' and that was it: I had an agent. This 'bidding war' was for my first interviews – there was a joint offer between the *News of the World* and *Heat* magazine, then there was another from the *Daily Star* and *OK!* magazine. John said, 'The *Star* and *OK!* are offering you six weeks' work, but that means you won't be able to do anything with anyone else during that time – no TV, nothing.' Then he said that the *News of the World* and *Heat* combined were only asking for half a day's work each and that their deal meant I could do other things. When they started to discuss money it went right over my head. I just thought, *What?* I didn't believe this was happening. It was like being in a dream. The thing was, we had to make the decision fast because the newspaper I decided to go with wanted me to do a photo shoot and interview that very day. It had to be printed in time to hit the news stands the following day, and if they were going to pay me that much money there were to be no other pictures taken of me beforehand – by *anyone* – because that would dilute the deal. Ruin the 'exclusive'. Once he realised I wasn't going to be much of a judge, John told me he thought I should go with the *News of the World/Heat* deal because, although it was a bit less money, it was better in the long run – it freed me up to capitalise on my fame and make more money elsewhere. Katherine mentioned that the *Sun* were also interested in doing a week's deal with me and she'd also had a call about me doing something for Graham Norton's Channel 4 show. So I agreed. John was the agent, what did I know? At that moment in time I didn't know my arse from my elbow.

John and Katherine walked me out of the hotel and over to an old white vintage car owned by John. It was rickety and falling apart. I'd literally just met this guy a few minutes ago, I didn't know him from Adam, and now I was driving with him in this clapped-out vehicle. But it was the maddest journey I've ever been on. There were paparazzi following us *everywhere*. From the minute we climbed in the car they were on our tail. Then, as we drove off, they chased us down the road in another car. It was like something out of a film. Picture the scene: I'm sat in the back of this cranky car, this guy is in the front driving. He's meant to be a 'good agent' and he's on the phone to these people who are offering me all this money just to *talk* to them and he's saying 'No', then hanging up. Then he starts talking to another person and he slams the phone down again. Next one – 'She ain't doing it for that' – slam, slam, down goes the phone each time. I was thinking, *What the fuck?!! Why are you turning down all this money?* But he was playing games, you see. He was pushing each of them because he knew he could. Because he knew they wanted me. Me, Jade Goody. This was The Rottweiler they were dealing with, after all.

The paparazzi (or paps, as they're known) were following us the whole way. We couldn't seem to shake them. Then we pulled up at some traffic lights and there were these guys at the side of the road – you know, the ones that wash your car windows. Almost instantly, John Noel leant out of his window, handed one of them a £50 note, and said, 'Wash their windows back there.' Just as the lights changed, we sped off, and as we looked back the paps were getting their windscreen washed, polished, scrubbed, the works – they couldn't move. We were all crying with laughter. They were just shaking their fists like something out of a *Police Academy* movie. It was brilliant.

We went straight to John's office so Katherine could sort out the contracts with the *News of the World,* the *Sun* and *Heat* magazine. After that we were driven to a studio and it was time for the *News of the World* photo shoot. I looked under the make-up table and underneath it, in this little baby seat, was Jordan's baby Harvey! The make-up artist was the same one Jordan has, her best friend Sally

Cairns. I picked Harvey up and gave him a cuddle, he was so cute. I couldn't believe I was holding Jordan's kid!

The photographer was this woman called Jeannie Savage, who was responsible for all Jordan's early glamour shots. She wanted to put me in a leopard-print bikini and loads of skimpy outfits but Katherine was having none of it. She kept saying, 'There's no way Jade's wearing that.' They wanted me in next to nothing, looking all saucy. In the end they compromised and I was wrapped in a sheet, Marilyn Monroe style, my hair flicking out, and I had my picture taken as if I was reading a paper looking shocked. Later that day, Jeannie gave me her business card and told me to call her, saying all this stuff about the fact that she'd worked with Jordan and could get me further than John Noel ever could. But by this time I knew I was with the right agent; there was no way I wanted to be a glamour model like Jordan.

After the shoot I was driven to an amazing hotel the *Sun* had organised. When we arrived I was told that I was to be in their care and would not leave their sight for a week. I panicked and said, 'I haven't got any clothes!' All I had was the stuff I'd been wearing in the house, and I was buggered if I was putting any of that on again. So someone went out and got me a few bits. That night they let me invite some of my friends to the hotel. Emily, Charlene, Georgia and Danielle – all my mates from Bermondsey – came round. But, unbeknownst to me, Emily had started seeing my ex, Danny, while I was in the house. Nobody told me. Emily had a new Christian Dior bag on her shoulder and I said, 'I love your bag, Em. Where did you get it from?' She answered, 'Oh, it's just a present,' and got really coy about it. That's because Danny had bought it for her out of the money he'd earned from selling a story on me. But somehow I had this woman's intuition: I just knew. So I said, 'You've been with Danny, haven't you?' and Charlene answered for her and said she had. Apparently all my mates had stopped talking to Emily because of it, but that night no one wanted to spoil things, not even me, so we just got on and had a laugh. It was the first time we'd been together for ages. We ordered loads of champagne, room service, watched films and had a proper laugh. What did I really care if she'd been with Danny? I hated him anyway.

After that it was the *BBLB* (*Big Brother's Little Brother*) reunion show. Dermot was giving out awards – I think I won two or three, one of which was for 'Most Comical Moment'. Well, I had had a few of them! It was held in the *Big Brother* house and it was quite odd to be back there. All the other housemates were looking at me strangely because I had bodyguards and I wasn't allowed to stay for as long as the rest of them, due to the constraints of my newspaper and magazine deal. A few of them had this look on their faces that said, 'Come on, Jade! You never even won!' I think that's what got on Kate's nerves in particular. Here was me, the girl who came fourth, with the biggest magazine deal out of the lot of them, bodyguards who wouldn't leave my side, and a Channel 4 camera crew following me about (by now we were also filming a show called *What Jade Did Next*). They must've thought, *Who does she think she is?* But it wasn't my choice. It's not like I'd demanded it. The reason I wasn't allowed to stay and get drunk with everyone else was in case I blabbed or starting talking to someone I shouldn't. I did feel a bit poncy, though. Before I left, Alison and Jonny were talking to me about what they'd done since they'd been out of the house and what interest they'd had in them. I didn't want to start talking about what I'd done because I felt stupid and I didn't want to show off, so I tried to play it down. But that only lasted a few minutes, then I blabbed the lot. Spencer was seeing Kate at this point, and they were about to be sent off on holiday by *OK!* magazine. I just looked at him and said, 'I don't know why you're with her but never mind.' He just shrugged: 'But I really like her.' As I mentioned earlier, though, he was really upset when they got back. He rang me up and said, 'She's used me.'

The next day I was on my own again. The *Sun* organised a bodyguard for me called Tony. There was so much 'public interest' that I wasn't allowed out alone. Tony took me shopping to get some more clothes (nothing fitted me any more, I'd eaten so much) and I was swamped. It was somewhere in Cambridge and I got mobbed. I couldn't get my head around the fact that I was signing autographs and that every single person I came across knew my name. I went into this shoe shop and the manager even had to close the doors because it got so hectic. I was actually a bit worried. Although people were shouting, 'We love you! We think you're wicked!' I just kept thinking, *Someone might not like me in a minute and what if that someone stabs me?* I knew that for every ten people who liked me, there could be one who hated me. It was such a weird scenario. Everywhere I went, there were whispers: 'Is that Jade? Is that Jade?' I was really aware of it then, whereas nowadays I'm oblivious. My mates always say, 'Did you just see that person staring at you?' and I'll say, 'What?' But back then

I was turning my head all the time. I had a stiff neck I was turning round so much.

I did my photo shoot for *Heat* that week too. I loved it. It was so light-hearted and fun. It was with a photographer called Nicky Johnston – a short, bald-headed gay man from Liverpool – and he was hilarious, so sarcastic about everything and everyone. They were such a great team, we had a real laugh and it was fun. I was saying, 'I'm going to be in *Heat!*' It was the biggest magazine out there. They got me dressed up with all this jewellery on and a bag of chips in my hand. I think I asked if I could eat the chips because I was hungry, but they were saying, 'No! They've been there for ages!' I was dressed as a devil and an angel to represent the two faces of me in the house – my nice side and my evil side. I had my interview and the lady from *Heat* asked, 'How does it feel to have already earned X amount of money?' I remember saying, 'Is that more than £70,000?' and she said, 'Awww, bless!' She couldn't believe I didn't know the value of what I'd earned. She also asked, 'How does it feel to have sold more *Heat* magazines than Victoria Beckham?' My mate phoned me up the next week when it came out and said, 'I cannot believe you're on the front of *Heat* magazine and Posh Spice is just squashed in the right-hand corner. And that has been going on for weeks, Jade. It's amazing!'

When I first saw myself on the front of *Heat* magazine I couldn't believe my eyes. I wanted to frame it. One thing I'd love to do is have a room in my house that's full of all my magazine covers on the walls. Since leaving the *Big Brother* house I've done loads of magazine covers for OK!. The favourite has to be when me and Jeff were sent on an amazing trip to Jamaica. My ugly mug has also been on the covers of *Now, Closer, New, Star* and *Reveal*. I don't mean to be big-headed, but it's an achievement for me. How many times do you get to see yourself on the front of a magazine and then to get told it's sold a record amount of copies when you were on the front?

That week I did my interviews with the *Sun*. They took me punting in Cambridge and then hired a big open–top bus and took me back to Bermondsey. I was really scared. I thought, *What if people hate me because they think I've changed? What if I see Danny?* I was so worried people might not like me or that they might be jealous, but it wasn't like that. It was unbelievable. I watched Arsenal years ago when they won the Premiership and remember seeing thousands of people crowded round their open-top bus, screaming at them. Well, that was what this felt like to me. I was saying, 'Shitting hell! They're screaming at me like they screamed at the Arsenal players!'

There were people wearing T-shirts saying, 'Jade, we love you' – it was like Jade-mania everywhere. My head was spinning. 'Jesus, I used to walk down the streets here and now people are shouting my name and I'm on my own bus!' I signed a few T-shirts and threw them over the side to the kids. My nan and granddad were there and they were nearly in tears, they were so proud, bless them. Then some woman got her tits out.

I wasn't allowed to go back to my mum's afterwards. I had to stay at my mate Charlene's instead. My mum's house was being bombarded with press. It was sad, because all I wanted to do was sleep in my own bed. I couldn't go back to where I'd grown up – not unless it was in a fancy open-top bus, anyway. I haven't actually spent a night in my mum's house since I left *Big Brother* in July 2002. How weird is that?

The next time I saw Kate Lawler was at the *Big Brother* book launch six days later. The Channel 4 camera crew were still following me about. Almost as soon as I got there, Kate shouted out in front of everyone, 'Apparently, Jade, you can't spell your name and I heard you're going to get spelling lessons?' She thought she was going to embarrass me, but I didn't care. I said, 'Well, I can spell my name actually, but, yes, I'm going to tuition lessons because I'd like to improve my reading and writing.' And I was. It was something John Noel suggested and I told him that I thought it would be a good idea to try and improve myself a bit. I wanted to learn about accounts and stuff like that too. I'd come into so much money and I didn't have a clue about the value of any of it. So I went round to this woman's house for a while. She had loads of cats, and she taught me to read and write properly. The first book I read was *Harry Potter*. When the rest of the housemates heard that they all said, 'Well done, Jade.' So Kate's catty comments had backfired.

The same night, I had been booked to go on Graham Norton's show. He'd written me into this sketch and I had to rehearse some lines, which was a bit scary. I was to introduce myself as Bond girl 'Lulu Galore'. Obviously there were also jokes about verrucas and all sorts.

I know Graham Norton was the first person in the media to call me a pig, but he liked me in the end, and I'm not one to bear grudges. I never ever thought badly of him because of what he'd said. I just thought he was funny. After that first show, he had me on for a regular slot until the series finished. I was always getting muddled up with my words, which he seemed to think was hilarious. I think I once told him I thought a ferret was a bird, so naturally he made a joke of that. I was never nervous when I was on TV, though. I felt at home. It was like no one could get me or hurt me in there. It was a warming feeling to be in a place where people were being nice to me and cheering me. Before *Big Brother* I'd had such a shit time – I wasn't getting on well with Mum, my boyfriend was horrible to me, and at one point I'd wanted to kill myself. But here I was safe.

That same week, Kate was reported to have slagged me off at her local pub. Then we were both asked to appear on SMTV as guests. I loved every minute of being on that show. Brian Dowling was the presenter and I was in loads of sketches with him. I was on a Mastermind-type quiz thing and I ended up having a Chipstick fight with him and Lee from Steps. I felt as though I could behave like a big kid again and I wouldn't get told off. I also met the Sugababes. I walked up to Mutya and said, 'I thought you'd be really rude and scary but you're actually nice.' They all cracked up laughing. Out of everyone I met that day, the only person who was truly up her own arse was Claire from Steps. She was so rude and snooty. I thought, *You've got issues, girl.* Kate didn't talk to me much either. Actually, she was a bit off with me. I don't think she was very happy because her sketches were slightly smaller than mine. I wasn't bothered whether I was in any sketches at all, though. I wouldn't have cared if I hadn't got to say a word. I was on SMTV, for God's sake!

'What's a Ferret? Is It a Bird?'

That was the last bit of TV I did for a while. John Noel said he wanted me to keep a low profile for a time. That way, the next time I appeared in the public eye, people would still be interested in me. I guess too much Goody isn't such a good thing.

So, what was my idea of keeping my head down? Going to the Embassy Club in London where the glamour model Linsey Dawn McKenzie was having her birthday party, getting pissed and papped all in one go. It was about two weeks since I'd come out of the *Big Brother* house and I was feeling like a caged rat. I needed to let my hair down. I just couldn't be cooped up any longer. I knew I wasn't really allowed to go out but I thought, *Fuck it, no one's going to find out.* So I went out with a couple of mates. I didn't know who Linsey Dawn McKenzie was, let alone that it was her birthday that night, I just happened to turn up there. She introduced herself to me and she had the biggest tits I'd ever seen. Suddenly I was being given VIP treatment and all these bottles of champagne were being delivered to my table. I didn't even really want to be treated like a VIP, I just wanted to be normal and mess about on the dance floor like I always did – you know, doing the Bermondsey Two-Step. But I soon realised I couldn't do anything like that, because people just kept coming up to me and putting their arms around me on the dance floor. They would ask if they could have their picture taken with me, if I'd sign autographs, if I'd speak to one of their mates on the phone. If I'd stayed there on the dance floor, I'd never have been able to spend any time with my own friends.

Unbeknownst to me, there was some sort of sex party

151

going on upstairs where there were girls doing stuff to each other! I was unaware of this, but the snappers and reporters outside weren't. When I left the club, I could never have expected what would happen next. The amount of paparazzi photographers standing outside was out of this world. They were like a swarm of bees, and from the minute I set foot outside they began buzzing all around. All around *me!* The more I ran, the more they chased me. I couldn't get away. I couldn't even see where I was going because there were so many flashbulbs going off in my face. There was no bodyguard with me this time, either. I wasn't meant to be going out, you see, so it was just me and my mates. Katherine had warned me previously in one of her pep talks that I was not allowed to get photographed because it might ruin any magazine deal she'd done on my behalf. She said to me that it was OK if I got papped walking down the street as long as I didn't stop and pose, so this was echoing in my mind throughout. And because I'd said to my mates that I wasn't allowed to get photographed, they suddenly threw their coats on my head, which obviously made it worse, because the next day that picture was printed alongside the headline: 'JADE'S A DIVA'.

I got in a cab, but because of all the paps zooming round his car, the driver said he wouldn't take us – he thought his car was going to get damaged. So we had to get out. Next, I managed to order another car from the same company that had been driving me around all week, but when they arrived they wouldn't take me either, for the same reasons. So we tried to walk down the road. It was insane. I felt like I couldn't turn in any direction without a camera clicking in my face. Finally, someone agreed to drive us, so we clambered into his car and as we were driving away a photographer appeared on a motorbike and sped along beside us taking pictures through the car window. It was terrifying.

I didn't want to go out again after that. I nervously phoned Katherine and said, 'I went out and someone put a coat over my head, I'm sorry!' The next day I was all over the papers – they were saying I was in a sex orgy and all sorts! Linsey Dawn McKenzie was even quoted as saying I was part of her porn party that had been going on upstairs, and that I was doing stuff with the girls and was a lesbian. Another paper said I was a prima donna and printed the photo of me with my coat on my head and captioned it by saying it was me on my way into the club, not coming out. I was so upset. Katherine laughed it off, though. It was one of many things she learnt to laugh at. The agency is used to it by now. They get phone calls from me saying things like, 'I'm in Barbados in a prison cell,' so they're used to the dramas. I'm the only one of their clients who ever rings them in the middle of the night or on a bank holiday saying, 'I'm in trouble! Help!'

There were so many stories materialising in the newspapers about me. One of them was from Danny's cousin, a 16-year-old girl called Hannah. She said I'd tried to get it on with her, and the article made out I was some sort of lesbian. I had to shrug it off. The following day, the phone rang, and it was Danny's mum. She said she was ringing to apologise for Hannah's behaviour. She said, 'Hannah did it for the money and has now disappeared off somewhere on holiday. She's gone wild.' I told her it was a bit embarrassing but it was fine. I just wanted to get off the phone in case Danny suddenly wanted a word.

I'm not going to lie; I did love the fact that I could go to any club I wanted and get treated like a princess. One thing I didn't do, though, was push my way to the front of the queue. I would never do that. But I did once phone a members' club in advance to see if they'd let me in. Thing is, I didn't want to tell them it was actually me talking because they might have thought I was being cheeky. So I put on this posh voice and said, 'Oh, hello, I'm just ringing up on behalf of Jade Goody...' I don't think they sussed me. Mind you; I've got suite a distinctive voice, even when I do try my hardest to put on a posh accent. Shortly after that I got called into John Noel's office and I was told, 'No more going out. You've got to knuckle down now.'

One day I was invited to visit a child daycare centre in Haringey, North London. It was for a young carers' charity called NCH (National Children's Homes), a charity aimed at looking out for the interests of young children who spend their whole lives looking after and caring for one of their parents. Rather than taking the children into care and splitting the family up, the NCH kept an eye on things and provided support where they could. The kids were all just so young, it choked me up. There they were, their little eyes staring at me all expectantly, and yet each of them had so much responsibility on their shoulders, looking after their mums or dads who were drug users, disabled or depressed. I know it was the same for me when I was growing up, which is obviously why they wanted me to visit them, but seeing it with my own eyes was heartbreaking. These little kids should have been at school playing with their friends, but they all had such a look of seriousness etched into their faces. It was as if they knew they had to be the strong ones, and that there was no one to care for them – they needed to be the adults. It opened my eyes so much. Those kids deserved an award. None of them were dressed in the best clothes, but they didn't mind because their sole concern was their parent. Throughout the whole day, this one little boy refused to leave his mum's side. It was like he was physically attached to her hip, as if he was scared that if he let go she might wither away.

A few weeks after I left the house I got my first taste of the world of celebrity awards at The National Television Awards. Walking up that red carpet was just overwhelming: cameras flashing, TV crews calling my name, everyone staring at me. Barbara Windsor from *EastEnders* came over to me to say hello – I nearly fell over. I said, 'Hello Peggy!' (Well, I couldn't remember her real name, could I?) In fact, all night, all these stars I'd grown up watching on TV were coming up to me and telling me they loved me and thought I was a legend. People from *Corrie, EastEnders, Hollyoaks*... Gary Lucy said he wanted to talk to me but couldn't while there were reporters around. I don't know what he actually wanted, though, he never did come and find me in the end.

8

He's the One

Something ridiculous happened: I was offered the chance to do a fitness video! But when I thought about it, I realised it might not be quite so stupid after all. I wanted (and needed) to lose weight anyway, so why not be paid to do it? John Noel looked after a personal trainer called Kevin Adams at the time, who later went on to be one of the coaches in BBC1's *Fame Academy*. I had to meet him at 7 a.m., five days a week, at a gym in Essex. I couldn't drive so I had to get chauffeured cars everywhere. The amount of money I spent on them was so unbelievable – I reckon I could've bought my own car lot.

When I first met Kevin he scared me. My first thought was, *You're a big black man with the biggest eyes I've ever seen in my life.* And he was so strict. I'd be on the treadmill and shouting, 'I feel sick,' and he'd shout, 'KEEP RUNNING!' and I'd be wheezing, 'I can't! I'm going to faint.' 'KEEP RUNNING!' he'd scream. It was *every day* and it was awful. If I'm honest, I wasn't paying much attention to all this exercise lark and the call of the shops was often too much for me to resist. This meant that instead of turning up at the crack of dawn like I was supposed to, I'd often spend the morning going shopping and getting my nails done, which meant I'd be really late for training. I'd arrive laden with shopping bags and Kevin would shout loudly at me, 'You're not taking this seriously!' He got so pissed off that he phoned John Noel and said he'd pull out if I didn't make more of an effort. I guess his reputation was on the line, because if I started doing a fitness video and it didn't look like I'd lost any weight it would be his fault. In the end, John Noel called me up and said, 'Kevin's got a spare room in his house. You're moving in with him.' That was the only way he could see I'd get any work done. And of course, it took me away from the shops.

About a week before I moved in, Kevin told me his flatmate wanted to meet me. He was called Jeff Brazier. I was invited to dinner with Kevin, his partner Helen, and Jeff. He'd already shown me a picture of Jeff and I'd thought, *He's a bit of all right, isn't he?*, so when I turned up at the house to meet them my stomach was sick with nerves. Naturally, I was about two hours late, but Kevin had been expecting that and, when I arrived, no one was ready. Helen and Kevin were upstairs and I was greeted by Jeff lying on the sofa in his football kit. I thought he was beautiful, but there was no way I was going to let him know that. I looked at him and said jokingly, 'I can't believe you're not ready! I don't like waiting around for people you know!' He laughed and said, 'Why should I

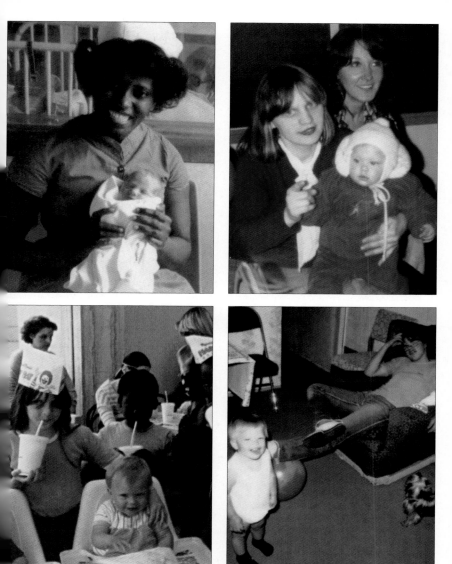

Above left: My first photo with the midwife, just after I was born.

Above right: Aged 1, with my mum. Doesn't she look young!

Below left: My first birthday party – at McDonald's, of course!

Below right: With my Uncle Martin – Budgie, who died in the motorbike crash that paralysed my mum's arm.

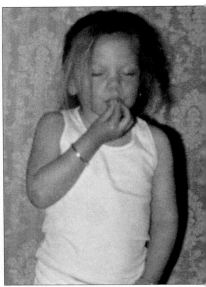

Above left: My dad (left) in his pimping days.

Above right: The famous photo of me taking my first puff of one of my mum's joints.

Below: Playing with my dad. Although he was in and out of prison, I did love him and I was devastated by his death.

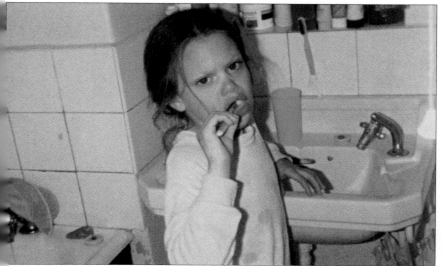

Above left: Posing for the camera, aged 4. I was always prancing about doing performances for my mum!

Above right: With my mate Zoe, a few days before I sold her my bed for £25.

Below: Aged 8, cleaning my teeth yet again!

Above: My mum with my half-brother, Brett. I thought he was a bit of an idiot but my mum was so pleased when he got in touch with her.

Below: In my first year at Bacon's College. I didn't half get up to some mischief there!

Above left: Going into the *Big Brother* house in 2002. I had no idea how much my life would change…

© *Rex Features*

Above right: A press shot taken after the *Big Brother* final. At this point everything was a total whirlwind and I had no idea what was going on!

© *Rex Features*

Below left: With Jeff – I'm pregnant with Bobby in this photo.

© *Ray Tang/Rex Features*

Below right: Just after Bobby was born – the birth was terrifying, as he was a month early.

© *Jason Mitchell/Rex Features*

Above: Pregnant again!
© *Richard Young/Rex Features*

Top right: With Bobby, when
he was four months old.
© *Ted Blackbrow/Rex Features*

Right: Tiny Freddy, just a few
weeks after he was born.
© *Rex Features*

Top left: Taking driving lessons – I eventually passed on my fourth attempt!

© *Jason Mitchell/Rex Features*

Below left: With Ryan Amoo – he was great, but unfortunately things didn't end too well.

© *Mark Campbell/Rex Features*

Right: Promoting *Jade's Salon*, the TV show I did with Living TV.

© *Rex Features*

Above left: At my friend and personal trainer Kevin Adams's wedding in 2005. Kevin put me through hell training for my fitness video, but he's a great guy. © *Mike Lawn/Rex Features*

Above right: Filming for another TV show about my life! It was hilarious having cameras following me to the supermarket. © *Jon Beretta/Rex Features*

Below left: Dressing up as Marilyn Monroe for a party – I love a good wig! © *Rex Features*

Below right: Doing the 2006 London Marathon. Everyone slated me but I did complete 21 miles! © *Jonathan Hordle/Rex Features*

start getting ready when you've only just bowled in two hours late?' We hit it off immediately and just started bantering and taking the piss out of each other. I fancied him so much, I wanted to get his pants off there and then.

We went to a restaurant called Browns in London. It was such a nice evening. Jeff told me he hated me in Big *Brother* because I was such a loudmouth. He'd recently been on TV himself, in a reality show called *Shipwrecked* on T4, so I kept asking things like, 'Er, Ship*what*? *Shit*wrecked?' We were both being really cheeky with each other and couldn't keep the grins off our faces. I stayed at Kevin's house that night, in the spare room. I wanted to be in Jeff's bed really, but I didn't think Jeff fancied me, not physically anyway.

After that I moved my stuff in. Jeff was working on a building site at the time, but he was still really fashionable and innovative. He would customise his clothes, his jeans in particular – I'd get home to see him painting or doing some graffitti on them. 'Mr Creative' I called him.

We became really close mates. Although I was always attracted to Jeff, I didn't think anything would happen between us, so I put it to the back of my mind. I'd never been such good friends with a guy like that before; it was a whole new experience for me. It was so comforting to know there was this person who liked me, worried about me and cared for me. There was a song in the charts at the time with NSync and Nelly called 'Girlfriend', and we'd always sing along to it in the house. But instead of singing the right lyrics, which were 'Will you be my girlfriend?', we would change the words to 'Will you be my *close* friend?' Kevin used to join in sometimes, but he'd sing it really sarcastically because he didn't believe we were just mates.

To him it was obvious something was going to happen between us.

I didn't know this at the time, but Jeff had a girlfriend before I moved in, and he finished with her once he'd met me. He told Kevin he liked me, but I never knew. We'd spend hours in Jeff's room together, just chatting or watching telly. I used to fall asleep on his bed and ended up kipping in there most nights. Nothing ever happened, we'd just cuddle. And I loved it.

The press started running stories that I'd moved in with Kevin and he was my boyfriend. I'm sure his girlfriend Helen was particularly chuffed about that, especially considering she was pregnant at the time. Then one day the doorbell rang and Jeff answered wearing just a pair of boxer shorts. I poked my head round the door behind him because I'm nosey and wanted to see who it was. There were hordes of paparazzi outside the house. So that was it: 'JADE'S GOT A NEW MAN'. After that we got papped everywhere we went: Tesco – the works. Nobody believed we were just mates.

Then, one night, we had sex. We'd been drinking and somehow started kissing. Then it just happened. The next morning I immediately thought, Shit! I didn't want things to get awkward between us and ruin our special friendship. But it was fine. We still bantered and carried on like it was before. I didn't even want it to happen again, because the closeness and the caring friendship we had was so much more important to me. I think Jeff felt the same because we didn't have sex again for ages after that. Not until we got together properly. And I wasn't even bothered because I knew he cared for me.

Besides, I don't think I had the energy to be getting up to any naughty business. I was working all the time. I'd be in the gym rehearsing for my fitness video for eight hours a day, then out at night doing personal appearances in nightclubs until the early hours of the morning. I was getting about three hours' sleep a night. I didn't have a life, I was just in and out all the time. I did a tour of about 70 nightclubs in all, sometimes two a night for six months. I was raking it in. The first club I went to was really nerve-racking. I was told that all I had to do was go inside, say hello and sign a few things. All I thought was, *What if I hear boos?* I was convinced everyone would throw things at me. Then I told myself not to be so stupid and that if people shouted nasty things I'd just have to get on with it. So I waltzed in there like Barry Big Time, strutted onto the stage and said, 'Hello everyone!' as confidently as I possibly could. There were a few boos but it was mainly cheers, and I soon realised that the more self-assured I behaved, the less likely the crowds were to boo. I think people can sense when you're scared and they prey on it. I ended up getting behind the bar and trying to serve drinks – I didn't want to leave.

In an attempt to be organised, I had four bank accounts: one to save up for a house, one for a car, one for spending and one for bills. I'd been applying for a credit card for years and until now I'd always been rejected, but in the end I was advised not to get one and to this day I still don't have one. Sensible me, eh?

My first extravagance was a car. I spent over £30,000 on a black Mercedes Kompressor. But I couldn't drive, so I told Jeff he could use it. I loved spoiling Jeff. I'd go shopping and buy him little presents. I bought him a pair of pumps that said 'Go Create' on the side, because of his nickname, Mr Creative. They were pretty disgusting actually, but he was so touched.

Then I got papped doing exercise in the park and I felt crushed. It was the first time I'd read something really nasty about myself and it really, really hurt. Mind you, I think I asked for it. I'd arrived to meet Kevin and was late (again) because I'd just been to the shops. I was wearing a pink Juicy Couture tracksuit, pink Chanel sunglasses, my nails had just been painted and I was carrying about 50 shopping bags. The headline was: 'IT'S A PORK IN THE PARK'. When I saw it, I sat on my bedroom floor and cried and cried. I hated the way I looked. I'd never been self-conscious before, but now I was just looking in the mirror and criticising everything about myself. Jeff came in and I said to him, 'When are they going to leave me alone? I'm trying to sort myself out and they're just knocking me, just like they did Kym Marsh.' Jeff thought what I'd said was hilarious and gave me a huge cuddle and told me it would all be forgotten about tomorrow, that the newspaper would just be someone else's fish and chip paper. Then he smiled and said, 'Babe, you have to admit; dressed in that get-up, you did kind of look like you weren't exactly taking it seriously.'

I was so upset about the pig thing that I didn't wear that tracksuit again. I thought, *Right, I'm going to show you,* and I was determined to lose weight and make myself look amazing. I knew I had to toughen up. And I knew I could do it too, because I had Jeff, and he made me feel safe. Jeff was such a rock for me. He would look at me and say, 'This is your time, enjoy it. Don't let anyone knock you.'

So I really worked hard. I was training every day, the fitness video was all coming together and my body was changing shape. My kebab belly was disappearing and I was getting fit. Even Kevin started to be proud of me.

I was also rehearsing for panto. All of a sudden I had untold amounts of work, all of which I was being paid for! I was still doing personal appearances in nightclubs until some stupid o'clock in the mornings and I was working all day long. It was non-stop. But it meant I didn't get to see Jeff as much as I'd have liked, which upset me, especially because there was a girl who used to ring him all the time. She was called Jen. Jeff told me they used to go out with each other when they were about 16 and that they were just mates. But she'd ring him all the time and ask him questions about his relationship with me. I found myself getting really jealous and saying, 'Who's this Jen? Who does she think she is, calling you all the time?' It got on my nerves. But Jen's actually one of my best friends now, I love her to bits – and she isn't a psycho.

Then Jeff and I both got invited to the *Esquire* Awards. Obviously the press had convinced the public we were a couple, so we were treated like one. Jeff didn't want to come at first – he was worried because he had nothing to wear. So when he was out at work one day, Kevin and I snuck into his room and looked in his wardrobe. I found out his sizes and I went out and bought him a pair of Prada boots, some Prada trousers and a black Prada shirt (although when I say it, it comes out as 'Parada'). I wrapped all the clothes up in tissue and left them on Jeff's bed. When he got home and saw them he was almost in tears. He looked so grateful. He couldn't believe I wanted him to come with me that much. So that was our first night out in public together, and we didn't leave each other's side all night.

Not long after that, I went on a girls' night out to Sugar Reef. I'd read about it in the papers because all the celebs hung out there. As soon as I got inside I spotted the actress Lucy Benjamin, who was still in *EastEnders* at the time playing Lisa. I didn't know Lucy was her real name, of course. She was pissed out of her head and staggered over to me saying, 'Jade, I love you, girl!' I just said, 'Oh, thanks, Lisa.' She kept buying me shots and at one point actually fell on top of me, so I was shouting, 'Lisa, you're squashing me!' Then I met Jordan (aka Katie Price). She knew who I was and came over for a chat. She was really sweet. Two male models came up to me as well. They were twins and were absolutely gorgeous – and they invited me back to their house! The thing is, it wouldn't have mattered if they'd been Brad Pitt because I only had eyes for Jeff. It was probably the one time in my life when I could've had the pick of the bunch and I should've had a really wild time; but I couldn't think about anyone except him.

Then we went to the Lake District together and everything changed. Kevin suggested it; he just thought it might be nice if we all went somewhere to get away from the hectic pace of London life. So it was me, Jeff, Kevin and his girlfriend Helen. And this was when it became pretty clear to me just how much I must have liked Jeff, because never in my whole life could I have imagined I would go on a hiking holiday. That is *not* my idea of fun. I broke my nails, my Gucci belt, ruined my Prada trainers, the lot. And all for Jeff.

I didn't even know where the hell the Lake District was, or what it was, for that matter. I was climbing, waist-deep in water, in my favourite shoes, and I got well and truly drenched. Soaked. Sodden. I was wearing a lovely pair of jeans, a Gucci belt and a really expensive shirt, and they were all getting ruined. Everything was going wrong. Jeff kept saying, 'Stop moaning and enjoy the view, will you? Just breathe in that fresh air!' I said, 'View?! *Fucking* view?! What about my nails? They're filthy!' Kevin and Helen were pissing themselves laughing. There I was, huffing and puffing, tramping along behind Jeff, saying, 'I can't believe I'm doing this!' We got to the top of a mountain and Jeff smiled and told me to look at the beautiful surroundings. I rolled my eyes and said, 'Breathtaking, isn't it, Jeff?'

We had such a wonderful time. Jeff and I were constantly bantering with each other, the flirty piss-taking was just going backwards and forwards. But throughout the whole weekend, Jen kept ringing and ringing Jeff's phone and I found myself getting really envious of her. I was thinking, *Who are you? What do you look like? And why do you keep ringing him?* I didn't even attempt to hide my feelings from Jeff – I'm not very subtle – so he was in no doubt as to how I was feeling about him.

When it came to sleeping arrangements, Helen and Kevin were together in one room and Kevin had booked it so that Jeff and I were in another. I guess he knew that I slept in Jeff's bed every night at home so he presumed I'd do the same here. But our feelings for each other were changing. We were getting closer and closer, and by the time it got to night-time and we were in the hotel room together, it was obvious that something was going to happen between us. One thing led to another and we had our 'first' night of passion. It was amazing.

Reading this back now, I can safely say that I chased Jeff. I did things that I would never normally do, just to get him to like me. I went hiking. I ruined my nails, my designer belt and shoes. Still, it worked.

When we got home, we carried on having sex. We were acting very much like a couple, but nothing was said between us. Neither of us really knew what was going on – the boundaries had blurred. Then one day Jeff looked at my phone and saw I had a text message from Matthew, one of the guys I used to go out with. It was perfectly innocent and just said something like 'How are you?', but Jeff got really jealous about it. He went quiet. I kept asking him what the matter was but he wouldn't tell me. Then he announced, 'I'm sleeping downstairs tonight', and I couldn't understand what he was playing at. Suddenly it all came blurting out: 'Fucking Matthew? Who's he? Why's he texting you? What's that all about?'

I flipped. 'What? Do you think I'm some sort of fucking trollop who sleeps with you, then goes and boshes someone else? I'm not being funny, Jeff, but you've got no right to tell me who I can see or talk to because you're not my fucking boyfriend. If you remember, all you wanted to call me was your "close" fucking friend. So what am I? Girlfriend or close friend? Make your mind up!' And I stormed out.

I don't think any girl had ever spoken to Jeff in that way before. None of his previous girlfriends had dared. He was used to girls fawning all over him: if he said 'Jump,' they'd say, 'How high?' But I wasn't like that, which I think he found quite refreshing. Nevertheless, I needed answers. What was happening? Were we together or not? All this 'close friends' bullshit was starting to do my nut in.

That was our first ever argument and Jeff slept on the sofa (the spare room was full of my stuff). Me? I couldn't sleep a wink. All the while, I was lying in bed upstairs thinking of him lying downstairs. I'd hardly slept on my own since moving into Kevin's and I missed him. I missed our closeness. At about midnight, I heard a car pull up outside the house. It was Jen. She'd come to pick Jeff up and take him out! Well, you can imagine what I was like. I was fuming. She was driving this little purple car and I was trying to get a look at her through the curtains but it was too dark. Once they'd driven off, it took so much willpower for me to not phone him up and demand to know what he was doing. But I didn't want to give him the satisfaction, so I went back to bed and did nothing. The next morning he had a really bad hangover, which gave me great pleasure. I walked into the kitchen and said, in a really sarky tone, 'Have a good night, did you?' He looked at me and nodded. 'Yes, I did, actually.'

We didn't speak for about five days after that. And to get back at him, I spent most of that time hanging out with this friend of his called Mason. I knew it would wind him up because Mason was minted. He drove a top-of-the-line Range Rover, had a swimming pool and an incredible house, basically, everything Jeff didn't have. It made Jeff insecure because he thought it was a lifestyle I'd always wanted. But what Mr Brazier didn't realise was that I wouldn't have cared whether Jeff was a dustbin man or a zoo-keeper, I wanted to be with him unconditionally.

That didn't stop me from wanting to teach him a lesson, though. I thought, *Bollocks! If you're going to go out in the middle of the night with girls I don't know then I'm going to play you at your own game. See how you like it.* After about a week, Jeff cracked and started speaking to me again. He offered to cook me dinner: salmon and broccoli it was. We sat down at the table and I said to him, 'We need to sort things out,' and he told me he didn't want to be my close friend any more: he wanted to be my boyfriend. Deep down we were both thinking about each other as far more than 'close friends', but neither of us wanted to be the first to admit it. I would never have marched up to Jeff and said 'I want you to be my boyfriend' – I'm far too proud for that. It took a full-blown argument before anything could happen between us.

I don't think I've ever been so happy. Not much changed between us really, but the thing that was different was the security of knowing we were properly together. I had a good-looking boyfriend, I was earning loads of money; life was great. I loved nothing more than making Jeff feel special too. One time he was in hospital having a knee operation, so while he was away I redecorated his whole bedroom. I bought new bed covers, painted the walls, and when he came home I'd left him a heart-shaped pillow saying 'Together'.

Jeff hadn't even met my mum yet. In fact, I was so busy I didn't get time to see her myself. I talked to her every day on the phone, but for about a year after leaving the *Big Brother* house I hardly went to Bermondsey at all. We'd gone from being a mother and daughter who never spent one day apart, to a mother and daughter who led totally separate lives. It was quite strange. One thing I always did, though, was make sure she was OK for money.

I still hadn't started making the fitness video yet. I'd just been rehearsing like a maniac. So, in a last-ditch attempt to get me fit and ready for the filming day, John Noel sent me to Brazil for a week. You might be thinking, *How very nice of him*, but it was the worst week of my life. Admittedly, I was staying in a beautiful location, but this was a detox holiday, designed to cleanse the soul and lose weight while you're at it. The instructor (or 'leader', as he seemed to prefer to be called) was called Michael. He thought he was God. We were treated like we were part of a non-eating, healthy-living cult. What's more, I was all on my own. OK, so there were others there, but no one I'd ever met before. Most of them were American, and I only liked about two of them.

Every day was the same. We had to get up at about 5 a.m., then we'd do yoga for an hour – which I thought was all very nice – then we'd be given a few blinkin' seeds for breakfast! After that we'd be told to go back upstairs, get our bikinis on, then we'd attempt to kayak across the sea for two hours! And I hated it. There were sharks in the sea, for God's sake. I ended up making everyone cry because I moaned so much. We reached the end of this mammoth kayak trip once we got to this little island. We'd then have to climb up a mountain, which took another two hours. I'm talking proper hiking like Jeff wouldn't even comprehend! We were allowed a few rations of food while we were walking. Yes, that's right: a few nuts and raisins. When we eventually got to the top of the hill, the instructor told us to have a look at the view, and we couldn't see a fucking thing because it was foggy and overcast. Only when we were there could we eat our lunch. And do you know what that was? Two flaming carrot sticks, a stick of celery and a boiled egg.

I was going mental. The first day we did it I started shouting, 'This is fucking bollocks!' I'm sure the instructor took great pleasure in telling me what was coming next: we had to kayak all the way back again.

The evening wasn't so bad, though, as we were allowed to sit in a hot tub. We had a massage too, but the woman doing mine tried to stick her finger up my bum (apparently that's part of the relaxation programme in Brazil). Of course, I wasn't having any of that, and told her what she could do with her finger. Then we had to do it all over again the next day. I left halfway through the week. I was missing Jeff like mad and I couldn't hack any more seeds, so I escaped into the town and stuffed my face with ice cream. It was the best ice cream I'd ever tasted.

When I got back, Jeff and I decided to go public. Because there was so much speculation in the media about whether we were a couple or not, my agent decided it was much easier if we went public in a magazine and set the record straight.

Jeff had been on telly before and had had a taste of fame, so he wasn't really fazed by it. He was happy, but at the same time he wouldn't have cared if the fame thing wasn't there at all. For a good few months, I can honestly say that

I knew Jeff was pleased to be with me whether I was 'Jade from *Big Brother*' or 'Jade, the girl who nobody knew'. Anyway, I wasn't even like the girl from *Big Brother* any more: I'd become quite a nice person. I had no reason to be rude or obnoxious because I wasn't surrounded by nasty people. I wasn't outrageously behaved, either, I was just living a normal life. The relationship I had with Jeff just got better and better. We were like soul mates and I was besotted by him. I'd never had that kind of relationship with a man before – it was perfect.

Then I got pregnant.

Finding out I was pregnant was a complete and utter surprise. I still don't know how it happened, because I was on the pill. I'd been getting pains in my stomach, so I went to the doctor. He made me do a pregnancy test, just to be on the safe side, and that's how I found out. I was supposed to be going to work that day – to rehearse for the fitness video – but I couldn't go anywhere. I was in utter shock and I burst out crying. I remember begging the doctor not to tell anyone, because my biggest fear was the papers finding out. I thought, *Fucking hell, I can't believe this has happened to me.* I rang Jeff straight away; he was at work. I was sobbing, 'Jeff, Jeff.' I could hardly get the words out. 'I'm pregnant.' There was a silence, then he just said, 'What?' I was crying and crying. Jeff didn't hesitate. 'I'm coming straight home,' he said. I didn't even register what his reaction was because I was too wrapped up in myself. I found out later that after he got off the phone he leapt out of his seat and was screaming 'Yes!' because he was so happy. But I wasn't. I didn't like it. I didn't want this to happen. I was on the pill. I'd used contraception.

Jade: How It All Began

I phoned my friend Charlene. I said to her, 'I want to stab my belly! I want to get rid of it! I want to make myself fall over!' I couldn't believe this was happening to me. I was 21 years old. I felt sick to the bottom of my stomach. I was also utterly scared about what Jeff was going to say. I didn't want him to think I was trying to trap him. We'd only been together for a few months and I was so frightened about his reaction. I remember just trembling, rocking backwards and forwards, holding my belly.

Jeff came through the front door and gave me a massive hug. I didn't have a clue how much he wanted the baby right then because his only concern was me. He said, 'Babe, I'm with you all the way – if you want to get rid of it, you can, and I'll support your decision. But if you decide to keep it, I'm 100 per cent there for you.'

I looked at him with tears in my eyes and wailed, 'I don't even *know* you! I wanted to get married before I had kids. I didn't plan it to be like this!' I told him I was scared that if I had the baby he'd end up leaving me, and I didn't want to be a single mum. Jeff smiled. 'I would *never* let that happen, Jade. I couldn't be happier. When you told me you were pregnant I felt like the luckiest man in the world.' I just stared at him blankly before sobbing again. 'I feel like the unluckiest woman in the world.' I kept crying and crying. What were people going to say? Things were just starting to go so well for me and now look what had happened. Jeff was so calm, he just cuddled me and said, 'It'll be OK, Jade. We'll work it out.'

At that moment I suddenly realised I had to keep our baby. I wanted to have our baby. What a great dad Jeff was going to make. He didn't even know me that well and here he was saying that he would be proud to have me as the mother of his child. I realised, what could be a more extraordinary feeling than that? I felt suddenly lifted, so I got straight back on the phone to Charlene and shouted, 'I'm going to have a baby! I'm so happy.' Charlene nearly dropped the receiver in shock. She said, 'Er, you just told me you wanted to stab yourself!' I said, 'I know, but I'm all right now.'

I tried ringing my mum but I couldn't get through to her. She's terrible with mobile phones – she either never answers it or leaves it at home and goes out. So I called John Noel's office and spoke to Katherine. She was shocked but excited, and told me how important it was to keep it quiet until we were ready to announce it in the press.

I didn't want it to get leaked until at least after the three-month safety period. It was tough, but somehow we managed to keep shtum. It's quite astounding really, because I was rehearsing for panto and doing my fitness video at the time and I had to keep running to the toilet to be sick. But, luckily, no one guessed. I still hadn't spoken to my mum about it, and in the end I decided not to tell her for a while either. Knowing her, she'd end up telling a journalist by mistake.

Then it came out. Katherine rang me and said she'd had a call from a reporter and that it was going to be in the papers the next day. So Jeff and I were madly trying to get through to our families to tell them the news – we didn't want them finding out they were going to be grandparents by reading about it over breakfast. When I finally got through to my mum she was stunned: 'I can't believe it,' she said. 'You *never* wanted to be a mum.' She was still over the moon though.

Jeff wanted the baby so much. His mum was really young when she gave birth to him, and everyone in her family had been against her having him. Jeff always says that it breaks his heart knowing there was a big chance he could've been terminated. He says, 'My family can't think of a world without me in it, and I would hate to think of a world without our child in it.' Jeff's background is very much like mine in that we both grew up looking after our parents. His dad left his mum when he was really young, so Jeff was the one who looked out for her. We were like the adults, growing up, and neither of us wanted our children to grow up the same way. I knew we'd make brilliant parents. I love my mum to bits, but I never wanted to make the same mistakes she had.

I was asked to take part in BBC1's *Comic Relief* in the autumn of 2002. They were planning a segment called *Celebrity Driving School* and they wanted me to be one of the contestants. Well, I still hadn't learnt how to drive so I thought I might as well give it a go. The driving instructor they gave me was called Ricky and had the worst breath I have ever smelt. He had dentures and I'm sure he never once took them out to brush them. It was disgusting. God knows why the BBC picked him to teach me: I did ask them once and they told me he had 'character'. Yeah, a big, fat, stinking one. I always used to say, 'Have a chewing gum, Rick,' and he'd tell me he was fine, thanks, and that he didn't need a chewing gum. I'd be thinking, *Yes you do, yes you fucking do!*

I used to get all hot in the car too. I was starting to get

bigger, which made getting behind the wheel a bit awkward, but I just wanted to drive so much. I desperately wanted my independence. Pregnancy wasn't panning out in quite the way I'd imagined. I was beginning to feel fat and horrible, and whenever Jeff left the house and drove off somewhere I found myself getting incredibly jealous. As a consequence I needed to feel like Jeff wasn't the only one who could leave the house and go where he wanted. I thought passing my test was the answer. I didn't pass first time, though; it took me until my fourth attempt. Most would say I shouldn't be on the road now, but I have my good old satellite navigation system, and that looks after me.

I decided to visit my dad in prison. I hadn't had any contact with him for as long as I could remember – I didn't even know what he was in for, but he was always in for either robbery or drugs. He'd sent me the odd letter in my teenage years, but as I got older they'd become less and less frequent until I hardly knew him any more. But, of course, the newspapers had dredged up our whole relationship and reporters had been to ask him questions since I'd been in *Big Brother*. He was always full of remorse and longing to see his daughter again. Deep down, beyond the drug problem, there was a caring, loving dad. But in the end, when it came down to it, drugs always took priority over his daughter.

It was a massive long ride all the way to the prison, but I don't remember feeling any emotion. It all felt a bit fake, if I'm honest. This was a man whom I hadn't seen for most of my life, and then, because I'd been on telly, he wanted to see me again. But I went. I can't even remember the name of the prison. I had so much on my mind that day, details like that were just a blur.

We chatted for half an hour about what I'd been up to since I'd been in the house, and he told me how he'd watched me every day from his prison cell, and how he loved showing off that I was his daughter to the rest of the inmates. Then he looked sad and started saying that some of them hadn't believed him because I hadn't been to see him for so long. He started telling me how excited he was to learn he was going to be a granddad. I immediately felt guilty. While there was a part of me that knew how important it would be for my baby to have contact with his family, I also had this overwhelming desire to protect my new family from my dad. I didn't want them to get hurt like I had been. Nevertheless, I tried to make more of an effort after that.

But then Dad stabbed me in the back again. I'd go to see him, and more or less the next day I'd pick up the paper and there'd be some story with quotes from him about me: he was selling stories to the papers. It was like nothing was sacred. When I confronted Dad about this he would always try to wriggle his way out of it, saying he didn't know they were reporters.

Then one day Dad asked, 'Will you buy Nanny a bed?' That really hurt. This was his mum he was talking about; his mum who'd never made any effort to see her granddaughter; his mum who was a drug addict, just like her son; his mum who could afford to buy her own bloody bed, thank you very much. It was like I was nothing more than a cash machine to him and his family. But I still did it.

He's the One

As soon as I left the prison, I went to the shops and dutifully purchased a new double bed. She probably sold it for a bit of crack as soon as it arrived. After that I stopped seeing my dad. I didn't want to be part of his seedy world. I wanted him to leave me alone.

I had been asked to appear in pantomime as the Wicked Queen Dumplina in *Snow White and the Seven Dwarfs*. Panto was one of the best things I've ever done. I met some truly fantastic people and we had such a hysterical time. One of my funniest memories was when I was late on stage. I was rushing in from the wings, muttering 'Fuck! Shit!' under my breath, but what I didn't realise was that I had a microphone on and that day the Brownies had come to watch. They were in the first row, listening to every word, which was blasting through the theatre on the Tannoy. Then, in my rush to get to the stage, I'd forgotten to do up my skirt at the back. When I turned around, the whole of the audience started cracking up laughing. All they could see under the lights was my big white bum beaming out at them.

My panto costume was getting a bit small for me too. When I first had the fitting I'd lost so much weight from training that they made my outfit a size 10–12, but by the end of the panto season I'd put on so much weight from the baby I could hardly fit into it. The only way I could get it on was to pull my skirt right up under my boobs.

I spent my whole Christmas of 2002 doing panto. While I was there, Jeff went on holiday to New Zealand for a few weeks. The way I saw it, I had hardly any time off so there was no point in him being around. He had mates over there, so I bought him his ticket and gave him some spending money. I really missed him though.

In December 2002 I was presented the award of Mouth Almighty at the *Smash Hits* Poll Winners' Party. It was so surreal because this was one of my favourite shows as a kid. It was hard to get my head round the fact that I was now on stage with the UK's most famous pop stars. I was happy to win it though. Well, I *have* got a mouth almighty. I met Jack Osbourne backstage. He fucking stank. Honestly, he smelt like the biggest, oldest person I've ever met in my life. You know, like the mouldy smell of old people's homes. He said, 'Hi Jade,' and gave me a hug. I nearly gagged. I walked off in shock. He's since said in interviews that he doesn't like me. That's fine, because I certainly don't like him. He says he thinks I'm annoying – I think he's a stinking rat-bag.

When Jeff returned he started working on this Channel 4 television programme called *Dirty Laundry*. He'd already started to get interest from TV companies when he met me because of his appearance on *Shipwrecked* (and probably because he's not exactly horrible to look at), but when we got together and he was forced into the public eye more, he was taken on by my agent who set up some auditions for him. He's got such a great character, it was only a matter of time before he was snapped up for some presenting work. And he already knew a lot about dirty laundry from living with me!

Jeff was working on this television show and I was still in panto for a few more weeks, so we were both working flat-out. I did get one day off a week, and it was on one of these days that I nearly blinded myself while he was at work. We'd moved out of Kevin's house by then and we were renting a little place near Lakeside in Essex, near to where I was in panto. We had an intercom in the house but it was hanging off the wall, so I tried to screw it back on with a pair of scissors (as you do). Inevitably, I slipped, and the scissors went straight into one of my eyeballs. I was screaming and wailing. I rang Jeff and he rushed back home in a panic and took me to the local hospital, and I was told by the doctors that I was two millimetres away from being permanently blind. What a div. When I got to the hospital they put a white bandage over my eye which I had to keep on for a week. I looked like something out of *The Mumrny*. I thought that was it – I was going to have to wear an eyepatch for life. The only panto character I'd be asked to play in the future would be a pirate.

My fitness video turned out to be the fastest-selling fitness video of 2003. There were 22 other exercise videos out for Christmas and mine beat all of them; even that Rosemary Conley woman. I was stunned. I can't watch it, though, it makes me cringe. I hate hearing the sound of my voice trying to teach those 'geezers' behind me how to dance. I swear that the only reason it sold well was because people bought it just so they could laugh at me. I reckon they get the video, sit on the sofa with a bar of chocolate, then laugh their heads off. One of my best mates, Kelly, bought Kate Lawler's workout video but refused to buy mine. I rang her up once and she answered the phone, huffing and puffing. I said, 'Why are you out of breath?' 'I'm doing

Kate Lawler,' she breathed. I was fuming. 'What? Where's mine?', but she said to me, 'I can't watch yours! I'd just piss myself laughing.'

In February 2003, Jeff took me to Prague for our first Valentine's Day together. I bought him a Cartier watch because I knew he wanted one, and (of course) I bought one for myself to match. I didn't have a clue he was taking me to Prague. He was working during that day (co-hosting *Dirty Laundry* on Channel 4), and whenever I called him he mysteriously refused to answer his phone. He just kept sending me little texts instead. He would say things like, 'Pack some warm stuff' and 'There's a car coming to pick you up at 4 p.m., get in it and I'll meet you at the other end.' I was texting back, 'Where are you taking me? What are we doing?' But it was really exciting. I got driven to the airport and I still didn't have a clue what we were doing. He came to meet me and gave me a huge hug and made me close my eyes as he guided me to the check-in desk. When I opened them I heard a lady say, 'Anyone for Prague?' 'Where's Prague?' I asked – well, you didn't seriously expect me to know where it was, did you?

When we arrived it was snowing. Jeff kept making me walk loads – I think he was trying to get me to be cultured – and it was beautiful: the buildings in Prague are gorgeous. We also went on a ghost-hunting walk, which was actually more funny than scary. It was romantic too. When I gave Jeff his watch he welled up and said, 'Every time I look at my watch, every second of every minute of every hour of every day, I'll remember how much I'm in love with you.'

9

'I F**king Hate You'

We were still living in the house near Lakeside until May 2003. We planned to move to another house in Harlow in Essex, but it was still being built (!) so we had to wait. But I hated waiting. It was one of the lowest points of my life. I had no independence, I couldn't drive, I was heavily pregnant and I have never felt so insecure. Jeff and I had suddenly changed from being the perfect pair, the golden couple, two soul mates who were so in love, to the most irritable, nit-picking, argumentative duo you could ever meet. To be fair, though, I think most of this was down to me and my hormones. They were all over the place. I felt so fat and ugly; I couldn't even do my shoelaces up.

Jeff used to come home from work and I'd be lying in the bath, in complete darkness except for a few candles flickering around me. Mariah Carey would be blaring from the stereo and I'd be bawling my eyes out. Jeff would look

181

at me and say, 'Why are you crying?' I'd stare at him for a few seconds then blub, 'I don't know!' I definitely wasn't the easiest person to live with at that time. He'd be out at the shops or doing some TV work, and I'd be on the phone to him saying, 'You're leaving me, aren't you? I'm pregnant and you don't care!' I became jealous of everything he did, and in the end I think that's what drove him further and further away from me.

Jeff started to go for nights out with his mates. I'd read about it the following day in the papers: 'JEFF CHEATS ON JADE!' But when I confronted him about it he'd always deny that he'd done anything with any other girl. He'd admit that there were girls around when he went out, but he said he only ever had a bit of banter with them and nothing else. I'd like to think nothing happened, and, knowing the kind of person he is, I honestly don't believe that he would've done the dirty on me. But you never truly know, do you? And considering who I'd become and the way I would talk to him, there's a small part of me that wouldn't really blame him if he had done something behind my back.

I became a horrible person. I'd never felt this insecure before and I didn't know how to deal with it. I'd read things in the paper, quotes from other girls saying things like, 'Jeff looked gorgeous in his Prada trousers and his Prada boots,' and I'd say, 'You fucking bastard, I bought you them!' Then they'd talk about the car he drove and I'd say, 'I bought you that car!' Every time he pissed me off or upset me I'd throw the money card back in his face. I was nasty to him and I've got an evil tongue. I'd hit him right where I knew it would hurt him the most: 'Get out of my fucking house! You're a scrounger, you're a ponce, you've got no independence. You drive my car as if it's yours. You think you're the man when you're out but you're not – you're a little boy with your bleached-blond fucking hair.' I could sting him with my words just like that, and he'd be distraught. I'd get violent too. I'd hit him. I was so aggressive. But you see, I didn't know how to be anything else. All my other relationships were fuelled by violence so I didn't know how else to behave.

The perfect relationship I thought I'd found suddenly didn't seem so perfect after all. I felt like I'd let my guard down with Jeff and now he was forcing me to put it back up again. So I pushed him further and further away. Jeff would always try to make me sit up and talk about it, and he'd attempt to reason with me. He would say, 'Do you realise what you're doing to me?' and even though I could see it, and that most of it was my fault, I'd just do it all again the next day. And so it got worse and worse. Every weekend there was a different story about Jeff and another girl. It did my head in. I'd confront him about it but there'd always be an excuse and he'd talk his way out of it. He was good at doing that and I'd feel bad that I hadn't believed him. Then when I tried to make it up to him, he'd be stubborn and refuse to let me. It went round and round like that in circles for weeks. I became convinced I was going to have my baby on my own and end up a single mum.

In the meantime we'd agreed to take part in a celebrity version of Channel 4's *Wife Swap* with Charles and Diana Ingram (the couple who hit the headlines for trying to pull a fast one on *Who Wants to Be a Millionaire?* when Charles was accused of cheating). I was about seven or eight months pregnant, and Jeff and I hadn't been getting on at all. But this was work, so we agreed we'd do it, smile for the camera and pretend everything was fine. But deep down neither of us was happy. We'd been fighting; I felt insecure. I kept pushing him away and he was finding me too much to take. There were the occasional nights when we'd sit on the sofa and he'd rub my belly lovingly and sing lullabies to my tummy and read it little stories. But then we'd ruin it and argue again.

So off I went to live with Charles Ingram for seven days, and Charles's wife Diana went to live with Jeff. During the filming we were told we weren't allowed to have any contact with our real partners, but I ignored that rule. I couldn't have coped if I wasn't allowed to talk to Jeff. Despite our differences he was still my boyfriend, the father of my unborn baby, and I was very, very hormonal!

I hated living with Charles (or Army Ingram, as I called him). His children, Rosie and Esther, were the only thing that got me through it and kept me going. They were adorable. But because Charles was so regimented and spot-on with every aspect of his life, it had rubbed off on his daughters, and they were obsessed with having to do things to order. I had to teach them to relax. I remember sitting with little Rosie on the sofa one day, teaching her to sing a hip-hop song, and she was joining in, in her posh little voice. It was hilarious.

The girls were the sweetest things ever and I felt sorry for them. All their money was being taken away from them because Charles had been sacked from the army after he was accused of cheating. And still he refused to admit it. I tried to tell him that if he'd only confess he could earn a fortune from magazine and newspaper deals by telling 'his story'. I was getting quite savvy in my old age and I knew that as far as the media were concerned, there was a price for everything. If only he'd listened to me, the Ingrams could've been living in a mansion by now.

I didn't learn anything at all from living with Charles. He just fucking pissed me off, if I'm honest. And spending time with him just made me realise what I had myself. When I saw Jeff again I was so happy to be home. I couldn't believe how much I'd missed him. Of course, our equilibrium didn't last for long. The four of us were filmed meeting up for a 'catch-up', after which I wanted to smack Jeff in the face. Diana had started criticising me for not having any curtains in our house and there being no salt and pepper. I naturally went off on one, but then Jeff started sticking up for her! When we got home we had a huge row and Jeff was furious with me for talking like that to an 'older lady'.

Then we moved into our new house in Harlow in Essex, and for a few weeks things got a bit better. The last place was always going to be nothing more than a temporary situation while we were waiting for our house in Harlow to be built – we didn't want to stay at Kevin's because I was pregnant – but the flat was tiny. With our new place it was like, new house, new start.

I was planning to have the baby in the Portland Hospital. The newspapers criticised me for choosing a posh place where all the celebrities have their kids, rather than a normal run-of-the-mill hospital. But although the Portland was expensive, it was also extremely private. I didn't want the media finding out every detail about the birth. It was going to cost £5000 in total and by June 2003 I'd already put down the £3000 deposit. But in the end, Bobby was born a month early, so all my plans (and my deposit) went kaput.

One night, when I was eight months pregnant, I had a few mates round to the house for a curry and to watch a horror movie. Jeff and I were due to visit the Portland to have a look around the next day, but in the morning I woke up in a pool of blood. I screamed my head off (naturally) and Jeff dashed about in a mad fluster before driving me to Harlow Hospital. I didn't have a bag packed or anything, so I turned up at the hospital looking like a pikey. I was wearing bikini bottoms because I couldn't find any proper pants (well, I only owned thongs) and I was dressed in one of Jeff's old T-shirts.

When we arrived, the doctor told me I was already seven centimetres dilated, which meant I'd been having my contractions in my sleep. Then they started coming thick and fast, but I didn't have a clue what to do – I wasn't due to start antenatal classes until the following week. The baby wasn't meant to be born for another month! I didn't have a clue what I was doing or what was going on, but the hospital was great, and they totally respected my privacy. When we got there they'd ushered us in the back door so no one could see it was us. I was shitting myself. I remember screaming, 'I don't like it, I don't want to be here – they don't know what they're doing!' I was on my knees, shouting at everyone. I needed to wee and poo and push – do everything at the same time. It was all so confusing.

Even though it was pain like I'd never felt in my life, I didn't want any drugs. I kept refusing. I wanted to experience the birth of my first child and actually be able to remember it afterwards. Jeff was constantly telling me, 'It's all right, it's all right,' and was wiping my head with a tissue. His mum had turned up by this point too. I wouldn't have cared if five thousand people were in there, I just needed to get it out. But I was being told I wasn't allowed to push because it wasn't ready yet. I shouted, 'I need to eat, then!' so someone ran off and got me a chicken sandwich. Well, I had two mouthfuls and that was it; it was now or never. I threw my sandwich away and pushed with all my might. I must've looked so attractive. Finally, after six hours, little Bobby was born, weighing in at 5 lb 7 oz. I didn't even know I'd had a boy until the midwife plopped him on my lap. It was the strangest thing: all of a sudden I was handed this little human being and it was wriggling around and making noises. Jeff and I were so overwhelmed we both cried, then Jeff cut the cord. I kept looking at Bobby and thinking, *Why has he got all this white slime all over him?* He was gorgeous, though.

It didn't take long before the press got wind of Bobby's arrival. Because he was born prematurely, he was kept in hospital for a good few weeks following the birth, and I stayed in there with him for most of the time. Reporters would camp outside day and night. The papers were desperate to get a shot of Bobby. They'd even tried to bribe hospital visitors to help them. People would walk inside and attempt to come and take a photo of him while he was in his incubator. They'd been told that a snap of our son was worth £10,000. When they couldn't get the shot they wanted, one of the papers kindly printed a picture of a pig in a blanket instead. Nice, eh!

Jade: How It All Began

Not long after Bobby was born, the *People* ran a kiss-and-tell from a girl called Lindsey Peel who claimed Jeff had romped with her under the covers in a hotel while I was at home pregnant. I didn't know what to think. If I could've gone and hunted her down, I would have; I swear, I'd have ripped her eyes out. Jeff denied he'd done anything remotely sexual with her. He still denies it to this day. I have no choice but to believe him really. After all, at the end of the day, would you ever truly know if your partner had cheated on you? And did I really want to know that this man, Jeff, who was such a massive part of my life, had slept with someone while I was pregnant? It would make me feel sick. I have to trust him, otherwise what's the point?

Bobby's first ever outfit was a Christian Dior babygro. He was given millions of presents – he was so spoilt. Spencer and PJ sent me a card saying 'Congratulations', which was really cute considering I hadn't spoken to them for about a year. Phil Edgar-Jones sent him a gorgeous silk and cashmere blanket. I've still got it now – it's obviously really expensive.

I didn't think about my dad once. I didn't want him to know anything about his grandchild. I wanted to blank him out.

A month after, we were invited to Jeff's friends Jade and Ed's wedding. This is where I finally met Jen, the ex-girlfriend from Jeff's past. Jennifer Smith is her name. We broke the ice almost as soon as Jeff and I arrived, and by the end of the wedding we were running around taking the piss out of people like we'd known each other for years.

She's an amazing, funny girl and now I'm proud to call her one of my best friends. Needless to say, I got quite drunk that day, and, as a result, Jeff and I ended up having a row. We'd driven to the wedding but had always planned to get a cab home because it was only local. We were standing outside – I can't even remember what we were arguing about – and Jeff was concerned that the neighbours could hear us, so we sat in the car. Then we put the keys in the ignition because it was getting chilly outside and we wanted to keep ourselves warm. Next thing I know there's a knock on the window – one of the neighbours had called the police. We were arrested for drink-driving! I was screaming, 'Are you having a joke, officer? Do you think we were driving anywhere? I haven't even got a fucking licence!' This went down brilliantly, as you can imagine. We were held in the station for hours. Jeff was hopelessly trying to calm things down while I was making things ten times worse: 'What are you going to do, handcuff me?' I'm surprised they didn't gag me. Lo and behold, it was in the papers the next day: 'JADE AND JEFF – ARRESTED FOR DRINK-DRIVING'

10

A Cry for Help

Once I'd stopped breast-feeding Bobby I was able to start my training again. There was a second fitness video in the pipeline and I wanted to get back to the shape I was in before I fell pregnant. I worked so hard and stuck to all my meal plans. I was eating healthily – things like grapefruit in the morning, salad for lunch, salmon and broccoli for tea. I was being really good and I got down to a size 12. I've never felt so confident in my life. I had a new house, a beautiful baby, I was going out and having a good time, and it was like a whole new me. I also dyed my hair caramel and got long hair extensions put in. I felt great. After all the shit in my life, things were going brilliantly again.

The press were even starting to be nice about me. Rather than comparing me to a photo of a pig, I started reading headlines like: 'IS JADE TURNING INTO LIZ HURLEY?' Fancy that! It was so refreshing to read magazines that said

I looked pretty and that were giving their readers tips on how to dress like me. I might come across as if I've got a tough exterior, but all those comparisons to a pig had really hurt me. The negative comments knocked my confidence so much. Once upon a time I'd never have looked at a dodgy photo of me and thought twice about it. I'd just shrug, 'It's the photo, it's a bad angle.' But now I was always analysing things, because that's what every paper does to me: I look at my body and always think I need to change a part of myself.

But now that I was happy with my looks, it was Jeff's turn to feel insecure. I was the happiest and most self-assured he'd ever known me. Gone was the needy, fat, pregnant moaner, and in her place was a whole new Jade. I didn't care that I could see him feeling low. I felt too good about myself. I'd always been the one feeling that way before, and I relished the fact that I no longer felt worried he was going to leave me.

Inevitably, though, there's a danger that comes with feeling so good about yourself, especially when you've previously felt self-doubt. You'll do anything in your power never to feel that bad again. And that's what happened to me.

It began one night when I was at home alone. I'd been so good up until now – eating low-fat food, sticking to my diet religiously – but that evening I desperately wanted to have a take-away. I wanted a Chinese. I told myself that surely I could treat myself after I'd worked so hard? So I ordered it and I ate it all in one go. Then I sat watching telly. A few minutes after I'd eaten it I felt this overwhelming sense of dirtiness: it was almost as if I could feel the grease from the Chinese swilling around in my stomach and I just needed to get it out. I had to get rid of it. I started to get hot and sweaty and thought, *I feel sick.* I went to the bathroom and brushed my teeth. As I was cleaning them, the brush accidentally knocked the back of my throat and I was sick. And sick. And sick. I've never been able to do that before – at school people would dare each other to make themselves sick and I just couldn't bring myself to go ahead with it. But now I had. I looked at myself in the mirror and I smiled. I'd actually enjoyed the feeling of being sick. I felt so much better. I'd eaten what I wanted, I'd got rid of it from my stomach and the bonus was that now I didn't feel hungry so I didn't need any more food. So that was it; I didn't stop after that. No matter what I ate, it could've been something as small as a biscuit, I would get rid of it afterwards. Jeff didn't know. Nobody knew. And it went on for months.

I'd go out for meals, then disappear off to the toilet and throw up. I'd always make sure I was carrying at least a couple of packets of chewing gum in my bag. If I was ever in my bathroom at home, I'd run a bath or the tap so I couldn't be heard when I was throwing up. It was like a carefully planned military operation and I learnt to be quite clever about it. Whenever people were in the house, I'd make sure I went to the loo upstairs so they couldn't hear me. To me, vomiting after a meal was an amazing, unexplainable feeling. I would think, *This is wicked!* I could sit and have a meal with everyone else, be all happy and jolly, and then go and throw it all up. No one would be any wiser.

But underneath it all I was deeply ashamed. I'd be all

alone, crouching in a toilet with my head down the loo. What kind of a person does that? What was worse was that I was still exercising like a mad woman. I'd eat breakfast, exercise, go home and throw up.

I knew it was getting out of control, and the jolt that really woke me up was when I was in a restaurant toilet and the woman in the cubicle next door could hear me being sick. She started knocking on the wall, saying, 'Are you all right, love?' and I replied, 'Yes, don't worry, I'm just feeling a bit ill.' But I felt so mortified. There was a voice in my head telling me it was wrong and I needed to do something about it. But I knew I couldn't do it by myself.

One evening, I was at home, and as I came out of the toilet after being sick I felt so unbelievably weak I could hardly stand. My lack of nutrition was starting to affect how I was with Bobby: I had so little energy I couldn't even lift him up. To make matters worse, my hair was dull and lifeless, and I'd noticed it was even starting to fall out in places. I knew I couldn't go on. I had to tell Jeff. So I went into the lounge, sat beside him on the sofa and broke down in tears as I told him. I admitted, 'I've been throwing up my meals for the last two months. I can't help myself.' He just sat there quietly, listening to every word. Once I'd finished telling him I added, 'I'm not exactly skin and bones, though, so I'm not bulimic.' He looked so sad as he held my face and stared straight into my eyes. 'Yes, you are, Jade,' he said. 'You might not be a size 6 but you've got to face facts. You're a bulimic.'

After that, Jeff followed me wherever I went. From the minute I told him, he was watching me like a hawk. He did everything in his power to make sure I wasn't sick. He was feeling apprehensive and unhappy himself, but he loved me and he wanted to protect me. I would sit outside the bathroom door begging him to let me be sick. I'd cry for hours. But he wouldn't let me in there alone, even when I'd be pleading with him to leave me just for a second. He'd make me sit on the toilet with the door open so he could watch me. And if he walked off and heard me running a tap, he'd be in the room with me like a shot.

Jeff had recently bought himself a sunbed shop – he wanted a nest egg in case the TV work dried up – and because he was trying to make a go of his business he couldn't always be at home to keep an eye on me during the daytime. So sometimes he'd have no choice but to leave me alone. The thing is, he knows I can't lie. If he ever called me up and asked if I'd been sick I'd have to admit the truth. And if I had, I knew he'd be disappointed and I'd feel guilty. But by not being sick I was starting to feel conscious about my looks again. I was beginning to think Jeff might not fancy me any more. It was a vicious circle. So our relationship started deteriorating once more. I was the one relying on him now. The tables had turned back again and I needed him more than I ever had before. It must've made him look at me with disgust. We'd go to a restaurant with friends and I'd desperately want to be sick, but of course I wasn't allowed to go to the toilet. I wanted to eat the food because it looked nice, but once it was inside me I felt unclean and needed to get it out.

Although I managed to control it, I still do it now sometimes. I don't think you can ever truly get over an illness like that. I have to admit that every now and then I still throw up. The difference these days is that I always tell

Jeff or my friends about it. I'll say, 'I'm going through that stage again,' because I know they'll look out for me. It's when I'm feeling uncertain about a situation that I want to do it – if I'm nervous or anxious about something. You'll be able to see when I'm agitated at a mealtime because I'll start twiddling with my hair or picking at things around me, then I'll say, 'I'm just going to the loo.'

If there's something in my life that's not going well, it'll happen again. Most things could be perfect but there only needs to be one thing to tip me over the edge. At the moment I think it's my dad. He's playing on my mind. I can't stop thinking about it. But back then I was making myself ill because I desperately wanted the papers to keep saying nice things about me.

When I told Jeff, he told my mum a few days later; and she'll be the first person he'll tell now whenever he suspects I'm going through 'a stage'. He'll phone her up and say, 'Make sure you keep an eye on her, will you? She's at it again.' As a consequence of being sick (and since having the boys) I've collapsed a few times. The papers always think that because I'm rushed to hospital or I've fainted that I'm pregnant again, but really it's down to the fact that I've burnt myself out, and not kept any food in my body for a while. It happened the first week my beauty salon opened. I was running on nothing and I'd worn myself out. The doctors have told me that as a result of throwing up all the time, my blood-clotting cells are really low. I had to have two blood transfusions after giving birth to Freddy.

I could never keep it up, though. I've seen what puking can do to your teeth. Whenever I start making myself sick, I remember what I used to be faced with when I was a dental nurse and it brings me back down to earth. I've always been proud of my gnashers and I know what it looks like when people don't look after them. You can tell immediately when someone's bulimic because it makes them go all see-through. The teeth become transparent at the bottom because of the acid from the stomach bile. It burns them away and they go thin and brittle.

In September 2003, the fighting between Jeff and me got so bad that he actually moved out for a couple of days. I started looking at his phone to see if he had any text messages. When I found one from a girl I didn't know I got really suspicious and scrolled through his sent messages to see what he'd been writing to her. Lo and behold, I found one that he'd sent to this girl, saying, 'Come down to the sunbed shop and I'll get on the bed with you.' How could Jeff possibly get himself out of that? When he came into the room I was standing there ironing, and he's lucky I didn't hit the iron over his head. I was fuming. But he said that it was just harmless fun, he was winding this girl up, that it was a joke and they were just having a bit of banter.

You can imagine what I said in response. I threw back at him – not for the first time – that he was living in my house, that he'd be nothing without me. I can be quite spiteful when I want to be. I knew I could hurt him that way because Jeff is a proud man. When we talk about it now he says I was being a bitch to him and that's what made him want to go out and talk to other girls, just to have a bit of a flirt and a laugh, and to feel like he was his own person, not just an extension of me.

Jeff used to write me loads of letters explaining how he

felt about me and why he thought things had gone wrong. He always said he had to write them because I'd never let him get a word in when he tried to speak to me – that way I couldn't go off on one. He's written me essays before, some of them are five or six pages long. This particular time it got too much and he packed a bag and went to stay at his aunt's. He left me a note telling me he loved me but that he couldn't cope any more. He said he felt like he walked in my shadow, that he didn't feel like a real person, that wherever he goes he gets recognised as 'Jade's boyfriend Jeff', not as a man in his own right. He said his friends had noticed a change in him, and that he was moping around all the time. That was a big blow for him. He's got a huge personality and it must've been hard to be referred to as merely someone's boyfriend. I think that's why he felt the need to chat to other girls – almost to prove there were people who wanted to talk to *him* and who would not just be interested in asking for my autograph. In a weird way I can see the justification. I did so want to be with him, and when I read his letters they made me cry and cry, but at the same time I was pushing him and pushing him to see if he would actually leave me. All my life I'd had horrible relationships with men and they'd only ever gone wrong. So when he left me that day I thought he'd turned out exactly the same. But after about two days he came back. He said he wanted me to recognise my mistakes, and I was so pleased to see him that I truly felt I had learnt my lesson. I wanted him back forever. Well, until the next pregnancy, the next bout of hormones and the next row.

Around this time, I started a beauty course at Brentwood Academy. I loved it there. I felt normal. No one referred to me as Jade from *Big Brother*. I was treated like one of them. What's more, I really wanted to be there, so I worked my socks off. I did all my coursework and stayed behind and did extra hours if I had to. My dream was to own a salon and I was determined it was going to happen. We'd practise waxing bikini lines on each other (Brazilian waxes didn't come until later, though, thank God). I waxed Jeff's leg once because I needed to practise, but I didn't trim the hairs beforehand, which meant they wouldn't come off in one go. I properly fucked it up and he went mental. He was screaming in pain. He wouldn't let me do any more after that and walked about with a bald patch on his shin.

My issues with food hadn't stopped, though. OK, so I was no longer throwing up, but I still felt the need to control my weight. So I bought slimming pills instead. My mate Laura got them for me from a little shop round the corner from our house (I couldn't do it myself in case I was papped coming out). These pills were so strong. They must've contained a derivative of speed because I was buzzing all day and my eyes were popping out of my head. I was literally whizzing around beauty school (no wonder I worked so hard). I passed my exams, though, with flying colours.

I was still taking the tablets when Jeff and I decided to have a fancy-dress Halloween party at our house. We really went to town and hired lavish costumes. Bobby was a pumpkin, and Jeff and I were the King and Queen of the Manor, but we were dead, obviously, so we painted our faces white and had fake blood dripping out of our mouths. Our relationship was going through a really good patch and we had such fun decorating the house with cobwebs and fake insects. We'd told our friends we were giving a prize for the best costume, but in the end we couldn't decide. Well, I was too pissed to choose by the end of the night. Bobby stayed the night at Jen's mum's house, which meant we could really let our hair down. I was drinking this green stuff called Absiss or Absinth – whatever it's called. It's lethal at the best of times, let alone if you're combining it with slimming tablets. I don't think I've ever been so out of it in my life. My mates were asking me for headache tablets and I was giving them all my slimming pills! One of them called me the next day saying, 'What did you give me, Jade? My heart was pounding and I couldn't sleep.' Oops. That night I also jumped into our hot tub (we had one built outside) fully clothed. My wig got soaked, then I tried to get undressed in the garden, battling against everyone else who was trying to cover me up. I was a mess. But Jeff still says that that night was the first time I properly spoke to him about how I felt – no barriers, no shouting, no spitefulness: I just opened up my heart to him. He still tells me it was one of the most meaningful talks we've ever had. He talks about it all the time, and when he does I just nod in agreement. Don't tell him, but really I can't remember a thing.

My dad got out of prison for a while and got in touch again. He asked if he could have some pictures of Bobby, which of course I gave to him. Then he sold them to the papers. I knew straight away it was so that he could get some money to buy smack. It really got to me. I would sit at home crying my eyes out; it felt like I was being used. I couldn't, and still can't, get my head around it. On the one hand he'd be saying he loved me and would plead for me to introduce him to his grandchild; then the next minute he'd sell photos of him for drugs. Where were his morals? I guess it's easy to judge an addict, but I'm not one, so I can't understand how their mind works. Maybe in some way it was like my addiction to making myself sick: I felt good when I was vomiting; he felt good when he had a hit. The thing was, he hurt a hell of a lot of people in the process.

Before our first Christmas as a family, Jeff and I went to the Maldives. It was just the pair of us, Bobby was at home with my mum, and we got on really well. One night we got really drunk and danced outside in the rain. It was very romantic. I missed Bobby like crazy, though. I'd sit on the beach reading my book while Jeff went off diving for fish in the sea, and I couldn't stop thinking about our son.

Jeff bought me loads of lovely little things for Christmas. Considering what a miserable bitch I'd been, he was very thoughtful. He wrapped everything individually with clues attached as to what was inside. One present was a keyring with a big diamond on the end. And on the tag he'd written, 'This is what you are – it sparkles just like you.'

New Year came and I was still enjoying life. One night, after finishing a photo shoot with *Heat* magazine, I went out with the girls, including Jeff's ex, Jen. I was feeling all lovely and pampered because *Heat* had given me a new set of hair extensions. We went to this nightclub called 195 in Epping. We had such a wicked time – downing shots, doing caterpillars on the dance floor – all sorts. Then, at about 2 a.m., we came out and went to get in Jen's car. But before we could drive off, Jen, being the busybody she is, saw an argument going on nearby and thought she recognised someone she knew. She went over and demanded to know what was going on. I was sitting in the car waiting for her but she was taking ages. So I got out and shouted, 'Jen, what's going on? Hurry up!' All of a sudden this girl looked at me and said, 'Eww! Jade from *Big Brother!*' and just whacked me in the face. Well, I saw red. I rushed back to the car, removed my Jimmy Choos (Jeff had bought them for me for Christmas and they'd already got a bit scuffed up when I was doing the caterpillar so I couldn't risk ruining them any more), put my Gucci handbag under the seat and stomped back to the scene of the fight. Then all hell broke loose. One of my mates was rolling about on the floor with a boy booting her in the face, so I jumped onto his back and smacked him round the head. Hair was being pulled, nails were being broken. It was comical, really.

Then the police arrived. Carly, my mate, who's always been the most sensible of the group, was a quick-thinker and immediately dragged me away from the scene and made me sit with her round the corner so it didn't look like I was involved. I sat against a wall, huffing and puffing, for a good few minutes. Then, despite her pleas not to, I decided to walk back round to see if the police had gone. They hadn't. Not only that, but the guy who'd been fighting my mate hadn't even been arrested. 'Hang about!' I said to one of the coppers. 'Look at the state of my mate's face! And you haven't even fucking arrested this drunk? What's all that about?' The boy in question looked at me with venom in his eyes and said, 'Oh, just shut up, Jade.' So I leant across the policeman and hooked him one. Next minute, the policeman tried to arrest me. I went nuts. There

I was, trying to punch and kick the boy while the policeman was holding me back. In the end we just got separated and I was taken to the hospital with my friend so they could sort her face out. Two days later I opened *Heat* magazine to see a picture of the very same boy holding a scraggly bit of hair in his hands, saying, 'I've got Jade Goody's hair extensions!' I had to laugh.

Jeff was starting to get jealous of any bloke I spoke to, the main culprit being Antony Costa from the band Blue. Antony lived round the corner from us in Harlow and I'd often bump into him on nights out and we ended up getting quite pally for a while. There's absolutely no way in the world I fancied him, though – he reminds me of one of the cartoon pigeons from the Tetley teabag adverts – so Jeff had nothing to worry about on that score. But one night Antony and I swapped numbers. It was completely harmless, but it was also the first boy's number I'd ever taken. Jeff had taken loads of girls' numbers before – hence all the slanging matches we had when they started texting him – but I never had. One day my phone beeped and Jeff looked at it. It was a text from Antony. It said something random about someone we'd been talking about the night before (I'd been out to a nightclub called Faces in Gants Hill in Essex and I'd seen him and chatted to him at the bar). I didn't realise Jeff had seen my phone, and when I came into the room he told me I'd got a text message and casually asked who it was from. As soon as he asked me I suddenly felt bad, even though nothing had happened and meé and Antony were just mates. I don't know why, but my knee-jerk reaction was to lie, and I said it was from someone else. Jeff flipped. I'd never ever fibbed to him before, so to him this meant I was hiding something. He kept saying, 'Why do you need to lie if you're not guilty of doing anything?' and I didn't know what to say. I guess I was scared that if I said the wrong thing I might lose him.

After that, Jeff's level of distrust shot off the scale and his insecurities kicked in. At one stage it got so bad that he took the dustbin we kept outside our house to work, just so he could rummage through it and see if there were any other boys' numbers in there. I wasn't very supportive; my attitude was 'get over it'. But when I'd been jealous of him and other girls he would always sit and convince me otherwise – he'd be patient, he'd tell me I was beautiful and that he was always there for me. But when he needed reassurance I didn't give it to him. I think there's a part of me that wanted to punish him, as if to say, 'Look at all the times you've done it to me.' But that's not the right attitude. I turned him into a weak man; it was like I had drained his personality from him. That's why he's so apprehensive about us ever getting back together again. He says he will never let a girl do that to him again. He wasn't the confident, bubbly Jeff who'd always looked after me and knew what to do. I didn't have the patience. I wasn't a good girlfriend, that's for sure.

Jeff and I celebrated Valentine's Day early that year. I'd signed up to appear in a new Channel 5 reality TV show called *Back to Reality*. There was me, Rik Waller from Pop Idol, Lizzie Bardsley from *Wife Swap*, James Hewitt and Josie D'Arby from *The Games*, Maureen Rees from *Driving School*, Ricardo from *The Salon*, Catalina Guirado and Uri Geller from *I'm a Celebrity, Get Me Out of Here*, and Craig Phillips from *Big Brother 1*. We were to stay in a house in a studio for three weeks while the public voted out the least popular.

A couple of nights before the show, Jeff took me for a meal in Smiths, a lovely fish restaurant in Ongar, Essex. There were paparazzi outside. We looked quite loved-up in the pictures, but we weren't. Our relationship was going through major problems. The night before I went on the show I didn't even see Jeff. We'd been arguing and he didn't want to stay the night with me, so I spent it in a hotel with my girlfriends instead. It was me, Kelly, Jen and Cath. We call ourselves the famous four. After the row with Jeff, I got on the phone and pleaded with them to come over and keep me company. None of them were dressed to go out (Jen had the greasiest hair in the world!) but they dropped everything they were doing and came to be with me. I dragged them to a Chinese restaurant in Soho, then we ended up in a sleazy Australian backpackers' pub called The Walkabout. By the end of the night we were pissed out of our nuts and throwing ourselves around the room. At one stage, the R.E.M. song 'Losing my Religion' came on, and every time the chorus was on I'd fling myself into the corner of the room and sing along to the words, 'That's me in the corner'. The others cracked up. Then we staggered along the road, back to the hotel, and a bus drove past us with a huge picture of me on the side. It was an advert for *Back to Reality*. The girls started running down the road shouting, 'That's you!' and chasing it round the bend. It brings it all home when I see things like that: one minute I'm like a normal pissed idiot squealing down the street, and the next minute I see my face on a giant poster.

Jade: How It All Began

When I got into the *Back to Reality* house I immediately bonded with Catalina and Josie. I thought Lizzie Bardsley was funny and Maureen was sweet – I used to put her socks on for her because she couldn't bend down. Ricardo, though? What a cock. He was nothing but bitchy and horrible. Rik Waller was dirty and he smelt. And I hated Craig Phillips because he thought he was always right. James Hewitt was lovely, which is probably why he won the show in the end. Uri Geller was fascinating – he would always sit there and have grand theories about things.

A few days into the show I started feeling really sick, and began complaining of stomach pains. It got so bad that the producers had to take me to hospital – and that's when I found out the cause of it. I was pregnant again. I was stunned. Not only was I not with Jeff at that time, but I was on national television so I couldn't even tell anyone. I said I was fine to go back into the house as long as I could make a private phone call. I didn't have a clue how Jeff would react so I just blurted out, 'I'm pregnant.' No matter how things were between us, there was never really any doubt as to whether I'd have it. When I told Jeff he said, 'That's brilliant news, Jade! I'm coming in to stay with you tomorrow anyway. I'm coming into the *Back to Reality* house.' Apparently the producers had booked him to come in as a surprise. I found it a bit weird, considering how we'd left things when I went in. But Jeff was happy that I was pregnant, and, in the end, him coming into the house was the best thing that could've happened. He was so comforting.

Despite Jeff's attitude towards the pregnancy being so positive, our relationship was still a mess, and I spent the following week seriously thinking about having an abortion. When I left the show the press were already all over the story and asking if I could confirm or deny the pregnancy rumours. It was a really difficult time as I didn't have a clear idea of what I wanted to do. I kept these feelings from Jeff and took some time out to think about things. If I hadn't already had Bobby, I might've had an abortion. But once you are a mother, things change. I couldn't ever deny Bobby the chance of having a brother or sister. I simply couldn't do it.

So things were looking up for us for a while, and we thought this addition to our family would make us stronger as a unit. But I was getting hormonal again and I was still feeling rubbish about myself. I even started getting mysterious phone calls from this girl, saying things like, 'Jeff's been cheating on you. I just want to let you know. I don't want you to be taken for a mug.' I would ask, 'Who are you?' and she'd reply, 'I don't really want to say.' But whether I believed this girl or not, she did a good job of playing silly buggers with my mind.

Then it happened. Our big break-up. It was May 2004 and I was about three months pregnant. No thanks to me, Jeff had started to build himself and his confidence back up again. He was going to the gym, doing his own thing, mixing with friends who made him feel good about himself. He'd started hanging about with this guy called Luke. Luke was only about 19, and looked up to Jeff like he was David Beckham or something. He worked in Jeff's sunbed shop, which I think he pretended he owned on a few occasions. I hated him because he was such an arse-licker and I thought he was false.

Jade: How It All Began

The night it happened, Jeff had been out filming all day. He was on an episode of the BBC's *The Weakest Link*. I'd been out all day too, and by the time I got back home he was still out. So I rang him up and asked him why he wasn't home yet. He just said he was out and would be back later, and all I could hear were girls' voices in the background. I kept ringing back and demanding to know where he was. It picked up but no one answered me; I could just hear all this background noise. I was shouting 'Jeff! Jeff!' and there was no reply. I didn't know what was going on. The next time I rang, a girl picked up the phone and said, 'Oh, who the fuck is that?' I was so angry. If I could've driven I would've got into the car, found wherever he was and dragged him out by his ear. I was shaking so much. All I could hear was him laughing in the background. I was just beside myself.

My mum was staying at our house at the time but was downstairs with Bobby so she didn't know what was going on. I was pacing up and down in my bedroom, thinking, *You fucking cunt!* I know they are awful words but I can't think of any other way to describe my anger and how upset I was. What was he playing at? There were so many horrible images running through my head. I rang him again and this time it went straight to answerphone. He'd switched his phone off!

That was it. I left him a message saying, 'Jeff. Don't come home. Don't set your foot back in my house.' I was boiling up. He'd made me feel like crap all over again. Within the space of a few hours it was like all the destructive relationships from my past had merged into one.

A Cry for Help

I lay in bed, not sleeping. Then in the early hours of the morning I heard the door open. There were a few giggles downstairs, but no girls' voices, only men. It was just Jeff and that Luke. Jeff walked upstairs and he was stinking of booze. I saw his silhouette coming over to the bed and he stopped and looked at me. Then he leant over, poked me in the arm and said 'Oi!' like an annoying kid at school. I tried my hardest to be calm, and gritted my teeth and said, 'Get out of the house, now.' I was shaking all over. Jeff just said, 'No. Fuck off, Jade. Why should I get out of my house?' Suddenly every insult I could possibly find lodged in my brain came spilling out, and I jumped out of bed and whacked him in the face. Then he pushed me against the wall. He went to run down the stairs but I grabbed him and hit him again as hard as I could.

Luke was downstairs but I didn't even think about the fact that I had no clothes on. I was starkers, flying around the landing, throwing punches all over the place. Arms were going everywhere, and we were both screaming at the top of our voices.

Then I fell down the stairs. Bobby was screaming and my mum woke up and tried to calm us down, but we were oblivious. I was shouting at her to get back into her room. Jeff and I were fighting – well, I was hitting him and he was trying to restrain me. We were properly going for it, as if we were bitter enemies. He pushed me against the banister so hard it started wobbling, then he went into the kitchen to get away from me. I opened a drawer and grabbed a spatula and whacked him with it: The scary thing is, if there had been a knife in there I probably would've grabbed that instead. Jeff had scratches all over his neck and I had a lump on my head. He pushed me, I punched him. It was horrible. But one thing that will always stick in my mind was the look on Luke's face as he stood there motionless, not even attempting to break up the fight. It was as if he was enjoying it. He was just gloating, and I'll never forget it. My mum kept screaming 'Stop it! Stop it!' She just didn't know what to do, so she called the police.

Jeff legged it out of the house before they arrived (I found out later that he was hiding in the forest next to our house because he was so scared the police would think he was a wife-beater). I just sat there shaking. When the police came I had to give a statement and I said it was just a little argument. I didn't want to get Jeff into trouble and I didn't want the police to run after him and nick him, so I kept my statement as short and minimalistic as possible. 'It was a domestic,' I said. 'Things got a bit out of hand. It's nothing to worry about.' But they didn't believe me for a second. The policeman said, 'We no longer deal with domestics in the way we used to...we have to investigate every situation thoroughly.'

Jeff's mate Luke was still in the house. Jeff had rung him but he wouldn't tell me or the police where he was. Luke was asked for a statement too – and of course, he went into every fucking detail. Then the police left, and suddenly I looked round and Luke had taken my car keys and gone out of the house. He'd gone to find Jeff.

The night just seemed to go on forever. Then Jeff's auntie came round to get some of his clothes. The next day, Jeff went down to the police station of his own accord. He'd obviously decided to tell his side of the story and hope for the best. I personally think he overexaggerated a bit. Not that he was lying or anything, just that I think he went into more detail than was necessary. I'd rather he'd kept it between us. I don't think he needed to go into all the details he did. He could've been brief, like I was. He told them I was bashing his head against the wall and had reached for a knife. But I guess you have more to prove as a man in a fight like that, and he felt he needed to make it clear that it wasn't him doing the beating.

11

I Can't Go On

The following day was horrific. I was dreading seeing the papers. I knew our fight would have found its way n there in some shape or form because once the police have been called things always seem to leak. I just didn't know what the headline would be. I could've guessed. The *People* ran with the story: 'JADE'S LOVER HELD FOR BEATING HER UP'. This was Jeff's worst nightmare, and the reason he subsequently decided to call them up and tell his version of events. If I'm being really honest, when I read the headline my first feeling was a sense of 'Ha! Serves you right.' But he's not a wife-beater, and it was unfair. And at the end of the day, this was my son's dad they were writing about. I knew he wasn't a violent man and I didn't want him to be portrayed in that way.

I called Katherine at John Noel and told her the whole story. I was sobbing. They were Jeff's agency at the time too – they'd taken him on after we got together and he'd started getting offers for TV work – so Katherine was concerned about both of us. She knew how fiery I could be and how placid and calm a person Jeff usually was. So for him to reach boiling point, she realised it must've been bloody bad. But just like everyone else, she thought it would be another one of our rows that would blow over eventually. No one realised the extent of the argument except me and Jeff. We hated each other. I didn't want to be with him and at that point he wouldn't have had me back in a million years.

Looking back, I can see how wrong I was in so many ways. I feel so completely different as a person compared to how I was back then. I'm still trying to convince Jeff that I haven't got a temper any more (which, unsurprisingly, is taking him a pretty long time to believe). I used to love having an argument and feeling like I was the winner in a fight, but I know that's not the answer now. Arguing is just damaging and it stressed me out. It makes me feel drained and exhausted. And at the end of it all there's nothing ever gained except negativity. Maybe I've grown up.

After reading what the press had written about him, Jeff rang the *People* himself and demanded that they listen to his side of the story. What a gift for them: someone actually offering to talk to them without even asking for payment! Jeff told me he didn't even get any money for his story; he couldn't care less about that kind of thing, he just wanted to clear his name. Meanwhile, I'd left the country. After reading the papers I just packed my bags and left. There were press buzzing around outside my house and I was feeling sick to the bottom of my stomach. Although I was still feeling angry and bitter towards Jeff, the thought that it was completely over between us was starting to sink in and I was hurting. To go through something like that and have it played out in the press like it's just some sort of pantomime is really hard. I had so many mixed emotions: I felt guilt, sadness, hate, regret. I wanted to go away and hide from everything. So I grabbed Bobby, turned my mobile off, got in a cab to Waterloo and got the Eurostar to Euro Disney.

It was probably one of the most heart-wrenching weeks of my life. Thinking about it now, Euro Disney is probably not the most therapeutic place to be when you've just split up with the love of your life (happy families everywhere!). We stayed there for the best part of a week. That was when it hit me; what life as a single mum would be like. Just getting myself onto the Eurostar was a struggle – bags, Bobby, a pram...how the hell was I going to cope with a second child and no Jeff?

We were staying in a hotel in Disney Village. I can't remember its name, but it was big and pink. When we got there it was raining. Everywhere I looked there seemed to be lovely couples kissing or cuddling. Going there was probably one of the worst things I could've done. I should've been with my friends, but I wanted – needed – to isolate myself. I'd get back to the hotel each night and cry my eyes out. I didn't ring or text anyone. With me, I hate putting my problems onto other people. It feels like I'm burdening them. I'd rather just take it, take it and take it until it gets too much. And when it does get too much, the only way I can control it is by making myself sick. That's how I deal with it. But my mate Jen tracked me down. She'd been so worried. One night I got back to the hotel room and there was a message from her on the answerphone: 'Ha! I've found you. Are you all right?' It was so good to hear her voice and it really cheered me up to realise that people did care after all. She'd rung every single hotel in Euro Disney until she found me. Mind you, I wasn't that hard to find because I'd checked in under my real name. I'd never be any good as a criminal.

Just to add to the great time I was having, the fucking fire alarm went off at 4 a.m. one morning. So there was me, humping my son down billions of flights of stairs, and it was pissing with rain outside. Bobby was sobbing and we stood there wrapped in these silver sheets that had been given to us to keep us warm. I was utterly miserable. A few people recognised me that week, but it was as if they knew what I'd been through and left me alone. Nobody tried to talk to me too much, or ask for my autograph – people just seemed to look at me with a sympathetic smile. One lady said, 'Are you all right, Jade?' and she said it in such a warm way that it almost made me break down there and then. It was as if the public were giving me breathing space. I just sat there most days, spinning round with Bobby on the teacup ride or watching Winnie the Pooh. It was my way of saying sorry to him for what had happened. And despite all the tears I cried, I could at least take some comfort in the fact that Bobby was giggling and having a good time. I needed to see him smile, because after the fight I was so fearful I'd done him some damage.

I never wanted my family home to be an aggressive place where my kids would sit cowering at the top of the stairs while their mum and dad were downstairs arguing. But that was what had happened. And it was unacceptable on both sides. Bobby, our son, had been in the house while we were ripping each other apart, and although he was too young to really know what was going on, I knew he must have been affected by it in some way. And we'd both sworn we wouldn't be the same kind of parents as we'd had. We'd said this would never happen. It still makes me upset to think about it now.

When I got back from Euro Disney, it hit me right in the fucking face. Reality. There were stories circulating everywhere. Reporters were doorstepping me, people were phoning my house, my mum was being hounded, everyone wanted my story. I hate it when journalists doorstep me because I'm not a horrible person so I can't say 'fuck off' to a total stranger, no matter what they want. This means I always get into an awkward position where they're trying to get things out of me and I'm sheepishly replying, 'I can't talk, you'll have to ask my agent.' Then I feel like a wanker for having to talk about having an agent. Journalists would knock on the door and bring me flowers and cards to try to coax me into opening up to them. But I kept my mouth shut.

Jeff and I despised each other. We would ring each other up to talk about Bobby and end up having huge, abusive arguments. Then it started coming down to money and Jeff said he wanted to take me to the cleaners. He started demanding half of everything, including the house. The thing is, I'd bought my half of the house outright and he had a mortgage on the other half, so I didn't think it was right that he could make out he owned half of it. But after all the times I'd accused him of being a sponger I suppose he just thought he might as well prove me right and act like one. He started saying, 'You're not doing any magazine shoots with my children. If you do, I want half of everything you earn.' I screeched, 'I'm not having this. I'm going to get myself a fucking lawyer because you're not going to take me for everything I've worked for. I'm not married to you. I've been with you for a year, and that's it. I'm certainly not giving half of everything I've earned to you.' I remember being at Jen's house one day and just sobbing down the phone. He shouted, 'I'm going to take you for everything you've fucking got.' Then I started telling him what I thought about his family (which wasn't very nice), I ripped his character to shreds, I said the most hateful, horrible, mean things.

However, there was one thing I never said, and that was, 'You're not seeing the kids.' I wouldn't do that to him. But because of how he felt towards me, it did feel for a little while that he didn't spend quite so much time with Bobby as he could have. I'm not blaming him, it's just that he hated me so much he couldn't stand to be near me or come to the house. And I can't really blame him.

I cried myself to sleep every night. I didn't know how to deal with it. I kept thinking, *What the hell am I going to do when the next one's born?* This was not how I had imagined my life would be: a lonely, angry, bitter single mum. To this day I thank God I had my friends around me, even though, ironically, these were the friends I had met through Jeff.

Weeks and months passed. I was having to fight with Jeff over money. I was talking with solicitors and I hadn't even known how to pronounce the word 'solicitor' before. In the end, though, Jeff didn't have a leg to stand on. He didn't, and couldn't, get half of my earnings, but he was entitled to some money from the house. The whole thing was horrible. Before he came round to get his clothes, I cut them up and put them in a bag. I put the scissors to one of his Gucci sandal straps and had a snip at some of the nice stuff I'd bought him. As you can imagine, that worked wonders for Jade–Jeff relations.

I was invited to dine in ITV1's *Hell's Kitchen*. It was the first series, the one with Gordon Ramsay on it. I didn't get to see him, though; because the kitchen staff were all really stressed and didn't let you near. I took Jen as my guest and remember having a few glasses of champagne. I know I shouldn't have been drinking while I was pregnant, but it helped me forget about things. When we walked out of the restaurant my heel got caught and I fell arse over tit. I fell backwards and my legs went right up in the air. It was all on camera too: Jordan was waiting to interview me for the ITV2 sister show, which she was presenting. She kept saying, 'Are you all right?' while trying her hardest not to laugh. The next day it was all over the papers. I thought, *Great, I'm going to have Jeff on the phone having a go at me in a minute*. And I was right. He rang me that morning and said that as far as he was concerned I was irresponsible and I was acting like an alcoholic.

When Jeff came round to pick up Bobby, we kept conversation to an absolute minimum. When I first saw him again after our huge fight I felt numb. I didn't fancy him, I didn't feel any love for him – I hated him. He'd come to the door, I'd give Bobby a kiss goodbye and they'd be off. Then, gradually, it started easing, and after a few weeks things became more amicable between us. We'd begin to exchange the odd civil word – he'd pat my bump and say, 'How's the baby doing?' and he'd come with me to the doctor's whenever I needed to go for scans.

After our big fight, Jeff's police statement didn't match mine, so I was called into the police station and given a caution for violence. They waffled on about not having strong enough evidence to put me away for beating Jeff up, so this was all they could do. I don't think it meant much though. Except that I obviously couldn't lay a finger on him again. I walked out of the station and got papped, which meant the next day's paper read: 'JADE'S BEEN DONE FOR BEATING UP JEFF'. So then, of course, I was a psycho bird who tried to stab people with a spatula.

I didn't really talk to my mum about Jeff because she had a tendency to make matters worse. She would never mean to, but she's very highly opinionated so she'd never be able to help herself. The problem is, she doesn't actually know what she's talking about most of the time so I always end up telling her to shut up. She knows what she's like, and says she'd rather just keep her distance and be there for me when I need her. Mum's always loved Jeff, though, which made it hard for her not to stick her oar in. She's a very good judge of character and could always see that Jeff's a good man.

12

My Wake-Up Call

Something Mum said one day made me take a good long look at myself. She sat me down and asked, 'How on earth are you ever going to hold down a decent relationship? You are fucking hard to live with, and unless you sort yourself out you're going to end up very lonely.' You might think this is a perfectly reasonable thing to say, but not for my mum. Never in my whole life has she criticised me. Ever. No matter what I've done or said in the past, she has stuck up for me, regardless. She's headbutted teachers, knocked people's teeth out, and she's been my number one supporter through thick and thin. She'd often think I was wrong, but she would never criticise me. So when she said that, I had to take notice. And that's when I started to change. I was determined to become a better person.

I went on a girlie holiday to Puerto Banus in Marbella. I'd booked it as a surprise for my friends – the ones who helped make up the famous four: Jen, Cath and Kel. I invited them round to my house and told them it was my treat, but our flights were leaving in two days' time, so they needed to get the time off work. I don't think I really took it into account that they had normal jobs. Two of them, Kel and Cath, even worked together at the same place, so it was lucky their boss was an understanding one! But thankfully they managed.

We stayed in a cheap hotel right on the port. It was probably one of the best holidays I've been on in my life, *and* I was pregnant. It was 'football season' out there, which means that the English Premier League teams had finished playing for a few months, and for a lot of them their first port of call was to have a big party in Spain. I personally don't care if someone works in a post office, a supermarket or kicks a ball about on a pitch, so it really meant nothing to me. I think Jen was excited about the prospect of mingling with a few footballers, though. By this stage I was heavily pregnant with Freddy – I was massive. There are pictures of me splashing about in the sea with my big fat belly hanging right out. But I didn't care.

On the second day of the holiday we met this massive group of boys, and to this day I'll say they're the best lads I've ever met (I'm still mates with most of them). Jen and I walked past them as we were going to the shop and they shouted, 'All right, girls?' Now, you might not think it, but I get really shy with new people, so I just looked down and didn't say anything. Later that day we saw them again; they were sitting at the bar near our hotel, so we went over to them and said hello. They were a good-looking bunch. I wasn't thinking I would pull any of them or anything like that (I was pregnant, so there was no way I thought they'd look twice at me), but I sat down and we ended up having a bit of banter. Every girl loves a flirt and I'm no different. They said, 'Oi, go and get us some playing cards, Jade,' and I started giving them lip back and saying, 'Don't pretend you know me cos you don't!' Still, I did go and get them some cards in the end. They introduced themselves (there were too many for me to name now but at least three of them were called Jay), and one of the group said his name was Lee Hendrie, although I didn't have a clue who he was, and that he was a footballer for Aston Villa. We sat there all afternoon and it was so much fun. They began playing drinking games, but I didn't join in, even though I was tempted.

That holiday was how the press speculation about me and Lee Hendrie came about, even though I think I spoke to the others more than I ever spoke to him for the whole holiday. The reason the boys were in Marbella in the first place was that they were on Lee's stag do – so as if I was going to do anything like that! Besides, I thought he looked like a little elf when I first saw him.

Lee was due to get married on my birthday: 5 June. But by the time we'd all returned to the UK, the papers had linked us together and as far as they were concerned I was having a budding new romance. All I could think about was his poor fiancée. I'd met him for all of about 20 minutes and now, according to the press, I was having rampant sex with him in a hotel room. I also worried about Jeff reading it. I didn't want him thinking I was someone who could go round having sex with men while I was pregnant. It really bothered me. I wanted to call Lee and tell him I was sorry for all the shit in the papers because I felt guilty, but at the end of the day it wasn't my fault. I kept in touch with some of the other lads, though, because we'd become quite good mates. Then, when I was having a meal with one of them – Little Jay – the papers got wind of that too, so he became my next new romance. It was all rubbish, though, and Jeff's never mentioned anything about it – I don't think he wants to know just in case it was true.

Bobby's first birthday was on 2 June. The theme for his party was footballers' wives. It was my idea, and all the little boys dressed up as footballers and the girls wore feather boas and fancy make-up. I hired out a big gym near where we lived, and Jeff came, which was a bit strange because the party was being covered by OK! and this was the first time we'd really been pictured since the fight. It was a bit awkward because his family were over one side of the room and mine were on the other. My family would play with Bobby for half an hour, then his would have him for another half-hour. There was still quite a bit of animosity there.

I got together with the lads from holiday again when it was Little Jay's birthday. They were all there, including Lee Hendrie, and we all had a meal together. It was the first time I met Ryan Amoo, but nothing happened between us that night. In fact, when I first looked at Ryan I thought *dork in a red coat* and that was it. It never once occurred to me that I'd end up living with him a few months later. The following day the paper was all about me and Lee again: 'JADE LINKS UP WITH HOLIDAY ROMANCE'. It felt like I couldn't go anywhere. Also, I knew what it was like feeling insecure and I didn't want Lee's new wife to feel the same. It just goes to show that you shouldn't believe everything you read in the papers, and it made me think about the stories that had come out in the past about Jeff and all those other girls. If I could be accused of doing something when I wasn't, surely he could too?

After that dinner with the lads, Ryan apparently told Lee that he really liked me. He, too, was wondering if something had gone on between us, and wanted to know if the coast was clear. Lee said, 'She's a good girl – go for it.' I later came to wish he hadn't bothered.

The next thing I knew it was in the papers that I was seeing a guy called Lee Howels – Bobby's godfather and Jeff's best mate. Again, it was ridiculous. Where did they get this stuff from? The papers just seemed desperate to link me with someone. Being single is almost as much of a curse as being in a couple! Another time I was doing a photo shoot and when I got out of the car a guy from the magazine came over to say hello and gave me a kiss on the cheek. It was in OK! magazine the following week – a double-page spread all about Jade's new man. Jesus Christ! His wife was probably sitting at home, thinking, *What's going on?*

My mate Angie was married to a guy called Mark. I met them both through Jeff and they were already married before I knew them. Jen had their wedding video at her house and one night I decided I wanted to put it on. I wanted to see what it was like because I hadn't been there. I bawled my heart out the whole way through. It even brings a lump to my throat when I think about it now. They just looked so completely in love. Every time she turned around, her eyes were glimmering at him and his were brimming with adoration for her. It was so romantic. Later that evening I sat and sobbed. That's all I wanted: someone to look at me with that unconditional love and affection. I was convinced I was never going to get anything close to that and it made me so sad. But, if I ever think of marriage, in the back of my mind I can only picture Jeff.

I didn't realise how not having a dad around all my life had affected me. Now I know it did. Especially now he's dead – it hurts so much inside. I wish he'd been a normal dad, I wish I could've been that 'Daddy's little girl' everyone talks about. I wish I could've had a normal relationship with him, even just for ten minutes. That's why I've always wanted to create that happy family unit for my kids. And although I hated Jeff at one point, deep down I never stopped wanting to be with him.

In August 2004, after my fourth attempt, I passed my driving test. Thank God for that. I thought I was doomed to a life of taxis and cars I couldn't drive. I've owned quite a few motors in my life, but never been able to drive them. Now I've got a BMW XS and a Smart car that advertises my salon, Ugly's, on the side. I bought one for my business partner Carly to zoom about in too.

After my holiday in Marbella I had a spring clean. I thought, *Right, Jade, you need to accept you're a single mum and get on with it*. I was about seven months pregnant and there I was, up and down ladders, decorating the house. Bobby's bedroom had wallpaper with characters from The Cartoon Network all over it and

I wanted to change it, so I went to B&Q and got all the gear. I stripped all the walls and painted them myself. I weeded the garden, tidied the house; I didn't stop. Everyone was telling me to take it easy – I think they were waiting for me to collapse, but I was probably the fittest I'd ever been. I had a big clearout too. One of the things I chucked out was my *Big Brother* suitcase – then the paparazzi took a picture of it and the papers got all deep and meaningful and said I was 'throwing away the past'. It was broken, for heaven's sake! I only ever chuck things if there's something wrong with them. All Bobby's old toys, all my old clothes, I give to hospitals or charity. I, more than anyone, know what it's like to grow up having to go without, so I never waste a thing.

As the bitterness lessened between Jeff and me, we began spending more time together. We'd make an effort to do things as a family and we'd go to dinner and take Bobby to the park. Jeff was getting more TV work, and he went on a programme called *Famous and Frightened* on Living TV (although I don't think any of the people on that show were particularly famous or frightened, to be honest). In one of the shows he was sat in bed with Adele Silva – an actress from *Emmerdale* – and they were really flirting. I didn't like it one bit, so I told him. My friends thought I had no right to say anything to Jeff about what he could and couldn't do, but that didn't stop me. I called him up and said, 'Are you fucking Adele Silva? What are you doing flirting with her on the telly? If you're going to go and do stuff like that I'll just have to live with it, but don't rub it in my face on national TV. I'm pregnant with your baby!' Jeff said he wasn't doing anything and that it looked far worse than it actually was. He said he didn't want to hurt me, so that made me feel better.

Then, in another magazine, I read that he'd said he fancied Abi Titmuss! I thought *fucking slag*. I was steaming. Whenever he mentioned any female in an interview I would immediately absolutely hate that person, even though they were probably really nice. Again, I called him and said, 'What are you saying that about Abi Titmuss for? She's a dirtbag!' Then I demanded to know if he'd tried to pull her. He just sighed and said, 'No, Jade,' so I said, 'Oh, all right then,' and was happy again. I was never one for playing games or pretending I felt OK when I didn't.

Even though we were starting to get on better as friends, it didn't make up for the fact we weren't a couple. As the birth of my second child grew nearer, I'd lie in bed staring at the ceiling, and I'd be so scared of what it was going to be like being on my own with two kids. Who would be there for me? Was I going to be able to cope?

About two months before Freddy was due to be born, I went to the Canary Islands with Charlene, her little boy Jack, and Bobby. We were just there for a short break and everything was fine for the first few days, until one afternoon we were sitting round the pool and I felt these twinges in my stomach. What I didn't realise was that they were contractions. (When I had Bobby I had all the contractions while I was asleep.) I tried to stand up to get in the pool, then all of a sudden my bikini bottoms filled with water. No, I hadn't wet myself – my waters had broken. I was in a right panic. Charlene tried to calm me down, but the pain got worse so we told the hotel and they directed us to a doctor's surgery round the corner. As soon as I got there I was rushed to hospital in an ambulance, but I was on my own because Charlene had to stay behind and look after the kids. I thought I was going to have the baby there and then, and I was thinking, *What the fuck is going to happen to me?* They could hardly speak any English, for a start. I looked at one of the doctors and tried to tell him I was allergic to both penicillin and plasters. Then he stuck a plaster on me, so I knew he hadn't understood a word I'd said. I was crying my eyes out and rolling around in pain. Then a nurse came over to me and said in this pidgin English, 'You may have to have baby!' I was shouting 'No!' but she shrugged. 'Too early, but maybe baby.' Then they started trying to tell me they'd have to get a helicopter to take me to another island because they didn't have the facilities to cope with a birth.

I was all over the place. I was terrified. Eventually they gave me some tablets, and even though I didn't have the foggiest idea what they were, I just swallowed them and hoped for the best. It turned out that they were meant to stop the contractions, which they did, thank God. Gradually, I calmed down, but I still had to stay in the hospital for a day or two. I called Jeff, who started saying he was going to fly out, but I told him not to be so stupid. Charlene and Bobby came up to visit me and found me pouring a bottle of vodka all over my legs. I was covered in bites from mosquitos and a woman in the hospital had told me that vodka stopped it from itching. I think Char thought I'd lost the plot. I wasn't allowed to fly, but all I wanted to do was go home. I needed my mum, my friends, and I needed Jeff. So I discharged myself and flew home regardless.

Jade: How It All Began

My waters broke about eight times over the course of the next month and I was in and out of hospital constantly. When your waters break you're meant to give birth straight away – but not me. The doctors couldn't understand it; my body just kept repairing itself again. I kept going for scans and I'd be told the waters had built themselves back up. The baby just wasn't ready to come.

Then it happened. I was at home and, thankfully, my mum was staying with me. I woke in the night in loads of pain, went to the toilet and all this water just gushed out. I couldn't get off the toilet after that. Mum rang the ambulance but it was taking fucking ages, so I rang Jeff and left him a message (he was out in Colchester for his brother's birthday). I think when Jeff heard the message he just thought it was another false alarm at first, though. All my friends had gone out in the city that night. I couldn't get hold of anyone. So I rang Lee Howels – Bobby's godfather – and he said he'd come straight round. I don't know what I would've done if Mum hadn't been in the house that evening, because when Lee came to take me to the hospital, she stayed to look after Bobby. Lee was panicking so much, bless him. He didn't have a clue what to do. He probably went the longest way in the world to the hospital. We must've gone over about 20 speed bumps at about 80 miles per hour. The whole time I was in the back of the car, wailing. He kept saying, 'It's all right, it's all right!' and I was replying, 'It's not! We're lost!' We got there eventually, and about an hour later Jeff arrived with Jen. They were both steaming drunk. I was lying in the hospital bed, with Jen to my right and Jeff on my left, and it was the worst thing in the world. Jeff stank of booze and Jen had just

230

eaten a curry! Jeff was slurring 'it'ssssss allllight – push!' but the only pushing I was doing was manoeuvring him away. He reeked! Still, they were both in the room when little Freddie was born. Jen was down the horrible end watching him come out, while Jeff was up my end holding my hand. Jeff shouted, 'It's got balls, Jade!' which was a bit of a shock because I was convinced it was going to be a girl. I'd bought a dress and everything.

I know I'd previously had my doubts about Jeff being there for the birth, but when it came to it he was the first person I called. It just wouldn't have been right if he hadn't been there, and it wouldn't be right if he's not there for the birth of the rest of my kids in the future, even if we're not together. I want my kids to have the same dad, so if I ever have another kid I'd want to use Jeff's sperm.

Jeff wasn't about for long immediately after Freddy's birth. He'd been booked to go on a Channel 5 reality show called *The Farm* with the likes of ex-Liverpool player Stan Collymore, ex-rapper Vanilla Ice, and David Beckham's infamous mistress Rebecca Loos. I knew I wasn't going to like Rebecca – what a slag. I knew she'd have a try with everyone, including Jeff, which she did, but I also knew she wouldn't be his type so I didn't worry.

I didn't watch it all the time when it started, but I would tune in every now and then to see how Jeff was getting on. I was more excited about Vanilla Ice being on it than Jeff, though. Jeff would sometimes talk about me on the show and it wound me up. He was never horrible but he would mention me and the kids a lot. I used to think, *Oh just shut up*. One of my mates told me they saw a conversation in which Vanilla Ice was talking to Jeff and was saying the pair of us should get back together. I thought that was nice of Vanilla, but he didn't know what he was on about, to be honest.

My dad had a suspected drug overdose in October 2004. I wasn't in contact with him or his family at all by then. The whole thing hurt far too much – he would just use me for drug money, and now that I had two children I didn't want him using them too. I found out about the overdose because someone contacted John Noel, and Katherine rang and told me. But I just blanked it out. I didn't care.

After Freddie's birth, I seemed to lose control of my senses a bit and I went on a week-long boozy bender. Until now – apart from when I was in the *Big Brother* house – I'd been careful never to let myself get into situations where there could be pictures taken of me appearing completely pissed out of my head, looking awful and spilling out of clubs. I used to drink a bit, but never that badly, and even when I was pictured going out I was never caught in that predicament. But post-birth number two, there was a period of a few days in which I was on a mission. It was exhausting looking after two little boys – getting up in the night, feeding one, putting the other one to sleep. I wanted to escape reality and let my hair down.

By now my mum had virtually moved into my house and was helping me out so much. I must admit, I took advantage of her. Over the course of a week I went out in London every night and pictures would appear in the papers the next day of me looking vile, horrible, and drunk as a skunk. There was one of me bending over to climb into a cab and it looked like I had cellulite (and that's one thing I don't have – orange peel!), my face was contorted and I looked so, so ugly. I would read the papers and sob every day. My self-esteem was so low. When most people get drunk and have a hideous photo taken they can rip it up and chuck it away. Mine goes into every single magazine and newspaper. I needed to get away. So I booked a flight to LA.

It turned out to be one of the best things I could've done. I'd decided to see Catalina, one of the girls I'd made friends with on *Back to Reality*. She was living in Los Angeles, trying to make it big in Hollywood. My seat was first class. I don't usually fly so swankily but I felt shit, I had the money, it was a long flight, and I didn't want to be hassled by people asking me to sign a photo of myself from one of the newspapers where I looked ugly, so I thought, *Why not?* When you fly first class there's a special lounge you're allowed to go in while you're waiting for the flight. It's all posh with free drink and food and anything you could possibly want. I saw this big tall black guy standing in there and I thought I recognised him but I couldn't work it out. I knew he was someone famous, though.

When I got onto the plane, I settled into my seat and the air hostess walked past me and smiled, 'You OK, Jade?' I grinned back at her. Then she leant over and whispered, 'Kate Moss is over there in front of you, Orlando Bloom is to your left, and Samuel L. Jackson is two rows in front!' She obviously knew I'd be excited. In an instant I was on that phone – the one that you can use midair – calling all my mates. 'You'll never guess who I'm on the plane with!' I'm sure they must've all heard me; I'm not exactly discreet.

Orlando Bloom was sitting there in a black jumper. He didn't say very much, just seemed to want to keep

233

himself to himself, but he did smile at me. He could probably feel my eyes boring into the side of his head, poor boy. Then I got up to go to the toilet and found myself stood in the queue with Kate Moss. She started chatting to me, asking how my boys were and stuff. I couldn't believe it – it was like I was in a parallel universe. I was asking her what she was doing and she told me she was doing a modelling job. It was just idle chit-chat, but it was with the world's biggest supermodel and me. She was lovely. She said, 'I'm not a good sleeper, Jade, but I'm going to try and go to sleep on this flight. If you're asleep and I'm not, I'm going to have to wake you up. Is that all right? I'll be bored otherwise.' I said, 'Yeah, all right,' and just smiled like a lemon.

I tried watching a few films but couldn't really concentrate. It was more interesting watching what was going on in first class. We got given a little bag with travel things in. At one point, Kate put the socks on and turned round to me, sticking her leg out. 'What d'you reckon about these, Jade? Look at these babies. Nice, eh?' We also got given these pyjamas which were plain grey, so I put them on. Kate didn't. Neither did Orlando. But a little while later, on the way to the toilet, I walked straight into Samuel L. Jackson and he was wearing his pyjamas too. We just looked at each other in our outfits and laughed. This was fucking mental! Then Kate went to sleep for a bit and so did I. When she woke up she looked so beautiful. I woke up with dribble all down my chin. No prizes for guessing which one Orlando was checking out.

Then, about an hour before the plane landed, I thought, *Fuck it, I've never asked for anyone's autograph in my life.*

I'm not going to get off this plane without getting Samuel L. Jackson's. Kate Moss and Orlando Bloom are such huge stars too, but Samuel L. Jackson? To me he's just a legend. I knew he was awake because I saw him go to the loo to get changed out of his pyjamas. I don't know where I got the bottle from, but I walked up to him and tapped him on the knee as he was staring out of the window. I said, 'Er, Samuel L.?' I didn't know what else to call him! Surely the L must be there for a reason? 'Samuel L.?' He turned round and I continued, 'I'm so sorry, I don't usually do this, but can I possibly have your autograph?' and he smiled and said, 'Yeah, of course you can.' I gave him my passport to sign. He looked at me quizzically and said, 'Is this legal?' I said, 'I don't care, just sign it.' Then, just before he started to write, I went to say who I was so he knew what name to put on it. Before I could open my mouth he said, 'Jade, isn't it?' My jaw dropped to the floor. I don't think it picked itself up again for a good few minutes after that either. 'You're Jade Goody, right? I read about you all the time in the magazines when I'm in England.' I was gobsmacked. This nervous laughter started coming out of my mouth because I didn't know what to say. I couldn't believe it. Then he smiled: 'You didn't look too good this week, did you, Miss Goody?' I said, 'That's why I'm going away! The pictures are awful!' and he started laughing. I asked him why he was over in LA and he said he was doing the voice for one of *The Incredibles* characters. I said thank you and walked back to my seat. I was in shock. I was thinking, *Did that just happen? Does that man know who I am?* I kept replaying the conversation over and over in my head. I couldn't stop grinning.

Jade: How It All Began

When we got off the flight I had to stop myself from loitering around to wait for him, but then I thought, *Don't be an egg – just get up and leave.* So I said 'See you later' to Kate and she said 'I hope you have a nice holiday', and I waved to Orlando. I began walking along the bit towards passport control and there were policemen and sniffer dogs all over the place, and I could hear footsteps behind me, running. I felt a tap on my shoulder and I looked round. It's only my mate, Samuel L.! He said, 'Don't worry about the dogs, Jade, they're just sniffing for peanuts.' Then he started walking along beside me. The queue split into two – one for US citizens and another for foreigners – and he looked at me and said, 'Do you know where you're going?' and I said I didn't have a clue, so he took me! Samuel L. Jackson walked right up to my queue with me and stood chatting for about five minutes! Everyone around must've thought we were genuine friends. I was desperate to say, 'Will you please take me to a Lakers game?' but I had to bite my lip. That wasn't cool. Then he walked off and said, 'You have a great time! Hopefully I'll see you again.' Wow. When I got to passport control, the man looked at me and said, 'Do you know him?' I smiled and replied, 'Yeah, he's me mate.'

I got to LA and met up with Catalina. I thought her house and lifestyle was going to be amazing but it was actually pretty pants and I felt sorry for her. I ended up having to pay her car tax for her because she had no money – otherwise we wouldn't have been able to drive round anywhere. She probably had no more than about ten pence in the bank, but she was there to try and get a big break. She had an agent and would go to castings every day, but it's so tough to get any kind of success in a place like LA. Everyone wants to do the same thing.

I went with Catalina to one of the castings and sat watching while she was among all these other girls waiting to go in for a reading. It was an audition for a film, and it was only for a small part. The amazing thing was that even all the way out there, people seemed to know who I was. A woman came out and called Catalina's name, then she looked at me and said, 'You're Jade Goody, right?' I nodded. 'Are you coming in for a screen test too?' I politely said no. I could see the look on Catalina's face and I don't think she would've been very happy about it if I'd nipped in and ended up getting a part. I didn't want to upset her, and I didn't really want to audition to be in a film in the first place. I can't act, for God's sake! Catalina's agent really liked me too and told her she wanted to 'do something' with me. But as far as I was concerned, I was just over for a holiday. Everyone else over there was a wannabe and I didn't want to be part of that. But still, it felt nice to be in demand. After all the shit I'd been going through, it was as if someone was looking down on me and doing everything in their power to make me feel better about myself. And it was working.

Catalina and I went to Hollywood, which I thought was going to be glamorous and amazing, but it was a shithole. We went to a couple of bars in the evenings but nothing mad. We also went to Las Vegas. I won about £800 on this game, at the craps table, even though I didn't have a clue what I was doing. Catalina didn't win anything – she must've loved me.

When I got home I had a big barney with Mum and told her to get out of my house. She'd been living at mine since before Freddy was born and I think she just got on my nerves. I'd left home when I moved into the *Big Brother* house and hadn't lived with her since, so to suddenly go back to living with her again and have her moaning because I hadn't tidied up my living room was just annoying. Our fall-out didn't last long, though. After she left I started sobbing, called her up and begged her to come back. I hate arguing with my mum, I love her to bits. She was probably gone for a couple of hours in all before my pleading worked and she returned.

I started exercising again, but the flab just didn't shift as quickly as it did after I'd had Bobby. No matter how hard I tried, I couldn't get rid of my belly. I've always had quite good legs but it's my midriff that's the problem area. Besides, it's not easy trying to keep up an exercise regime when you've got two kids to look after. I'd lose a little bit of weight, do the odd photo shoot, then the pounds would pile back on again. I didn't start making myself sick again, though. Things were going well in my life, I was feeling secure and I was happy.

It was at that point that Jeff came to me and told me he wanted me back. But I couldn't be with him. I'd become so strong, I felt so independent, I didn't want to do anything that might rock the boat. Jeff was renting a place across the road from where I lived with the boys, so we saw each other quite a bit. On this day, I'd gone round to his house and I was sitting there chatting on his bed when he asked me. He told me he wanted to try and make another go of it and I just started sobbing. 'No,' I replied. I didn't want to be with him and I was upset because I felt sorry that I didn't have that feeling any more. I'd always wanted him before and now I didn't, and it broke my heart to see him hurting like that. He begged me to get back together with him but I just couldn't say yes; too much had happened. I couldn't put myself in that situation again. I felt like I'd found a balance in my life where my emotions were stable. OK, so they weren't particularly up, but they definitely weren't down either. I wasn't insecure, I wasn't unhappy, I'd got the house sorted: everything was falling into place and I didn't want to upset that. It seemed too soon to go back. Jeff was gutted, though, and it made me feel horrendous. I think it really hit him hard, and, if I'm honest, I think he still holds it against me a bit. I also knew that by doing this I was risking him going out with someone else, but I had to put up with it.

For Christmas 2004 I was asked to be in a three-week TV special called *The Big Brother Panto*. There was a mixture of ex-*Big Brother* housemates from across the different series and we all had to rehearse for a pantomime, which would then be performed live on E4. We also had to live together in the same house for a while. I loved the whole pantomime aspect of the show, but I didn't love all the other *Big Brother* contestants. I thought Mel Hill from *Big Brother 1* was a contradicting little cock who was always busybodying around and didn't know what she was talking about. Kitten from *Big Brother 5* was an arsehole – she called me a cunt, so I nearly knocked her out. Anouska was a jealous little bitch who was angry because she never got to be Cinderella and I did. Spencer was there, though, and to see him again was just brilliant. We had such a fun time being together again. I really missed Freddy and Bobby, though, I always do when I'm away from them, but at the end of the day it's work. That's how I earn my money, so I just had to get on with it.

One day, out of the blue, I received this text and I didn't know who it was from. It said, 'Hi, Jade, how are you? Do you want to meet up for a drink?' So I replied, 'What do you look like?' Then another one came and it said he'd met me before at a meal with Lee Hendrie and the other boys. Somehow I guessed it was Ryan Amoo, so I said, 'Are you the dork in the red jacket?' He was so narked. He replied, 'What do you mean?' and we had a bit of banter. His texts made me laugh. I thought he had something about him, plus it was nice that someone was showing a bit of interest in me. We arranged to go out for a drink with Jen and her boyfriend Anthony, but nothing happened – we never even kissed or anything. Then he sent me a Christmas present – it was a Christian Dior bag. I texted him and said 'You're a bit keen!' I'd bought him a belt.

Jeff came round on Christmas Day and so did my mum. Things were initially a bit strained after I'd told Jeff I couldn't get back together with him, but he'd come to accept it. When you've got two kids together you haven't got much choice really. At first he thought that I'd found someone else, although I hadn't, but then I met Ryan, so Jeff just presumed that was the reason and he'd been right all along. It wasn't, but it seemed to make him feel better.

In the new year, Ryan started getting in touch even more, and slowly we began to see each other. He played football for Northampton Town at the time, although that didn't seem to last long. I'm not sure he was much good at it really. Looking back, though, there wasn't any mind-blowing, amazing romance between me and Ryan; it was just something to do. I didn't even sleep with him straight away. He was more like a mate to me, and that's how I preferred it.

13

Boobs and Boys

A few months after Freddy was born, I had my boobs done. I'd wanted to have breast implants ever since I'd given birth to Bobby, but Jeff would always try and talk me out of it. He says I've got an addictive personality and he was worried that if I had one thing done I'd end up having everything done. But after Freddy, I just kept looking down at my chest and all I would see was saggy old tits. They looked like empty chicken fillets – it was disgusting. Nobody could see there was anything wrong with them because I always wore a bra with padding, but I didn't feel feminine, I was too self-conscious to go topless on the beach. I certainly didn't want to be taking my top off in front of a new man, so I booked myself an appointment with a doctor that was recommended to me by my nail technician. Dr Frame, his name was. When I first made the call I panicked, though. I couldn't just say, 'Hi, I'm Jade Goody, I want a boob job,' could I? What if the papers got hold of it? So when the receptionist asked me for my name I suddenly blurted out, 'Er...Katie Price.' So I basically told them I was Jordan. Now, 'JORDAN HAS YET ANOTHER BOOB JOB' would've made a much more interesting read. Thank God it didn't get out.

When I met Dr Frame I just sat in his office and said, 'I want the works.' I wanted him to turn me into a completely different person. I wanted my bum lifted, my cheeks sucked in, liposuction on my stomach, and my boobs done. He simply looked at me and said matter-of-factly, 'You're not having any of that. You don't need it. If you were my daughter I wouldn't let you have anything done at all.' Then he paused and said, 'The thing I would suggest you have done you haven't even mentioned.' I was screaming, 'Well, what is that?' but he wouldn't tell me. He still hasn't told me to this day. Every time I try to ask him he says, 'When you decide you need it yourself, then I'll tell you.' God knows what it is. He probably thinks my mouth should be stitched up or something.

I told him I wanted boobs like Victoria Beckham to start with, but he just pulled a face and said, 'They don't look real. Why would you want boobs that are up to your neck?' After I'd thought about it I had to agree (sorry Victoria!), Then he started asking me if I'd seen Daniella Westbrook's, to which I replied, 'I can't have them! They're massive!', but Dr Frame pointed out that if you look closely they look more natural because they move with her body.

He asked me what size I wanted to go to. I said I didn't want to look like Jordan with great big balloons, I just wanted my Baggy bits to be filled out. Then he opened a drawer and showed me all these different implants – they just looked like funny little wobbly sacks to me. He started explaining the different names, like 'teardrops', which kind of hang down, and which he said I couldn't have because mine were so droopy anyway. Cheek! I lost interest after that. Most of it went in one ear and out the other, to be honest. I just said, 'You decide what you think looks best.' So that's what he did.

In the end I went from a 36C to a 36DD/E. Dr Frame said he took a load of different implants down to the operating table to see what suited my body most when he was there. My mate Charlene came with me to the hospital. I couldn't have gone on my own. When it came to the actual day I was shitting myself. I was shaking. I was mostly worried about the anaesthetic because I react quite badly to it. I freak out and start trying to rip my face off.

We got to the hospital at about 6.30 a.m. or some ridiculous o'clock like that. Being the muppet I am, I hadn't packed any pyjamas or clothes to wear after the operation. For some reason, I'd just brought eight tight vest tops and two thongs. I obviously thought I was going to be whisked off to a glamour shoot on the beach straight after the op. I hadn't even paid for it yet either, because I'd had some problem with my bank card, so almost immediately I was asked to hand over a cheque – it came to about £3000 in total. I hadn't been allowed to eat anything for 24 hours and I was starving. Charlene kindly had some toast.

It wasn't until the doctor came in at around 10 a.m. and started drawing all over my boobs with a big fat marker pen that it properly sank in what I was about to do to my body. Shit. What if it went disastrously wrong and I ended up looking like Dolly Parton? Or worse – like Alicia

Douvall (hers were so big they ended up morphing together)! By 10.45 a.m. I was dressed in a gown and told to lie down on the trolley. I could've walked to the operating theatre, but the gown has a gap at the back and because I was wearing nothing but a thong I would've frightened my fellow patients. I was sobbing all the way there. I was so scared. Charlene came with me and held my hand, saying, 'It's going to be OK.' We got into this white room and I felt the needle go into my hand. The last thing I remember saying was, 'Next time you see me I'm going to have massive boobs!'

The whole thing lasted about two or three hours. Next thing I knew, I was in bed, propped up by about six pillows. I was wrapped up like a mummy. I had a sports bra thing on and over the top of that I had two big bandages. I couldn't really breathe. It felt like my tits were in my throat. It ached so much it was like I'd just completed the biggest workout ever.

The next day I was allowed to take the bandages off and my boobs looked hideous. The nurse told me I shouldn't be alarmed by the size of them because there would be a lot of swelling. Well, that was the understatement of the year. I burst out crying. I felt like a freak. To make matters worse, the papers had got hold of the story and had printed a picture of a pig's face on my body and said I'd had liposuction and that I'd asked the doctors to make me look like Marilyn Monroe. I was in bits. When was I ever going to get away from this whole pig thing? It really, really got to me.

Thankfully, though, the swelling did go down. So much so that by the time my mate Jen had come to visit me, I'd decided that my boobs weren't quite big enough! She'd popped in with Ryan and I said to her, 'Your tits are still bigger than mine. It's not fair.' I made her pull her top up and stand there next to me in front of Ryan and I told him to tell us whose were the largest. He just sighed and said, 'Jade, yours are bigger by a mile. Now can Jen put her top down, please?'

Ryan moved in with me after that. I didn't actually invite him to, but he made himself indispensable because I couldn't lift things around the house because of the stitches, especially not the boys. He was like my little helping hand. Then he just refused to go home.

I was invited to the TV Quick Awards again, and Nadia from *Big Brother 4* was there too. We all had to put £20 in for a raffle, but I didn't have any money on me so I had to borrow it from Nadia. I signed the back of it, then put it in the tombola, and mine was the note that got drawn out. I won a holiday to Barbados. When I got the prize I did a speech and said, 'Cheers, Nadia! I'll give you 20 quid tomorrow.'

I took my mum on the holiday as a treat. When we got to Barbados we met up with a couple of friends – David, who I used to go to school with, and his girlfriend Tasha. A couple of days before we were due to come home, I was sat chatting to David as he was having a puff on the beach. Then he saw a guy videoing us with his camcorder and got paranoid. I wasn't bothered myself, I just ignore it if anyone takes pictures of me – my theory is, you can't spend your whole life worrying, otherwise you'll never be able to do anything. But David went up to him and said, 'Why are you videoing Jade?' The guy replied that he didn't know who I was, so David asked to have a look at the footage. The only way he'd agree was if David gave him some cash first, so he gave him £50. When David looked at the recording, he saw that this guy had zoomed right in on me and David chatting: there were loads of close-ups. It was blatantly obvious he was going to try and sell it and make out David was my latest lover.

Just as David was playing back the tape, this guy reached into David's pocket to try and get more money. David used to be a boxer, so his reaction was to push him away. He didn't even need to punch him because he was so strong, the guy just fell to the ground, and David grabbed the camera and ran off down the beach. Suddenly, Tasha and I were surrounded by all these local guys. My mum was upstairs sunbathing on the hotel balcony and didn't have a clue what was going on. We were circled by ten black Bajan men and they wouldn't let us go. It turned out that this guy with the video wasn't a tourist, he knew the locals, and they were all sticking up for him. The guy started shouting things at me like, 'I know where you live in London! I know you've got kids! I'm going to blow your kids up and your house!' I was begging, 'Please just leave me alone. Have I nicked your camera? No! I didn't do anything, I don't know what's going on.' Then he started pushing himself against me. Somehow or other we managed to escape to the hotel complex, and because it was private property they weren't allowed to come in.

The next day we had to go to the police station and give a statement. I called Katherine at John Noel and said, 'I'm in a police station in Barbados! Help!' I don't even think she was surprised. The next day we had to go to court (they're fast workers out there) and it turned out that this guy was on the run from the police in the UK. He lived in Brixton and had got nicked for drugs and jumped bail. So they stopped his passport so he couldn't go home. I hope he's still behind bars now – he scared me so much.

Ryan told me he loved me during the first week of our relationship. He wanted to marry me by the second week and by the third he wanted kids with me. He was a real keeno. He didn't have any independence either. He didn't have his job as a footballer for long, so I ended up paying for everything, and he wouldn't ever leave my side. Sometimes I'd just want my space and I'd tell him to go home to his house but he wouldn't listen. My mum hated Ryan: she thought he was dirty and lazy, because he never used to clean the microwave. She didn't stay at the house much when he was there.

Ryan bought me a horse for Valentine's Day. He'd been asking me what I wanted and I said I didn't really need anything. Then, in passing, I told him I was planning to buy myself a horse soon: I'd always ridden when I was younger, and I wanted to get some of my youth back. Next thing I knew, he'd gone and bought me one. He said, 'That's the best Valentine's present in the world, isn't it?' He always needed reassurance. He was right, though, it was a bloody nice present and he'd got me the exact colour I wanted too. The horse was called Artino (I don't know if that's how you spell it, I just always thought it sounded like Valentino with an R). I kept it in some stables a little way from where we lived. It was a bit of a mission to get there but I loved going. Then Ryan took it back when we split up.

I don't know how Jeff felt when he found out about me and Ryan, he's never really spoken about it. He told me he was happy that I'd found someone who was good with the kids and who seemed like a good person. Jeff had started to date other girls too. I first found out because I went to his house and saw one of them through his kitchen window, but I didn't feel jealous because I knew none of them were serious. Also, I was seeing Ryan, so I didn't really have a leg to stand on.

By April 2005, the Granada film crew for Living TV had started filming me for a documentary about me setting up my own beauty salon. I'd been thinking about setting up my own business for about a year previously, but I was always too busy. Then Living TV heard about it and asked if they could film me doing it. My main concern was that I didn't want them to dictate anything. It had been my dream ever since I was a kid, so all the decisions had to come from me. They did help me find the designer, though, whose name was Derek. He was a good designer but we clashed a few times. The producer of the show also recommended my builders, one of whom was called Jason. They were the best group of builders I could have ever had. They stayed up working until the crack of dawn every day just to make sure it was open on time. I thought Jason was gay when I first met him because he was wearing a satchel. In actual fact, he had a wife who was five months pregnant.

It was when Jeff got a more serious girlfriend that it began to affect me. She was called Clare, and by then things had started to change between the pair of us. It took my mates to point it out to me, but once they did, there was no denying I still had feelings for him. They noticed it when a whole group of us had gone to Chessington for Carly's birthday. Ryan was there and so was Jeff and all our mutual friends. When we got back that evening, one of them said to me, 'Jesus Christ! There's something there still between you and Jeff. You've not stopped looking at each other all day.' I hadn't recognised it. So that got me thinking.

Then another of our mates had a barbeque and I called Jeff to see if he was going. He hesitated a bit before saying he was meant to be going on a date with Clare. So I said, 'Bring her!' I didn't really want him to, but Ryan was going to be there so I thought, *Why not?* I wanted to test myself to see if what my mates were saying was true, to see for myself whether I still had those feelings for Jeff.

Jeff and Clare rocked up just when I was stood in my bikini bottoms and a dodgy T-shirt playing with Bobby in the garden pool. Great. I said hello to her and was as polite as I could be. She wasn't ugly but I didn't think she was all that. She had fake tan on and I remember thinking, *Oh my God, you've not put it on right!* It was all orange around her ankles and in between her fingers. She was a lot older than Jeff too, but apparently they liked each other. However, I watched them together and he didn't seem to be that attentive, which made me feel slightly better. Then I went to the shop with one of my friends to get her some cigarettes and I found myself saying, 'I don't like seeing Jeff with Clare.' And from that moment on I began to question myself. Was I with Ryan because it was just a habit? Did I really care about him?

Then I went on a hen do to Marbella with 20 of my mates and my feelings for Jeff became increasingly obvious.

Jade: How It All Began

Ryan saw me off at the airport all lovingly, but when I was there, slumped at the bar while drunk in some nightclub, it was Jeff I called, not Ryan; it was Jeff I wanted to speak to. I vaguely recall being drunk one night and blurting out that I loved him down the phone. He just told me to stop drinking and said, 'Talk to me when you get back.'

14

I Want You Back

I had to be honest and tell Ryan and Jeff how I felt. And for me to be so open with both of them was a real step. I'm quite a wimp really. I'm never very good at admitting my feelings.

Ryan was upset, but I think he convinced himself that if he gave me a bit of time I'd eventually come back to him. I don't think he believed it was over. Jeff was still going out with Clare when I told him. I went over to his house and told him I needed to talk to him. I made him sit down in the bedroom and I said, 'I know you probably don't want to hear this and that it's just going to confuse you, but I am in love with you, Jeff, and I didn't realise until I noticed you with Clare and all my mates pointed out to me the way I look at you. And I've finished with Ryan.'

I could tell Jeff liked what I was saying to him. After all, he'd been wanting to hear it for a long time. But now it was his turn to protect himself, and he must have thought, *Shit, this means I could get hurt again. Has she changed? Or is she going to go back to the old, angry, evil Jade she once was?* But I knew I'd changed as a person, and I was convinced I could make a go of it with Jeff. I didn't want to row any more. I hadn't even really argued with Ryan (which was amazing at times). I wanted the easy life. I was a different person to the girl Jeff first went out with. I was the person he always knew I was deep down. He admitted he knew something was different about me because I would never in a million years have been so upfront before. I told him everything: that I wanted to be with him and nobody else, that I knew it might not happen straight away but that I'd prove to him he could trust me. I was prepared to do anything it took to win him back again, even if it meant waiting years and years.

Jeff finished with Clare straight away, but we decided to take it slow and see where it went. It wasn't a sexual relationship at first, just togetherness. I've always fancied him, of course, and there's often sexual tension when we're alone together: we simply didn't want to confuse ourselves by moving too quickly. Jeff said it was about proving we could be friends, first and foremost.

Ryan reappeared a week after we broke up. It was a beautiful summery day, so Jeff and I had decided to take the family for a day out to this fête in Essex. After the fête, I told Jeff to go on ahead to our mate Kelly's house with Bobby and Freddy and wait for me there because she'd invited us all to a barbeque. I had to scoot home and give my mum a bit of money, and then Mum was going back to Bermondsey. When I pulled up at the house I could see someone in the living room but I knew instantly it wasn't my mum; it was Ryan. He was sitting on a sofa; Mum must have let him in. When I got inside I said, 'What are you doing here?' and without even looking at my face he answered, 'I've come down to see you. I thought I'd stay the night.' I was stunned. 'You can't, I'm afraid, I'm going round Kel's for a barbeque.'

'I'm coming.'

'Er, no you're not, Ryan.'

Mum poked her head around the door and told me she was leaving, so I said goodbye to her. Ryan and I were alone. I didn't think it was a problem to start with, but he started watching me oddly. I went to leave the room and, without hesitating, he pushed me back onto the settee. It really took me by surprise because it wasn't like Ryan to do something like that. Normally in that situation I'd have hit him myself – I'm a big girl, probably bigger than him – but there was something sinister about the way he was behaving.

'Fuck off, Ryan.'

'No, you're not going anywhere. I need to talk to you.'

He moved so that he was sitting in front of me. I was on the sofa, he was on the coffee table. He kept his eyes firmly fixed on mine. 'You can't do this to me, Jade. You're not leaving me. You can't take my friends away from me.' I was in shock. *His* friends? They were *my* friends! He'd only known them a few months, and that was because *I'd* introduced them.

'If they want to see you, Ryan, they'll see you and that's fine by me, but this is my house and I don't want you here, so get out.'

255

'No, you're not going anywhere, Jade.'

He grabbed my keys from the side and locked the patio door, then he picked up both my mobile phone and my house phone (he'd obviously seen where I put everything when I'd arrived because he knew where they all were instantly). I tried to grab my mobile back but he was too quick for me. He told me he was texting Jeff. I tried to move again.

'Shut the fuck up,' he said. He'd lost it and I was scared. He wasn't even raising his voice, he was calm, which made it more eerie. He'd texted Jeff: 'Take the kids to Kel's mum's instead. I'm running late.'

I was sitting there shaking by the window, willing someone to walk past and notice something was wrong. Then Ryan leant towards me and began stroking my face, saying, 'It's all right, sweetheart, it's all right.' He leant in further and tried to stick his tongue down my throat. 'Jade, I love you. Please let me stay.' I was motionless. He put his hands on my head and began pushing me down onto the settee as if he was trying to bury me in it. He'd say, 'Jade, please don't take my friends away from me!' then he'd stop pushing and stroke my face again, purring, 'It's all right, sweetheart.'

He gave me a folder that he'd made. It was full of pictures of me and him and he'd stuck lovehearts and glitter round the edges, and it said, 'Jade and Ryan together forever'. It was so creepy. It contained loads of press cuttings too, photographs of me from the papers that came out way before he ever knew me. He'd been collecting them ever since I'd come out of *Big Brother*. I was panicking now.

I tried to go to the toilet but he forced me back into the room. 'You're not fucking going to the toilet. I'm in control now, not you.' He would only let me go to the loo if I left the door open, so I said I wouldn't bother. I've never been so scared in my life. Then he led me out of the lounge, until we were stood near the bottom of the stairs. He jarred my head towards the steps, saying, 'Get upstairs!' I was certain he was going to rape me. I managed to free myself and I ran back into the front room. Then he clenched his fist and forced it against my mouth, saying, 'Don't leave me, Jade.' His fist was so hard against my teeth, it made my lip bleed. Then, when he saw the blood, he stopped and pulled away. I think that's what made him leave: he saw the blood and freaked out. All of a sudden he muttered, 'I don't know what I'm doing,' dropped my keys and my phones on the floor and walked out.

I was quivering all over. I was about to ring Jeff, but then he appeared through the back door. He must've missed Ryan by literally a second. Jeff was really angry because he'd turned up at Kel's mum's house with the boys, thinking I'd arranged it, and she hadn't known what on earth he was doing there. Jeff took one look at me, and I was as white as a sheet.

'My God, what's the matter, Jade?'

Jeff was livid when I told him what had happened. He wanted to find Ryan and beat the crap out of him there and then. Then he went outside and rang him. I don't know what he said but I can imagine. Kel came round soon after, and she said she's never seen me looking so scared in her whole life. She says I was like a frail, frightened little mouse. And no one's ever described me as a mouse before.

Jeff and I slept at my house that night, in the same bed. Nothing happened – we just cuddled – but I was too scared to be left alone. The next day he took the boys out and I stayed at home. I'd never locked my back door before, never been worried about it either. But once I had got in the shower, all of a sudden panic shot through my veins: *Shit! What if Ryan comes round again?* I flew down the stairs and bolted the door. I couldn't stay in the house after that. I drove round and round the streets until Jeff and the boys returned home.

Ryan did turn up again, though, the day after that. Stupidly; I hadn't locked the back door again. I'd been in the garden and by the time I got back inside, he was stood in my dining room.

'What the fuck are you doing here, Ryan?'

'I need money. Something's happened to my sister. I need to get home to Leicester. Come with me, Jade. I need you to be with me. Don't leave me.'

I had £500 in the drawer so I gave it to him without even blinking. I just wanted to get rid of him. After telling me he loved me about ten times, he took it and left. But once he'd gone, things just didn't add up. If he'd been so bothered about his sister then why hadn't he just borrowed the money from his parents? Why was Ryan still here, begging me to get back with him? Besides, I didn't even know he *had* a sister.

The next day, Derek, the designer of my beauty salon, took me to Paris on the Eurostar for the day. We were going to look around flea markets for inspiration, except that when we got there they were all closed, so we looked around a few art galleries instead. Derek kept asking me all these questions about who painted certain things. I told him I thought the guy who painted the Mona Lisa was called Pistachio. He didn't stop laughing for about half an hour. Well, I didn't know it was a nut.

On the way back I got a phone call from Ryan. 'My sister's dead. She died in a car crash. Will you be with me, Jade? I need you.'

I was so confused. If his sister had really died I couldn't be horrible to him. But at the same time, how was she ill yesterday and suddenly in a car crash today?

'Jade, I need you now more than ever. Will you be with me?' Why was he still so bothered about me if his sister was dead? My love life would be the last thing on my mind if something had happened to a member of my family. But he went into such detail – she'd been driving to work when it happened and he said he was speaking to me from the hospital. Then he really stuck the nail in: 'Before my sister died, she said to me, "Where's Jade?" I had to try and explain to her that you didn't love us any more. That's what upset me the most.'

I flipped. 'Your sister has never even fucking met me, Ryan! How dare you start saying stuff like that? Look, I'm sorry if she has died but don't start throwing that at me. If she's never met me before then why the hell would she be calling my name on her deathbed?'

I put the phone down. What the fuck was he doing? A few days later a girl rang me. To this day I still don't know who it was, but she said, 'Don't take any notice of anything Ryan says to you. He's done it before. He told one of his exes that his mum was dying of cancer and that he needed her with him. Don't believe anything he tells you and don't let him put that pressure on your shoulders.'

Ryan still kept ringing and texting but I ignored him. I made sure I always locked my back door after that. He left a message informing me that he was going to sell his story to the papers. 'Fine,' I said. This consisted of a two-parter in the *People* newspaper. Week one featured a photo of Ryan looking all remorseful alongside a catalogue of abuse that he'd subjected me to. What an idiot – admitting he'd threatened me! What did he think he was going to get: a medal? Week two was Ryan talking about how insatiable I was in the sack. He made out that we'd had rampant sex in a service station on the way to Birmingham, which we never did. (For the record, I did have a romp with Jeff on a motorway once but not with Ryan.)

The last contact I had with Ryan Amoo was when he rang me threatening to write a book about me. He'd been with me for six months, what was he going to write? 'Met Jade, she took the piss out of me, I looked after her kids, I acted like a tit, then she dumped me...'? Great read that'd be. I told him I was sure it'd be a bestseller.

I was asked to appear on *The Weakest Link* because they were recording a 'reality TV special'. I was so nervous. I thought Anne Robinson was going to hammer the life out of me. I sat there for ages beforehand, thinking of witty answers that I could chuck back at her. None of them were very inspired, though. In the end, she was so nice and pleasant to me that I needn't have worried. She told me she was probably one of my biggest fans and I came away that day *loving* her. Throughout the show she had to keep doing retakes because she kept laughing at my answers so much. She said, 'I've got to do it again, Jade, because I'm meant to be saying mean things to you, not smiling!' I did all right in the end: I lasted for about five rounds. Stan Collymore got voted off before me and was furious. Anne wrote me a letter a week later; it was written on headed paper from the hotel she was staying in during filming, and she said it had been a pleasure having me on her show.

Plans for the salon were coming along nicely. I had to advertise for staff, which frightened me a bit. Shit, this was actually happening! I was going to be someone's boss! Carly, my business partner, and I wrote loads of little ads requesting 'Goody's Girls' and stuck them in shop windows. When we interviewed people, I really wasn't much use to anyone though. I was hungover because I'd been out on the lash the night before and I stank of booze. Good first impression, eh? It was really hard telling people they hadn't got the job, but we've got ourselves a really good bunch of workers now. Thank God Carly is the manager and not me. I work there too, but I'm not the most reliable of people. But, hey, I've put in £100,000 of my own money, so it had better work.

15

Endings and Beginnings

We decided on calling the salon Ugly's. Carly came up with the idea – you know, someone thinks, 'I'm feeling ugly because I've got no make-up on, no nails and hairy legs,' then they come into our salon and we make them beautiful. When Carly told me the name I thought I was going to get battered in the papers: 'JADE PICKS THE PERFECT NAME FOR HER SALON' – but I didn't. I guess I got there with the insult first.

Before we opened the salon, I was taught how to do a Brazilian wax. Ewww! Carly and I went to visit this woman in London because she was allegedly the best waxer in the world. It orginates from Cleopatra, supposedly, because she thought it was more hygienic to be hair-free. The waxing woman hated me before she'd even met me because I kept cancelling appointments. Then when we did turn up, I was late. It was the most intimate thing ever and it was disgusting. I had to do it on Carly and she had to do it on me. I feel like I've seen more of her insides now than her boyfriend has. I worked up the biggest sweat because I was so nervous about doing it. You literally have to put your hands inside someone's la la! I bruised Carly, poor girl. Now the salon's open I don't do them if I can help it. I had one booked in the other day but I turned up late, so I made one of the other girls do it.

Around that time I received an invitation to Jordan and Peter's wedding. It was a scroll design, white and silver and full of glitter; the most over-the-top invite you've ever seen. I knew I wouldn't be able to go because it clashed with the salon opening but the envelope will go in my memory box forever. I didn't know Jordan that well, not as a proper mate or anything, but to get asked to one of the biggest showbiz weddings of the century was just phenomenal. They had a deal with OK! magazine, the reality of which means that the more celebs you get to turn up, the more you get paid, but I didn't care. I wasn't under any illusions that I was her special friend (she invited Orlaith from *Big Brother 6*, for God's sake) but it meant a lot to me. After it happened, people knocked her because the whole ceremony was so lavish and extravagant. I think she looked wicked, just like a fairytale princess.

The last weekend in August 2005 was the V Festival in Chelmsford. I went with my mates Charlene, Jen and Angie. We were so excited. It was the first time I'd been to a festival and actually camped, even though we went without a tent. Jeff was going with some of his mates too, and he had a spare one he said I could have, as long as I put it up myself. But when I got there I couldn't be bothered putting up a tent, I just wanted to have a good time and get drunk. I spent most of my time in the VIP area because the drink was free there. I chatted with Charlotte Church about Jordan's wedding. I told her I'd heard she was going to sing there and asked if it was true, but she said she couldn't make it.

I saw Jeff in the bar later and said hello, but we made sure we weren't stuck to each other like glue or anything because we'd gone there separately. The papers said afterwards that I'd snogged one of his mates and someone from *Hollyoaks* or something. Rubbish! We did meet some of the *Hollyoaks* boys, though: Marcus Patrick who plays Ben was there, and so was Alex Carter who plays Lee Hunter. I loved Lee on *Hollyoaks,* and Alex was just as funny as he is on telly. We ended up watching the Prodigy with them. It was hysterical; they all had their tops off and were jumping up and down, beer was going everywhere. I ended up sleeping in Jeff's tent with him that night – my mates slept in the *Hollyoaks* tent because it was huge. Before you ask, nothing happened with me and Jeff, though. Are you joking? It took us about 20 hours to find the tent and it was freezing cold. Even if we'd wanted to have a little fiddle we couldn't have because our fingers would have fallen off.

On the way home from the festival our driver said that a man had died at V Festival in the toilet: apparently he'd taken an overdose. I thought, *How awful for his poor family.* The next day Living TV had set up a few press interviews for *Jade's Salon,* so I went into London. I'd just finished an interview when I was told the police were there to see me. They came into the room and one of them looked directly at me and said, 'We need to talk to you, Jade. We've got something to say.' I'd never had anything like this happen to me in my life. The police asked if I wanted to sit down. The first thing that went through my head was Jeff and the kids. My heart was pounding.

'Is it Jeff and my kids? Has anything happened to them?'

'No, Jade, they're all fine.'

'Oh my God, my mum?'

'No, Jade. We're really sorry to tell you but your dad's died of an overdose. He was found in a toilet in Kentucky Fried Chicken in Bournemouth.'

It was strange. I felt a wave of relief that it wasn't Jeff, it wasn't my boys and it wasn't my mum, but then I felt incredibly nauseous and just flat. I asked if someone could take me home. The next couple of days are a bit of a blur. I was in pieces. I called Mum and told her, and she was upset too but I don't think she was shocked: she'd been half expecting it for the last 23 years. What worried her more was how it was going to affect me. I'd never talked about my feelings towards my dad, I'd never shown him any kind of forgiveness – I'd barely acknowledged his existence. For my mum to hear me sobbing uncontrollably and not being able to speak made her feel helpless. I went to see Jeff and said, 'I don't know what to do or how to feel.' I felt guilty that my first thought had been relief. I felt self-reproach that I'd never taken my children to see their granddad. Jeff said, 'You must never ever blame yourself. You did what you thought was best.'

Then the coroners were on the phone telling me I had to pay for my dad's funeral. I didn't want to have anything to do with his family. I didn't want to go to his funeral and I didn't want to be part of it. Why should I have to associate myself with people I didn't particularly like or know? Why should I have to pay for it all and sort out the funeral when his own mum was still alive? The coroners only knew how to get hold of me because I was 'Jade Goody' – but they could bloody well track down his real family. I didn't want to have to bury anyone, especially not my dad. I felt like I shouldn't have to put myself through all that for someone who'd never been there for me.

Mum called me when the date of the funeral came round and tentatively asked if I wanted to go. I'd started acting all hard about it at first, but I think she knew I needed to say goodbye. But I wasn't ready then. It's only now that I really feel shit and helpless about the whole thing. I think I need to go to his grave, or do something at least. I need to put my mind at rest. All I've ever wanted was for my daddy to love me, even if it was only for a little while. He always said I was his little angel and he'd do anything for me, but words are meaningless. Do you know that my dad died without one vein in his body? In the end he'd injected every single part of it and all his veins had collapsed – even the ones in his penis. He was on heroin for so long that he'd simply run out of veins – they'd disappeared. The last time I saw him, his hands had been like big balloons. That's how I know when other people are addicts. I can't name names but there are certain celebrities I've met where I have instantly been able to tell when they've gone back to their habit again. There's one female celeb in particular. When I saw her last, her hands looked all puffy. I wanted to shake her and make her see sense. It's such a waste of a life.

A week prior to Ugly's opening we held a launch party for the press at The Embassy nightclub in London. So much was going on in my head about my dad, but I just had to get on with things and block it out. I was really scared that no one would come. My confidence went out of the window and I was supposed to arrive on a motorbike! The police had blocked the road off and everything.

I felt like a pillock in a pink dress going to a party. I felt so anxious. But when we pulled up, there were lights flashing everywhere and reporters shouting my name. Phew! All my mates had come down from Essex. I didn't think Jeff was going to make it, but he did, and that, made it all so much more special. We danced together most of the night and the papers ran stories that we were back together. I was caught at one stage with my hand on his bum, so I can hardly blame them.

There was another Living TV press launch too, this time to celebrate all their new shows. *Jade's Salon* was one of them, as was a show about ghosts called *Dead Famous,* hosted by Gail Porter. I'd always thought she was such a pretty girl. I was sat having my make-up done and she walked in. I didn't recognise her, so I was staring, thinking, *I'm sure I know your face.* She smiled and said, 'Yes, my hair fell out.' She was completely bald, except for a tiny pink tuft of hair in the middle of her head like a mohican. She'd been suffering from alopecia, the condition that makes your hair fall out when you're under severe stress. I thought she had cancer at first. I said, 'Oh my God, sorry Gail, I didn't even notice. I just was confused about where I knew you from.' Gail started sobbing; she was so scared. In a few minutes she would have to go out on a stage with me and face the British press for the first time and they didn't even know about her condition. I said, 'Look, girl, you're walking out there and nobody can knock you or slag you off because you're brave. You're not going out there hiding it, you're not going out with a headscarf on, you're not going out with a wig on. You're going out and admitting you've got a problem and you're dealing with it. You're saying, "I'm getting on with my life." People will look up to you for that, Gail.' But I felt so sorry for her, she was so nervous. To have that amount of stress in your life that your hair falls out? That must be some angst she was under. But she's dealing with it now in her own way and I have so much admiration for her. I rang her the other day and on her answer machine it says, 'Hi, Miss Baldy here. Sorry I can't get to the phone...'

Jade's Salon got the Jonathan Ross seal of approval too. I was invited on his Friday night chat show on BBC1. I'd never been interviewed by Jonathan Ross before, and for me to be asked on as a guest three years after I was first on *Big Brother* was pretty good going, I thought. Sitting in his greenroom, waiting to go on, I felt so much more than just an ex-housemate from *Big Brother*. I was surrounded by photographs of all his previous guests and they were all so incredibly famous. There was Kylie Minogue, 50 Cent, Samuel L. Jackson (my mate!), U2...The place was just filled with the most famous faces in the world. I was so honoured to be sitting on the same settee as all these people. Stephen Fry was a guest on the same show as me. I don't really like most intelligent people because they're usually patronising, but he was adorable and seemed genuinely interested in what I had to say.

As for Jonathan, I'd met him a few times before at awards ceremonies and parties, but only very briefly. He'd always been nice to me so I wasn't worried about him slagging me off. But I knew he could be very cheeky, so I thought ahead and sweetened him up beforehand with some doughnuts, after someone told me he loved them. I had a few butterflies before I went on, but, with me, once I'm out there in front of an audience, I feel at home. I got so comfortable, I think I had my feet up at one point. I videoed the show at home as a bit of a memento, because it was quite a big deal for me.

Around this time I went to see a tarot-card reader and had my fortune told. I thought it'd just be a load of codswallop but it really freaked me out. The man, who had a funny beard, asked me to give him something I was wearing so he could speak to the spirits. I gave him my ring and he suddenly started saying, 'Who's Andrew? Is he in the spirit world?' It made me well right up. That was my dad's name and he'd literally just died. He also said I was a working-class hero and that I'd be helping lots of people through my opportunities and doorways or something. But what he said about my dad was pretty distressing. When I'd been shuffling the tarot cards I was thinking, *I'm a bit confused about my dad*. I also wanted to know whether my business would be a success. This guy said, 'The angels have guided you to your opportunities and you will be successful.' He said I was an angel too, which was quite a nice thing to say. It was weird though.

But as far as the press were concerned, I wasn't an angel: I was a thief. It all came about because I'd been shopping in Asda and spotted a denim waistcoat for £16 (which I thought was a right bargain). When I put it on the counter with the rest of my stuff, the cashier didn't scan it and I didn't notice. I'd bought some other bits like sushi and a magazine but when I tapped in my number I didn't look at the price, I just knew that there was enough on my card to cover it. I walked out of the shop and it bleeped, so I ran back in and shouted, 'Oh my God, someone thinks I'm nicking this!' really loudly. The security guard directed me over to a supervisor lady and when I told her it had been bleeping she said, 'Oh, that's all right, Jade,' and removed the tag. I couldn't find the receipt when she asked about it so I told her what till I'd been on. She smiled: 'OK, not to worry. Take care, Jade, see you later.'

The next day I was summoned to the police station! I got a call at the salon telling me I needed to go to the station because I'd been accused of theft. I raced down there and raged to the policeman, 'I've got a good mind to go back into that store and pick up about 20 things and say, "Now come and nick me!"' He turned to me and paused before saying, 'Now you won't do that really, will you, Jade?' A week later *Heat* magazine ran a story saying that sales of that waistcoat had gone up by 26 per cent. I should get some commission.

Jade: How It All Began

Two days before Ugly's was due to open, Gazza – Paul Gascoigne – came into the salon. I was so starstruck, and so were the builders working there. The funny thing was, when I saw him he was really shaking and he told me he was starstruck to meet me! He was cuddling me and saying things like, 'I think your salon's beautiful, gal.' Then he started asking about me and Jeff and said, 'I missed the boat on that one, didn't I? That could've been me with your kids!' He gave me his number but I didn't fancy him. I'm sure he didn't mean it like that anyway.

The night before we opened I was sweeping the floor at 2.20 a.m. and I just started crying. I felt so emotional that I'd actually achieved something in my life. I looked around at this swanky new salon and thought, *This was all done by me.*

I soon came back down to earth with a bump, though, when I got into work the next day to admire the price list for our treatments and saw there were about ten spelling mistakes. Instead of 'sparkling eyes' it read 'sparking eyes', 'eyebrow tint' said 'eyebrown tint', and customers wanting a 'deluxe manicure' would've been asking for a 'duluxe manicure' instead. Mind you, people would probably expect that coming into my salon.

The first three days in the salon were a bit of a worry because we didn't get many customers, so we had an open day to try and get people through the door – basically we gave out free champagne and canapés. That got the punters in all right and they've been coming back ever since. I still can't believe there are people willing to pay me to make them look better! But I haven't had any complaints yet, touch wood.

Endings and Beginnings

I collapsed in the salon toilet the first week after it opened. The newspapers started saying it was because I was pregnant (that would've been a miracle because I hadn't had sex for months). The truth was I'd just been rushing about too much. And if I'm honest, I hadn't been eating properly again; probably as a result of thinking about my dad.

Epilogue: This is Me

I sit staring at the sky sometimes and it makes me cry. I seem to think my dad's up there, in the stars, watching me. I need to make peace with him, and with myself. I feel like maybe I should have helped him more or introduced my boys to him. I've got so much emotion inside me, so much stuff that's all churned up about him, but I don't know how to get it out. I think I should really talk to someone about it because I don't know how to channel my emotions – I've kept them pent up for so long. Was I wrong not to let him get to know my kids? If I could go back in time, would I behave differently? I've also been thinking how I'd love to find my younger brother Miles. He probably hasn't got a clue I'm his sister, but I just want to see how he is and talk to him. He must be a teenager by now.

Around Christmas time of last year (2005), Jeff and I finally decided to bite the bullet and give it another go. We didn't move back in together but we began sleeping with each other again (finally!) and going on dates, just like the old days. We loved each other, we didn't want anyone else, so it should work between us, right? Well, no, actually. For the first few weeks it was amazing and we couldn't get enough of each other, but it didn't take much time before the same old problems began to rear their ugly heads. We were both really busy – me with the salon and him with panto – and we weren't spending enough quality time together. Aside from that, once I'd started getting comfortable about the fact that he was my boyfriend again, I found myself making less of an effort. I should've been wanting to spend every waking hour with him and the kids, but I kept wanting to go out with the girls and enjoy myself. I've now realised that it's just not meant to be between us. Jeff saw this in the end and one morning he came over to my house and said 'Jade, you don't care about this do you?' and I couldn't give him the answer he wanted. He didn't get angry though, or upset – we're past all that. But both he and I now know it's not meant to be. I do love him, I will always love him, but I'm not in love with him and I've realised that at this stage in my life I need to live the life of a 24 year old. I've acted the grown up all my life – first with Mum, then with my kids – and now I need space to be young again. Of course, I will never regret being a mum, and Freddy and Bobby will always be my priority, but as for Jeff and me? It seems we are just destined to be 'close friends' after all. I think it might do me good to be single. Until Brad Pitt comes knocking on my door anyway.

As for me making myself sick, I might not be completely

cured but if I ever feel tempted to do it again at least I have the courage to tell friends what I'm thinking. I can recognise it's not a good thing and I need them to look out for me.

The day before I left the *Big Brother* house I went into the diary room and was asked how I'd like to be remembered. I said: 'As the person who let everybody see every single side of her, and they either liked her or they didn't.' Well, I think I've achieved my aim. I might be young, but I've learnt a hell of a lot over the last 24 years. I'll leave you with three of those things:

Don't shoplift (not in Selfridges anyway!).

Always lock your back door.

And never ever be afraid to talk about your feelings.

Goody Glossary

Absiss
Highly alcoholic green drink (*aka absinth*)

Barry Big Time
Person of fame or high celebrity standing

Beg-a-friend
Person whose behaviour denotes neediness

Bermondsey Two-step
Type of dance where an individual takes one step forward and two steps to the side, followed by one step back and two steps to the opposite side

Caterpillar
Type of dance move involving rolling the body along the floor

Jade: How It All Began

Chickpea
Small brown legume, possibly made from chicken

Chipstick
Person whose actions denote silliness or foolishness (*aka dipstick*); also a brand of potato chip

Continents
Salt and pepper (*aka condiments*)

Doughnut
Person of limited intelligence

East Angular
Group of counties in south-east of England

Escalope
Cut of meat, either chicken or camel

Escape goat
Person made to take the blame for others

Ferret
Breed of bird

Kebab belly
British midriff, occurring due to the excess consumption of alcoholic beverages, fast food and limited exercise

Keeno
Person who appears to be excessively enthusiastic or eager

Goody Glossary

La la
Intimate part of the female anatomy

Lingwo
Foreign or unfamiliar language or jargon (*aka lingo*)

Lu lu
see la la

Mentalist
Person whose actions denote mental illness

Minger
adj. minging Person of below average attractiveness or personal hygiene

Muppet
Person of limited intelligence

Nugget
Person of limited intelligence

Nuts, the
Something of extreme merit

Overall
Area in South London (*aka Oval*)

Parada Fashion designer

Jade: How It All Began

Pistachio
Famous Italian artist who painted the Mona Lisa

Portuganese
Language spoken in Portugal

Queen Burberry
Woman who wears a lot of items by the designer label Burberry

Sausage
Attractive woman

Right frigid, a
Person averse to, or frightened of, sexual activity

Sharpest tool in the sandwich box
Person of extreme intelligence

Sort
Attractive man

Stupid o'clock
Early hour in the morning

Tictacticals
Manoeuvres used or plans followed to achieve a particular short-term aim (*aka tactics*)

Tog
Person of limited intelligence or extreme naïvity

Goody Glossary

Tunisia
Country near India

Warning
Solemn or ceremonial vigil (*aka wake*)

Jade: Fighting to the End
- My Autobiography
1981 - 2009

Jade Goody

The moment Jade Goody stepped into the Big Brother house in 2002, her life changed forever. The glitz and glamour of Jade's sudden fame was a far cry from the real-life drama of the estate where she made her start. Behind the bubbly exterior, though, there was a tough and fiercely determined lady. But when she was diagnosed with cervical cancer in 2008, she faced her toughest battle of her life, in the full glare of the national media. Jade fought with dignity and unbelievable strength of character, never giving up hope and always striving to do the best she could for her beloved boys, Bobby and Freddy.

In this, the second instalment of her autobiography, Jade spares no detail as she reveals all about her time in therapy, her tempestuous relationship with the love of her life, Jack Tweed (who she married in February 2009) and the trauma of her cancer diagnosis. Funny, moving and disarmingly honest, *Fighting to the End* truly is a fitting tribute to one of Britain's best loved celebrities.

ISBN 978-1-84454-813-2   PB   £7.99

John Blake Publishing Ltd

Out Now

TO ORDER SIMPLY CALL THIS NUMBER
+ 44 (0) 207 381 0666

Or visit our website www.johnblakepublishing.co.uk

Prices and availability subject to change without notice